EXTRASTATECRAFT

EXTRASTATECRAFT

The Power of Infrastructure Space

Keller Easterling

VERSO

London • New York

The author would like to thank the Graham Foundation for Advanced
Studies in the Fine Arts for its generous assistance

First published by Verso 2014
© Keller Easterling 2014

Every effort has been made to trace copyright holders and to obtain permission for
the use of copyright material for the illustrations herein. The publisher apologizes
for any errors or omissions and would be grateful if notified of any corrections that
should be incorporated in future reprints or editions of this book.

1 3 5 7 9 10 8 6 4 2

Verso
UK: 6 Meard Street, London W1F 0EG
US: 20 Jay Street, Suite 1010, Brooklyn, NY 11201
www.versobooks.com

Verso is the imprint of New Left Books

ISBN-13: 978-1-78168-587-7
eISBN-13: 978-1-78168-588-4 (US)
eISBN-13: 978-1-78168-780-2 (UK)

British Library Cataloguing in Publication Data
A catalogue record for this book is available from the British Library

Library of Congress Cataloging-in-Publication Data

Easterling, Keller, 1959-
Extrastatecraft : the power of infrastructure space / Keller Easterling.
pages cm
Includes bibliographical references and index.
ISBN 978-1-78168-587-7 (hardback)—ISBN 978-1-78168-588-4 (e)
1. Space (Architecture)—Social aspects. 2. Power (Social sciences) I. Title.
NA2765.E23 2014
720.1ʹ03—dc23
2014012812

Typeset in Minion Pro by Hewer Text UK Ltd, Edinburgh, Scotland
Printed in the US by Maple Press

Contents

Acknowledgements   7

Introduction   11

1. Zone   25

2. Disposition   71

3. Broadband   95

4. Stories   137

5. Quality   171

6. Extrastatecraft   211

Afterword   239

Index   243

Acknowledgements

Verso, and especially editor Leo Hollis, deserve sincere thanks. The care and good cheer with which he edited the text for a general audience prompted not only clarifications but also discoveries for which the author could not be more grateful. Thanks also go to Mark Martin, Tim Clark, and designers Andy Pressman and Michael Oswell at Verso. Like a parallel text, the notes hopefully account for debts to ongoing scholarly discourses that a general audience may not wish to parse.

Yale University's Gustav Ranis Prize, the Graham Foundation for Advanced Studies in the Fine Arts, the Cornell Society for the Humanities, and the Jan van Eyck Academie provided funding for portions of the research and production of this book.

Colleagues and friends read drafts of the manuscript in progress: Ljiljana Blagojevic, Roger Conover, Stephen Graham, Michelle Komie, Nancy Levinson, Mitch McEwen, Brian McGrath, Susanna Newbury, Dara Orenstein, Vyjayanthi Rao, Andreas Ruby, and Ilka Ruby.

Several projects or collective research efforts contributed to segments of the book.

Research on the free zone was assembled for the 2007 Architecture Biennale in Rotterdam (Head of Programme Christine de Baan). Material for the chapter titled "Zone" was first published as a chapter in the book *Visionary Power* (2007).

A number of people assisted me in my research in Kenya including Mwangi Gathinji, Brian Herlihy, Professor Kigara Kamweru, John Mugabe, Pamela Odero, Simon Olawo, Dr. Bitange Ndemo, John Sihra, Steve Song, and Kai Wolff.

Material from the chapter titled "Broadband" was first published as "Cable" in *New Geographies* (2009). The research for this chapter was prepared to supplement the work of a research unit at the Jan van Eyck Academie that included Santiago del

Hierro, Gary Leggett, Dubravka Sekulić, Vesna Tomse, and Nadar Vossoughian. A website set up to present some of the research was designed by Tomas Celizna, with video by Min Oh and Celizna.

The final segment of the book, on alternative activist techniques, was first developed in 2008 for a master class and public lecture at the Berlage Institute at the invitation of Vedran Mimica and Saloman Frausto. Material for the chapter titled "Extrastatecraft" was first published in *Hunch 12: Bureaucracy* (2009). A collaborative exhibition at Storefront for Art and Architecture in 2008 titled *Some True Stories* experimented with some of these activist techniques. The team of collaborators included Gaby Brainard, Ashima Chitre, Neil Donnelly, Mwangi Gathinji, Santiago del Hierro, Mustapha Jundi, Rustam Mehta, Thom Moran, Jacob Reidel, and Carol Ruiz.

The book has benefited enormously from the intelligence of editors who have published portions of it. I am grateful to Justin McGuirk for publishing an ebook essay *The Action Is the Form* (Strelka Press, 2012) and to Nancy Levinson for publishing "Zone: The Spatial Softwares of Extrastatecraft" in *Design Observer* (2012)—two previews of the present book. Joseph Grima, first as the director of Storefront for Art and Architecture and then as the editor of *Domus*, has supported the work, as have Mark Wigley and Jeffrey Inaba for *C-Lab* and *Volume*. The journal *Perspecta* also published related research, and thanks are due to Dean Robert A.M. Stern and editors Kanu Agrawal, Gaby Brainard, Melanie Domino, Iben Falconer, Rustam Mehta, Thom Moran, Matthew Roman, Tal Schori, and Brad Walters. Other editors to whom I am indebted include Marc Angélil, Shumon Basar, Helen Castle, Dana Cuff, Cynthia Davidson, Peggy Deamer, Alexander Eisenschmidt, Daniela Fabricious, Homa Fajardi, Rania Gosn, Deborah Hauptmann, Aaron Levy, Sina Najafi, Warren Neidich, Amanda Reeser, Mark Shepard, Ashley Schafer, Lola Sheppard, Roger Sherman, Andreas and Ilke Ruby, Neyran Turan, Markus Miessen, Maya Przybylski, Daniel van der Velden, Marina Vishmidt, Srdjan Jovanovich Weiss, and Mason White.

Friends who provided support or reflection on the work include Arjun Appadurai, Julieta Aranda, Jonathan Bach, Shumon Basar, Chloe Bass, Ursula Beimann, Markley Boyer, Lindsay Bremner, Jordan Carver, Benedict Clouette, Beatriz Colomina, Jordan Crandall, Teddy Cruz, Shiela and Peter DeBretteville, Santiago del Hierro, Tina di Carlo, Elizabeth Diller, Edward Dimendberg, Kodwo Eshun, Homa Fajardi, Renate Ferro, Annette Fierro, Ray Gastil, Jordan Geiger, Eva Franc-Gilibert, Sara Goldsmith, Claudia Gould, Paul Gunther, Dolores Hayden, Molly Hickock, Nikolaus Hirsch, Jeffrey Inaba, Susan Jonas, Branden Joseph, Tom Keenan, Laura Kurgan, Jesse LeCavalier, Siddhartha Lokanandi, Marcell Mars, Reinhold Martin, Ana Miljacki, Mohsen Mostafavi, Tim Murray, John Palmesino, Satya Pemmaraju, Alan Plattus, Irit Rogoff, Ann-Sofi Rönnskog, Jenny Sabin, Joel Sanders, Fred Scharmen, Felicity D. Scott, Dubravka Sekulic, Michael Serino, Brett Steele, Daniel van der Velden, Misa Miodrag Vujošević, Mark Wasiuta, Eyal Weizman, Ines Weizman, Mark Wigley, Darien Williams, Brian Kuan Wood, and Gwendolyn Wright.

Several students—Ann-Marie Armstrong, A.J. Artemel, E. Sean Bailey, Swarnabh Ghosh, Brandon Hall, Gary Leggett, Rustam Mehta, Craig Rosman, and Ian Starling—provided research assistance. And too many students to name, in both seminars and lecture courses, contributed their wisdom and curiosity.

The book is dedicated to the memory of Detlef Mertins.

Introduction

Microwaves bounce between billions of cell phones. Computers synchronize. Shipping containers stack, lock, and calibrate the global transportation and production of goods. Credit cards, all sized 0.76mm, slip through the slots in cash machines anywhere in the world. All of these ubiquitous and seemingly innocuous features of our world are evidence of global infrastructure.

The word "infrastructure" typically conjures associations with physical networks for transportation, communication, or utilities. Infrastructure is considered to be a hidden substrate— the binding medium or current between objects of positive consequence, shape, and law. Yet today, more than grids of pipes and wires, infrastructure includes pools of microwaves beaming from satellites and populations of atomized electronic devices that we hold in our hands. The shared standards and ideas that control everything from technical objects to management styles also constitute an infrastructure. Far from hidden, infrastructure is now the overt point of contact and access between us all—the rules governing the space of everyday life.

Picture the places where we live: the parking places, skyscrapers, turning radii, garages, street lights, driveways, airport lounges, highway exits, big boxes, strip malls, shopping malls, small boxes, free zones, casinos, retail outlets, fast food restaurants, hotels, cash machines, tract housing, container ports, industrial parks, call centers, golf courses, suburbs, office buildings, business parks, resorts. In the retinal afterglow is a soupy matrix of details and repeatable formulas that generate most of the space in the world—what we might call *infrastructure space*.

Buildings are often no longer singularly crafted enclosures, uniquely imagined by an architect, but reproducible products set within similar urban arrangements. As repeatable phenomena engineered around logistics and the bottom line they constitute an infrastructural technology with elaborate routines and schedules for organizing consumption. Ironically, the more rationalized these *spatial products* become the better suited they are to irrational fictions of branding, complete with costumes and a patois of managementese.[1] This familiar confetti of brightly colored boxes nestling in black asphalt and bright green grass—the same in Texas or Taiwan—weaves elaborate, emotional stories about Starbucks coffee, Beard Papa cream puffs, and Arnold Palmer golf communities.

Now not only buildings and business parks but also entire world cities are constructed according to a formula—an infrastructural technology. We no longer build cities by accumulating singular masterpiece buildings. Instead the most prevalent formula replicates Shenzhen or Dubai anywhere in the world with a drumbeat of generic skyscrapers. Computer-generated videos that fly through shining skylines have become a standard signal of aspirations to enter the global marketplace. Here, manifest in these stock specifications, infrastructure is then not the urban substructure, but the urban structure itself—the very parameters of global urbanism.

Operating System

In *Notre-Dame de Paris*, Victor Hugo famously observed that "architecture [like that of the cathedral] was developed in proportion with human thought; it became a giant with a thousand heads and a thousand arms, and fixed all this floating symbolism in an eternal, visible, palpable form." The novel proposed that Gutenberg's new technology threatened the giant; the printed word usurped architecture as the vessel of cultural imagination and stole its supernatural power. Hugo prophesied, "This will kill that. The book will kill the edifice."

---

1 For a discussion of spatial products, see Keller Easterling, *Enduring Innocence: Global Architecture and Its Political Masquerades* (Cambridge, MA: MIT Press, 2005).

While evidence of infrastructure space within the contemporary city might appear to confirm the death of architecture, perhaps it really only demonstrates that the giant is alive again. Architecture makes unique objects—like stones in the water—while a constant flow of repeatable spatial formulas constructs a sea of urban spaces. Architects and urbanists typically characterize this state of affairs as disempowering, but if architecture was indeed killed by the book, perhaps it is reincarnate as something more powerful—as information itself. Infrastructure space has become a medium of information. The information resides in invisible, powerful activities that determine how objects and content are organized and circulated. Infrastructure space, with the power and currency of software, is an operating system for shaping the city.

That operating system is something like the "medium" in Marshall McLuhan's famous dictum "the medium is the message." McLuhan highlighted the difference between the declared content of media—music on the radio or videos on the internet—and the means by which the content was delivered. The content, he argued, is like the "juicy piece of meat carried by the burglar to distract the watchdog of the mind."[2] In other words, what the medium is saying sometimes prevents us from seeing what the medium is doing. In the urban context, we can identify the singularly crafted building—the stone in the water—as the declared content. Yet, the activity of the medium or infrastructural matrix—what it is doing rather than what it is saying—is sometimes difficult to detect.

We might not think of space as an information technology unless it is embedded with sensors and digital media, and there is digital software to generate and analyze urban arrangements. Yet infrastructure space, even without media enhancement, behaves like spatial software. And while we also do not typically think of static objects and volumes in urban space as having agency,

---

2   Marshall McLuhan, *Understanding Media: The Extensions of Man* (New York: McGraw-Hill and London: Routledge & Kegan Paul, 1964, 2001), 19: "For the 'content' of the medium is like the juicy piece of meat carried by the burglar to distract the watchdog of the mind."

infrastructure space is *doing something*. Like an operating system, the medium of infrastructure space makes certain things possible and other things impossible. It is not the declared content but rather the content manager dictating the rules of the game in the urban milieu.

Infrastructure space is a form, but not like a building is a form; it is an updating platform unfolding in time to handle new circumstances, encoding the relationships between buildings, or dictating logistics. There are object forms like buildings and active forms like bits of code in the software that organizes building. Information resides in the, often undeclared, activities of this software—the protocols, routines, schedules, and choices it manifests in space. McLuhan's meme, transposed to infrastructure space, might be: the action is the form.

Dubai, 2005

Extrastatecraft

Contemporary infrastructure space is the secret weapon of the most powerful people in the world precisely because it orchestrates activities that can remain unstated but are nevertheless consequential. Some of the most radical changes to the globalizing world are being written, not in the language of law and diplomacy, but in these spatial, infrastructural technologies—often because market promotions or prevailing political ideologies lubricate their movement through the world. These stories foreground content to disguise or distract from what the organization is actually *doing*.

Far removed from familiar legislative processes, dynamic systems of space, information, and power generate de facto forms of polity faster than even quasi-official forms of governance can legislate them. Large-scale spatial organizations like infrastructure projects (e.g., US rail in the nineteenth century, or global submarine cable networks) have long created the need for an administrative authority comparable to that of the state, and they continue to require direction from new constellations of international, intergovernmental, and nongovernmental players. As a site of multiple, overlapping, or nested forms of sovereignty, where domestic and transnational jurisdictions collide, infrastructure *space* becomes a medium of what might be called *extrastatecraft*—a portmanteau describing the often undisclosed activities outside of, in addition to, and sometimes even in partnership with statecraft.

For example, the world has dominant software for making urban space: the free zone—the formula that generates Shenzhens and Dubais all around the world. Some version of the zone is found in King Abdullah Economic City in Saudi Arabia, New Songdo City in South Korea, Cyberjaya in Malaysia, HITEC City in Hyderabad, and everywhere in between. Operating under authorities independent from the domestic laws of its host country, the zone typically provides premium utilities and a set of incentives—tax exemptions, foreign ownership of property, streamlined customs, cheap labor, and deregulation of labor or environmental laws—to entice business. The world has become addicted to incentivized urbanism, and it is the site of

Ordos, Inner Mongolia, 2008

headquartering and sheltering for most global power players. So contagious is this spatial technology that every country in the world wants its own free zone skyline.

While promoted as relaxed, open, and free from inefficient state bureaucracy, the politics written into the zone's spaces and activities often diverges from the declared intent. It is usually an isomorphic exurban enclave that, exempt from law, can easily banish the circumstances and protections common in richer forms of urbanity. Labor and environmental abuse can proceed unchecked by political process. Moreover, given its popularity, the zone has become a self-perpetuating agent in the growth of extrastate urban space—space beyond the reach of state jurisdictions. Yet, at the same time, it has also become an essential partner for the state as it attempts to navigate and profit from the very same shadow economies. In this form of extrastatecraft, far from overwhelming state power, the zone is a new partner that strengthens the state by serving as its proxy or camouflage.

In addition to the zone, the global networks of broadband computing and mobile telephony are another pervasive and consequential field of infrastructure space. Mobile telephony is the "world's largest distribution platform," and the broadband infrastructure that supports it is touted as a resource as important as water. Between 2000 and 2013, the global number of cell phone subscriptions went from 740 million to 6.8 billion phones with over three-quarters of the phones in the developing world.[3] East African countries like Kenya have only recently received international fiber-optic submarine cable. They are nevertheless using their large populations of mobile phone users to develop the world's newest business models. M-PESA, an app developed in Kenya that uses the mobile phone for exchanges of money, has become a global banking phenomenon. Advertisements for Safaricom and other telecoms in the region typically show Masai warriors, in full tribal garb, standing out in the savannah with a spear in one hand and a cell phone in the other, able to remotely access the world with an airborne technology.

Still, there is a disconnect between the stories and promises associated with the technology and what the urban space is actually doing. Both urban space and telecommunications are technologies and mediums of information. Fiber-optic cable buried in the ground gives land a new value much like a highway or railroad. Mobile telephony, while atomized and airborne, must nevertheless tap into that physical broadband network, and at these or any other switching points, a bottleneck or

---

3 "A 2010 Leadership Imperative: The Future Built on Broadband" (ITU, The Broadband Commission for Digital Development, 2010); Mohsen Khalil, Philippe Dongier, and Christine Zhen Wei Qiang, "Overview," in *Information and Communications for Development: Extending Reach and Increasing Impact*, ed. World Bank Development Data Group and World Bank Global Information & Communication Technologies Dept. (Washington, DC: World Bank, 2009); ITU, "World Telecommunications/ICT Indicators Database, 17th Edition," June 17, 2013, at itu.int.

monopoly can develop. The position of the fiber in urban and rural areas or the character of new enclaves and roads are all spatial factors with the power to either amplify or diminish the access to information.

As Kenya has become an investment field for global telecoms, the state must also convene a ballooning number of other non-state actors—intergovernmental institutions, consultancies, and nongovernmental institutions. All are hovering, advising, funding, researching, investing, and potentially controlling the urban space—offering expertise as well as outmoded forms that may foreclose on the real innovations to broadband urbanism. While Kenya is uniquely poised to make those innovations, its version of extrastatecraft must make spatial and digital software work together to enrich rather than obstruct information both realms.

Yet another field of infrastructure space, at once more immaterial and more ubiquitous, is able to contact any kind of infrastructure space anywhere in the world. If law is the currency of governments, standards are the currency of international organizations and multinational enterprises. ISO (International Organization for Standardization) is an extrastate parliament of this global standard-making activity. A private nongovernmental organization, convening both private companies and national representatives, ISO oversees global technical standards for everything from credit card thickness to dashboard pictograms, computer protocols, and the pitch of screw threads. Enhancing the influence of a raft of global organizations (e.g., The ITU [International Telecommunications Union], the IEC [International Electrotechnical Commission], the ICAO [International Civil Aviation Authority], NATO, the World Bank, the IMF, and the WTO), standards create a "soft law" of global exchanges.[4]

---

4   Nils Brunsson and Bengt Jacobsson, "The Pros and Cons of Standardization—An Epilogue," in Brusson and Jacobsson eds., *A World of Standards* (London: Oxford University Press, 2000), 171; Peter Mendel, "The Making and Expansion of International Management Standards: The Global Diffusion of ISO 9000 Quality Management Certificates," in J. W. Meyer, G. S. Drori, and H. Hwang, *Globalization*

ISO's seemingly innocuous technical specifications dictate the world's critical dimensions, yet their most popular standard, ISO 9000, is a management standard that promotes the ritualized incantations of something called "quality." Quality standards do not dictate specifications for a product but rather offer management guidelines for a *process* or quality system that may address everything from the environment to governance itself. ISO 9000 has been adopted as an essential credential in most countries of the world. ISO compliance is even a condition for the trading partners of EU countries. The whole world now speaks a dialect of ISO Esperanto, one that often resembles the hilarious, upbeat argot of self-help gurus.

While lacking any specific content or binding requirement, ISO is a perfect conduit of undeclared activities and intentions with potentially dangerous consequences. Companies may be certified as responsible players with regard to labor or the environment without having to abide by any global compact regarding, for instance, worker safety or dangerous emissions. Of all the things ISO addresses, remarkably the organization offers almost no standards that directly address the conflicted global frontiers of infrastructure space—where formulaic urban space confronts sensitive landscapes, failed economies, and complex political situations. Yet both the failure of ISO to create more consequential standards as well as its success in shaping global habits inspires a rehearsal of *spatial* protocols that join the bargains and offsets of contemporary global governance.

Space

While space may be enormously consequential in these infrastructure developments, private enterprise and other forces of extrastatecraft often speak in other technical languages. The financial industry quants format the housing landscapes, the

---

and Organization: World Society and Organizational Change (Oxford: Oxford University Press, 2006), 137–66.

carbon market regulates rain forest landscapes, informatic specialists shape the mobile telephony technoscape, McKinsey consultants offer econometrics, and ISO intones management jargon. Political and economic data come cloaked in the rationality of science even though they may really present false logics or systems of belief. Despite its relative physical durability—infrastructure space is often only regarded as a byproduct of more volatile markets and political games. Who is treating space itself as information? Who is writing the software or the protocols in which spatial variables take the lead?

The interaction of people and technology in the development of social/technical networks like infrastructure already calls on several areas of theory and scholarship, among these: social sciences, arts, business history, science and technology studies, history of science, organization studies, informatics, media and communication studies, architecture, and urbanism. Some of the most innovative thinkers in these disciplines now insist on stretching disciplinary habits to question the authority of their science or the purity of their master narratives. Rather than reinforcing the presumptions of theory, they want to discover what is actually happening on the ground. Not only the sciences, but also the *arts* of architecture and urbanism contribute to the conversation at this juncture. In the search for a more complex context, infrastructure space may be a fresh and potent field of evidence.

This book visits three different strata of infrastructure space: the free zone phenomenon, broadband mobile telephony in Kenya, and ISO's global management standards. Each is a crossroads of transportation, communication, management, trade, and development networks. Each addresses a pressing contemporary issue in infrastructure space while also harking back to the late nineteenth century when the growth of international infrastructure, organizations, and corporations began to accelerate and global travel and communication times began to shrink (the Suez Canal and the US transcontinental railroad were both completed in 1869). Each visits infrastructure space in developing countries to find new intelligence on the flip side of this early infrastructure history. And each is a potential test bed for spatial software.

Exposing evidence of the infrastructural operating system is as important as acquiring some special skills to hack into it. Interspersed between evidentiary chapters are more contemplative chapters. Ranging more freely over other examples of infrastructure like rail, internet, and mass-produced suburbs, these chapters dwell on an expanded repertoire of form-making, history-telling, and activism. Together they consider the art of designing interplay between spatial variables—an interplay powerful enough to leverage the politics of extrastatecraft.

Mark Twain, once a steamboat captain on the Mississippi, developed techniques for navigating the river. While the passengers saw "pretty pictures" of landscape scenes, he was extracting information from the changing "face of the water." A little ripple, eddy, or "faint dimple" signaled turbulence or obstacles in a complex and potentially dangerous organization below the surface. These were markers of unfolding potentials or inherent agency in the river—what can only be called its *disposition*. Disposition is the character or propensity of an organization that results from all its activity. It is the medium, not the message. It is not the pattern printed on the fabric but the way the fabric floats. It is not the shape of the game piece but the way the game piece plays. It is not the text but the constantly updating software that manages the text. Not the object form, but the active form.

For each technology in infrastructure space, to distinguish between what the organization is saying and what it is doing— the pretty landscape versus the fluid dynamics of the river—is to read the difference between a declared intent and an underlying disposition. The activities of a technology may be difficult to see even though, given the ubiquity of infrastructure space, they are hidden in plain sight. Examining each one, each active form— like each dimple or ripple on the water or each bit of code in the software—makes it more palpable. Detecting and developing the active forms that shape disposition is an essential skill of the urbanist in infrastructure space, and it is the topic of a chapter following the discussion of free zones.

Examining the power of the stories, persuasions, or ideologies that accompany a technology also helps in detecting disposition. For instance, infrastructure has often been groomed as either an instrument of militarism, liberalism, or universal rationalization. Yet we might question the dominance of these stories in organizing history. The pyrotechnics of war may distract from other more insidious forms of violence; theories of economic liberalism may ironically generate profound constraints on freedom; and dreams of universal rationality may sponsor their own special forms of irrationality. Well-rehearsed theories, like those related to Capital or neoliberalism continue to send us to the same places to search for dangers while other concentrations of authoritarian power escape scrutiny. Moreover, the less dramatic or upstaged histories—regarding the growth of international organizations, the division of the radio spectrum, or the creation of satellite, fiber-optic, and mobile telephony networks—have often been treated as bureaucratic or technical footnotes, despite the long-term impact these developments have had on our lives. Shaping and managing the story is then also an essential skill in infrastructure space. A chapter about these persistent ideological stories follows the examination of broadband.[5]

Following the discussion of ISO, the final chapter considers an enhanced repertoire for political activism tuned to more effectively address the powers of infrastructure space. The most familiar forms of political activism demand declaration. Yet, while there are moments in which to stand up and give it a name, dissent is often fooled by the sneaky way the world works, as the real power players maintain a currency in undeclared activities. Infrastructure space constitutes a wilder mongrel than any familiar Leviathan for which we have a well-rehearsed political response. The things that make infrastructure space powerful— its multipliers (e.g., zones, cell phones, spatial products), its

5   This discussion of the stories that attach to infrastructure space gestures to a few terms (e.g., script and narrative) already in play in a highly developed discourse about the reciprocity between social and technical networks—one that will be more fully engaged in the course of the book. For just two of many titles that contribute to this discourse, see Bruno Latour, *Reassembling the Social: An Introduction to Actor-Network Theory* (Oxford: Oxford University Press, 2005) and David E. Nye, *Electrifying America: Social Meanings of a New Technology* (Cambridge, MA: MIT Press, 1990).

irrational fictions, or its undeclared but consequential activities—are perhaps the very things that make it immune to
righteous declaration and prescription. The rational, resolute,
and righteous, while cornerstones of dissent, are sometimes less
consequential than the discrepant, fictional, or sly. Infrastructure
space tutors a shrewder, cagier counter to the lubricated agility of
most global powers—an alternative extrastatecraft.

CHAPTER 1

Zone

Promotional videos for the free zone invariably follow the same template. A zoom from outer space locates a spot on the globe. Graphics indicating flight times to major cities argue that this spot, wherever it is, is the center of all global activity. While the soundtrack for low-budget versions of these videos may be a tinny, canned fanfare, many have high production values. Stirring music, appropriate for an adventure film or a western, is ethnically inflected to suit the culture at hand. A deep movie-trailer voice describes the requisite infrastructure. As the zoom continues, clouds part to reveal multiple digital sun flares and a sparkling new skyscraper metropolis.

The zone has not always been the world's global urban addiction. Once relegated to the backstage, it has, in the space of a few years, evolved from a fenced-off enclave for warehousing and manufacturing to a world-city template. Yet the wild mutations of the form over the last thirty years only make it seem penetrable to further manipulation.

Free ports have handled global trade for centuries, but the mid-twentieth-century development of the Export Processing Zone, or EPZ, as a more formalized economic and administrative instrument, marks the beginning of the modern zone. With persuasive arguments about nation-building and free trade, the United Nations and the World Bank promoted the EPZ as a tool that developing countries should use to enter the global marketplace and attract foreign investment with incentives like tax holidays and cheap labor. Although intended as a temporary experiment and judged to be a suboptimal economic instrument, the zone spread widely during the 1970s even as it also spread new waves of labor exploitation. There were, however, unexpected consequences: rather than dissolving into the domestic economy, as was originally intended, the EPZ absorbed more and more of that economy into the enclave.

The next generations of the form, incubated in China or the Middle East, essentially became entire cities or city-states, rendering urbanism as a service industry. In the late-1970s, China's experiment with the zone as a free market tool was so successful that it generated its own global trading networks, which in turn accelerated zone growth worldwide. For Dubai, the zone was a fresh form of entrepôt not unlike those that had figured in its longer history. As zones multiplied they also upgraded, breeding with other increasingly prevalent urban forms like the campus or office park. Merging industrial and knowledge economies, the zone has begun to incorporate a full complement of residential, resort, educational, commercial, and administrative programs—a warm pool to spatial products that easily migrate around the world, thriving on incentivized urbanism.

Having swallowed the city whole, the zone is now the germ of a city-building epidemic that reproduces glittering mimics of Dubai, Singapore, and Hong Kong. While in the 1960s there were a handful of zones in the world, today there are thousands—some measured in hectares, some in square kilometers. No longer in the shadow of the global city as financial center (New York, London, Tokyo, São Paulo), the zone as corporate enclave is the most popular model for the contemporary global city, offering a "clean slate" and a "one-stop" entry into the economy of a foreign country. Now major cities and even national capitals, supposedly the centers of law, have created their own zone doppelgängers, like Navi Mumbai; Astana, the newly minted capital of Kazakhstan; or New Songdo City, a Seoul double that developer Stanley Gale considers to be a repeatable "city in a box." Economic analysts chase after scores of zone variants, even as they mutate on the ground, oscillating between visibility and invisibility, identity and anonymity.

As the zone mutates, it also resembles history's various intentional communities with their mixtures of withdrawal and aspiration—mixing ecstatic expressions of urbanity with a complex and sometimes violent form of lawlessness. Maintaining autonomous control over a closed loop of compatible circumstances, the isomorphic zone rejects most of the circumstance and contradiction that are the hallmark of more familiar forms of urbanity. In its sweatshops and dormitories it often remains a clandestine site of labor abuse.

For all of its efforts to be apolitical, the zone is often a powerful political pawn. While extolled as an instrument of economic liberalism, it trades state bureaucracy for even more complex layers of extrastate governance, market manipulation, and regulation. For all its intentions to be a tool of economic rationalization, it is often a perfect crucible of irrationality and fantasy. And while as spatial software, the zone is relatively dumb—the urban equivalent of MS-DOS—it has quickly spread around the world. Yet, for all these reasons, the zone is ripe for manipulation, and its popularity makes it a potential multiplier or carrier of alternative technologies, urbanities, and politics.

The Zone Is Ancient and New

The zone is heir to the mystique of ancient free ports, pirate enclaves, and other entrepôts of maritime trade. The Roman port of Delos in Greece is frequently cited as the primordial moment of the free port.[1] The Mediterranean fostered free ports for trade along Italian, Phoenician, Armenian, and Muslim trade routes. From the thirteenth to the seventeenth century in the Baltic and the North Sea, the Hanseatic League established a network of "free cities." Fiercely independent, the Hansa traders created a quasi-monastic society, living and dining together in their trading halls and factories where, in foreign cities, they were also sometimes confined. Hansa cities like Hamburg and Bremen traded with London, Lübeck, Rostock, Gdańsk, Königsberg, Brügge, Köln, and Novgorod.[2] In the Mediterranean, Marseille,

---

1   Guangwen Meng, "The Theory and Practice of Free Economic Zones: a Case Study of Tianjin, People's Republic of China" (PhD diss., Ruprecht-Karls University of Heidelberg, 2003), 25; Guangwen Meng, "Evolutionary Model of Free Economic Zones—Different Generations and Structural Features," *Chinese Geographical Science* 15, no. 2 (2005), 1; R. J. McCalla, "The Geographical Spread of Free Zones Associated with Ports," *Geoforum* 21, no. 1 (1990), 122; D. L. U. Jayawardena, "Free-Trade Zones," *Journal of World Trade* 17, no. 5 (1983), 427.

2   See Helen Zimmern, *The Hansa Towns*, 2nd ed. (London: T. Fisher Unwin, 1889).

Genoa, and Livorno were early free ports. By the seventeenth century, the European free cities or free ports included Naples, Venice, Trieste, Porto, Dunkirk, and Copenhagen. Hamburg would remain a prominent free port for centuries, able to evade the jurisdictional power of monarchies and national regulation.[3]

In the late eighteenth and early nineteenth centuries, as trade began to include the Americas in a truly global network, Spain, Portugal, Holland, and Great Britain established free ports in South America and the Caribbean. British and French free ports in Hong Kong (1841), Singapore (1819), Djibouti (1859), and Aden (1853) followed.[4] While the usefulness of the Caribbean ports declined, the Asian ports, notably Hong Kong, endured, and both Hong Kong and Hamburg continued to be global models into the twentieth century. When Hamburg joined the German Empire in 1871, the city refused to become a member of the German Customs Union, for fear of losing its various trading freedoms, and only joined in 1888, when it was allowed to fence off an area that remained outside of the union's control. Within this area, the city was granted increased freedom for sorting, manipulating, and manufacturing warehoused goods before re-export.[5]

In 1934, after sending delegations to Copenhagen and Hamburg, the United States passed the Foreign Trade Zone Act. Based in part on the Hamburg model, Foreign Trade Zones (FTZs) allowed for the sorting and manipulation of goods.[6] The first FTZs

---

3   Meng, "The Theory and Practice of Free Economic Zones," 29.

4   Meng, "Evolutionary Model of Free Economic Zones," 105. By 1900, there were, by some counts, eleven free ports in the world. In the first half of the twentieth century, eighteen more free ports were created in Europe, primarily in Sweden and Switzerland. See McCalla, "The Geographical Spread of Free Zones Associated with Ports," 123; and Meng, "The Theory and Practice of Free Economic Zones," 27. Of the eight created in Latin America, five were *puertos libres* created after Mexico established free port laws in 1924. See Dara Orenstein, "Foreign-Trade Zones and the Cultural Logic of Frictionless Production," *Radical History Review* 109 (Winter 2011), 36–61. Free zones were also established in Africa and Asia. See McCalla, "The Geographical Spread of Free Zones Associated with Ports," 127.

5   McCalla, "The Geographical Spread of Free Zones Associated with Ports," 125, 127.

6   Approaching manufacturing, this "manipulation" often involved refining or curing processes. The manipulation of goods made zones distinct from the bonded

in the United States were in New York, New Orleans, San Francisco, and Seattle. In 1950, FTZ law was amended to allow for manufacturing. Yet until the 1970s only three more zones—in Toledo, Ohio; Honolulu, Hawaii; and Mayagüez, Puerto Rico—were created.[7]

A number of installations, specially tailored to enable manufacturing, appeared around the world after World War II and served as forerunners of the Export Processing Zone—the formula that arguably spawned a global proliferation of zones. Although diminished after World War II and the Korean War, Hong Kong rebounded as a member of this new species of free port in part because of its own high volume of exported goods.[8] When Shannon Airport in Ireland was no longer needed for refueling, it began a deliberate campaign to attract both manufacturing and service industries with laws that established a Customs Free Airport (1947) and the Shannon Duty Free Airport Development Company (1959).[9]

In 1947, Puerto Rico, already a duty-free supplier for the United States during wartime, ventured to build manufacturing and warehousing facilities tailored to US businesses. A ten-year tax holiday and prebuilt modular buildings attracted almost 500 US firms by 1963. One promoter of the program characterized it as the "first significant effort to alleviate human suffering in the Caribbean." The development organization staff were trained to deliver clients to their new building, turn on the lights, step aside, and say "This is your factory, señor."[10]

The Colón Free Trade Zone in the Republic of Panama, established in 1948, was also designed to take advantage of

warehouses already permitted in the United States since 1846. See Orenstein, "Foreign-Trade Zones and the Cultural Logic of Frictionless Production," 7.

7   McCalla, "The Geographical Spread of Free Zones Associated with Ports," 130.

8   Hong Kong is now a Special Administrative Region (SAR) of the People's Republic of China.

9   McCalla, "The Geographical Spread of Free Zones Associated with Ports," 128–9.

10   Richard L. Bolin, "What Puerto Rico Faced in Being First to Create EPZs in 1947 . . . And Its Huge Success" (paper presented at the Award Ceremony during the conference of the Latin American Free Trade Zones Committee, San Juan, Puerto Rico, 2004).

existing relationships with the United States that had been forged during World War II. Plans for an international free zone had been discussed since 1917, three years after the opening of the Panama Canal, and investors from New York were interested in financing the project. By 1946, Panama had hired the executive secretary of the US Foreign-Trade Zones Board, Thomas E. Lyons, to study the feasibility of the project.[11]

In 1964, Mexico inaugurated the Border Industrial Program (BIP) just as the US-Mexican Bracero (or guest-worker) program was expiring.[12] The BIP allowed foreign companies to operate maquiladoras (or factories) within a twenty-mile strip along the border between Mexico and the United States, and by 1972 these factories could be established anywhere in the country. Taking advantage of cheap, mostly female labor, these zones were essentially inexpensive twins of factories in the home country.

These early outposts prompted experiments in other countries. Hong Kong and Shannon were models for Taiwan's Kaohsiung Export Processing Zone in 1965. All of these served as templates for zones in Africa, South America, the Middle East, and other parts of Asia.[13] South Korea established six free-trade zones, three in Seoul and three in Incheon in 1965.[14] India established Kandla in the same year.[15] Brazil established Manaus in

---

11   See colonfreetradezone.com; and Thomas E. Lyons, "Report on Proposal to Create a Foreign-Trade Zone in the Republic of Panama: An Analysis of Some of the Many Direct and Indirect Benefits Which Would Accrue to the Republic of Panama by the Establishment of a Foreign-Trade Zone," Washington, DC: US Dept. of Commerce, 1946. Despite installations that precede them, both Puerto Rico and Colón claim to be the first free trade zone.

12   Jean-Paul Marhoz and Marcela Szymanski, "Trade Union Campaign for a Social Clause, Behind the Wire: Anti-Union Repression in the Export Processing Zones" (1996), at http://actrav.itcilo.org

13   The countries using Kaohsiung as a model included: Ivory Coast, Liberia, Mauritania, Jordan, Columbia, Panama, Costa Rica, South Korea, South Vietnam, The Philippines, Indonesia, and India. See McCalla, "The Geographical Spread of Free Zones Associated with Ports," 129.

14   D. L. U. Jayawardena, "Free-Trade Zones," *Journal of World Trade* 17, no. 5 (1983), 433.

15   McCalla, "The Geographical Spread of Free Zones Associated with Ports," 132. It was not until 1978 that a zone was established in Sri Lanka. Bangladesh and Pakistan did not develop zones until 1980.

1967.[16] Prefiguring their later use as a market experiment in China, in 1963 the socialist country of Yugoslavia legislated trade zones along the Danube.[17]

Although descended from historic free ports, since the 1970s the zone had become a more thoroughly abstracted and formulaic instrument now distinct from the maritime spaces that had previously shaped trade. As container shipping became the global standard, wherever a plane could land or a truck could travel, new diasporic centers of global trade could develop—even in inland areas, borderlands, and backwaters that would never have sponsored the cosmopolitanism typically associated with global trade. Yet, as it opened its door to manufacturing and to new populations of workers, the zone also began to develop its own peculiar form of urbanity.

Maquiladoras, Tijuana, 2009

Keller Easterling

16   Walter H. Diamond and Dorothy B. Diamond, *Tax-Free Trade Zones of the World* (New York: Matthew Bender, 1986).

17   McCalla, "The Geographical Spread of Free Zones Associated with Ports," 129–30.

The Zone Is Extrastatecraft

Perhaps the most important factor contributing to the exponential growth of zones in the 1970s was an endorsement from the United Nations Industrial Development Organization (UNIDO). Established in 1966, UNIDO began to study and disseminate data and economic statistics about the zone as a prescription for developing countries. It established a Free Zone Unit to work with the Shannon Free Airport Development Company, Kaohsiung, and the World Bank to instruct potential zone developers. Shannon and Kaohsiung held seminars on EPZ formation around the world. By 1971, UNIDO claimed that "more than 30 developing countries" were seeking the "technical assistance services of UNIDO" in creating zones.[18] The zone was becoming a global contagion—a widely copied legal and economic template.

UNIDO characterized the zone as a temporary phenomenon that could jump-start economies. When no longer useful in one country, it would be taken up by another on the threshold of the global market. UNIDO even hoped to create an international "federation of free trade zones" that would convene representatives of governments around the world.[19]

---

18   Tsuchiya Takeo, "Introduction," *AMPO: Japan-Asia Quarterly Review, Special Issue on Free Trade Zones and Industrialization of Asia* (1977), 4. While Takeo refers to an organization with the acronym WIFZA, the World Economic Processing Zone Association (WEPZA) claims these same origins with 1978 as an inaugural year. In 1980, although there were other free zones of various types in both developing and developed countries, UNIDO listed the following developing countries as operating what it regarded to be export processing zones: Liberia, Malta, Mauritius, Senegal, and Tunisia in Africa; India, Malaysia, The Philippines, South Korea, Singapore, Sri Lanka, and Taiwan in Asia; Barbados, Belize, Brazil, Chile, Columbia, Dominican Republic, El Salvador, Guatemala, Haiti, Honduras, Jamaica, Mexico, Nicaragua, and Puerto Rico in Latin America; Egypt, Jordan, and Syria in the Middle East; and Western Samoa. See "Export Processing Zones in Developing Countries," in *UNIDO Working Papers on Structural Changes*, International Centre for Industrial Studies Global and Conceptual Studies Section (UNIDO, 1980).

19   Takeo, "Introduction," 4; and wepza.org. While initially established by UNIDO as an organization of governments, when WEPZA privatized in 1985 it was managed as an independent non-profit research organization. The director, Richard Bolin, had helped to prepare a 1964 study for the Mexican government that influenced the maquiladora program. As the WEPZA described itself, "the Institute is also active in educating governments, international organizations, and regional

Zone growth accelerated throughout the 1970s. In the United States alone, there was a dramatic increase from fewer than ten in 1970 to 118 by 1986.[20] Counting the number of free zones globally is, however, fraught with difficulty, since the form has been mutating as it migrates around the world. The Organization for Economic Cooperation and Development (OECD) and others often repeat the International Labor Organization (ILO) figures with tallies that reflect the recent exponential growth. In 1975, there were twenty-five countries and a global total of seventy-nine EPZs employing 800,000. By 1986, those numbers had nearly doubled. In 1997, 93 countries hosted 845 zones employing 22.5 million. In 2002, 116 countries hosted 3,000 zones employing 43 million. In 2006, 130 countries hosted 3,500 zones employing 66 million.[21]

As a legal and economic instrument, the zone presides over a cocktail of enticements and legal exemptions that are sometimes mixed together with domestic civil laws, sometimes manipulated by business to create international law, and sometimes adopted by the nation in its entirety. Incentives vary in every location but might include: holidays from income or sales taxes, dedicated utilities like electricity or broadband, deregulation of labor laws, prohibition of labor unions and strikes, deregulation of

and global trade organizations on the efficiency of EPZs in attracting Foreign Direct Investment to poor countries and the importance of their economic freedoms in many aspects of national and global development." The WEPZA was perhaps characteristic of the so-called "neoliberal" shift in global organizations from intergovernmental organizations with member nations to nongovernmental organizations with membership from private enterprises.

20   McCalla, "The Geographical Spread of Free Zones Associated with Ports," 131–2.

21   In 1986, forty-seven countries hosted 176 EPZs. See Michael Engman, Osama Onodera, and Enrico Pinali, "Export Processing Zones: Past and Future Role in Trade and Development," in *OECD Trade Policy Working Papers* (OECD Publishing, 2007), 12; Takayoshi Kusago and Zafiris Tzannatos, *Export Processing Zones: A Review in Need of Update* (Washington, DC: Social Protection Group, Human Development Network, World Bank, 1998), 5; Jean-Pierre Singa Boyenge, "ILO Database on Export Processing Zones" (Geneva: International Labour Office, 2007), 1, at ilo.org; and Thomas Farole and Gokhan Akinci, eds., *Special Economic Zones: Progress, Emerging Challenges and Future Directions* (Washington, DC: The World Bank, 2011).

environmental laws, streamlined customs and access to cheap imported or domestic labor, cheap land and foreign ownership of property, exemption from import/export duties, foreign language services, or relaxed licensing requirements.[22]

The host state also creates a legal entity, the zone authority, that has the power to negotiate with businesses and foreign governments. As an early free zone analyst wrote: "The exemptions granted to FTZ operators by these entities are exhaustive enough to strip the most stringent code of civil law of substance; in fact in most countries the FTZ investors cannot be sued in ordinary domestic courts by individuals." The FTZ thus often supplants "domestic ministries, courts, revenue offices, central banks, planning authorities, etc."[23]

A country may have strict laws regulating labor, the environment, sanitation, health and safety, or human rights, and it may be a signatory to global compacts. Yet the zone authority frequently has the power, in individual deals, to grant exception from any law. In other zones, the local government may help to manage the zone in exchange for a majority share, and, in theory, a state ministry for labor, environment, or economic affairs can work with the zone authority in implementing selective regulation. In communist countries and Middle Eastern kingdoms the state may retain even more control.[24]

While UNIDO initially promoted the EPZ, a 1980 report expressed caution about treating the format as anything other than a temporary catalyst. UNIDO evaluated a number of factors, from gender roles to the benefits of introducing new technologies into developing countries. They first determined that the form was attractive for both host and foreign countries because it strengthened collaboration between them and frequently created conditions better than those outside the zone. Yet the report also highlighted the dangers posed by the zone as it

---

22   Kusago and Tzannatos, *Export Processing Zones*, 6–7.

23   Jayawardena, "Free-Trade Zones," 428.

24   Xiangming Chen, "The Evolution of Free Economic Zones and the Recent Development of Cross-National Growth Zones," *International Journal of Urban and Regional Research* 19, no. 4 (1995), 595–6.

redirected national resources that might have been used to improve infrastructure, business platforms, and other potential relationships with foreign interests within the regular territory of the state. They argued that "the disadvantages of the EPZ would appear to lie in the continuation of their enclavistic nature. The choice facing host governments is whether to retain the enclave or to remove it. Perpetuation of the enclave will retain the problems, the social and economic costs, without the obvious off-set of further benefits." UNIDO recognized that the zone would be a losing proposition if it remained distinct from the rest of the host economy, yet it realized that the form would likely persist.[25]

OECD and World Bank publications similarly acknowledged that, rather than an EPZ, simple investment in a domestic economy was the best way to encourage trade and prosperity. Considering the associated infrastructure investments and lost tax revenue, the zone approach as opposed to the "enterprise approach" did not always yield significant value or "spill over" effects in the host country. The OECD characterized EPZs as "a suboptimal policy from an economic point of view."[26]

China's more powerful version of the zone would, however, soon turbocharge zone growth and turn it into a self-fulfilling prophecy.[27] In China, the zone often represented the first growth of a communist-style free market. As part of Deng Xiaoping's "Open Door" economic policies, the first five Special Economic

----

25   UNIDO, "Export Processing Zones in Developing Countries," 40–1. While UNIDO may have envisioned the zone as a temporary catalytic agent in a changing market environment, the zone authority was even able to issue legal guarantees that the host nation would not reabsorb zone territories.

26   See Engman, Onodera, and Pinali, "Export Processing Zones: Past and Future Role in Trade and Development," 6, 25, "Improvement of the business environment through trade and investment liberalization, establishment of good infrastructure, rule of law and administrative simplification remains the optimal policy option to promote investment, employment and growth." Kusago and Tzannatos, *Export Processing Zones*, 16–22. Labor representatives have called the zone a "health and environment 'time-bomb.'" See Jesper Nielsen, "Export Processing Zones or Free Zones—The Experience Seen from a Trade Union Point of View," at labour-inspection.org.

27   Gary Gereffi, "Development Models and Industrial Upgrading in China and Mexico," *European Sociological Review* 25, no. 1 (2009), 37, 40–1, 46–9.

Zones (SEZs) of the 1980s—Shenzhen, Xiamen, Shangtou, Zhuhai, and the entire province of Hainan—were planned as experiments with market economies. By 1984, China had created sixteen more zones. Since then, the country has established a multitude of special zones of various types, most of which diverge from the typical EPZ formula. An SEZ like Shenzhen is an entire city, including both business and residential programs. As the ILO tracked the zone in 2006, of the 66 million workers in the world's EPZs, only 26 million were employed outside of China. The country had generated it own category of zone phenomena.[28]

The Zone Is Breeding

As interest in the early EPZ form waned in 1980s and '90s, the zone began to breed more promiscuously with other enclave formats, or "parks," merging with container ports, offshore financial areas, tourist compounds, knowledge villages, IT campuses, and even museums and universities. It did not dissolve into the general business and industrial climate of its host country, but rather became a persistent yet mutable instrument, transforming as it absorbed more and more of the general economy within its boundaries. Reconsidering the role that their domestic labor was forced to play in the typical EPZ, many countries began to "upgrade" their zones, offering, instead of manufactured goods, services related to IT or finance.

Adapting to the growing knowledge economy, many of the early upgraded zones took the form of Science Industrial Parks (SIPs), based on the research park or campus.[29] Palo Alto's Stanford Research Park, established in 1951, was the model for scores of such parks in the United Saates, including Research Triangle Park in North Carolina (established in 1959 and becoming an FTZ in 1983), Cummings Research Park in Alabama

28   Engman, Onodera, and Pinali, "Export Processing Zones: Past and Future Role in Trade and Development," 8; and Boyenge, "ILO Database on Export Processing Zones," 1, at ilo.org.

29   Manuel Castells and Peter Hall, *Technopoles of the World: The Making of Twenty-First-Century Industrial Complexes* (London: Routledge, 1994).

(1962), and the Austin Technology Incubator in Texas (1989).[30]
The USSR built one of the first science cities in Siberia in 1957—
Akademgorodok (the Academic City), near Novosibirsk—but
more recent science cities have been based on the Asian SIPs.[31]
Japan developed Kyushu Silicon Island in 1965 and Tsukuba
Science City in 1968, along with fourteen other SIPs before the
1990s. Taiwan and South Korea, upgrading from processing
industries dependent on cheap labor, were also early adopters of
SIPs.[32] A number of high-tech parks for IT, electronics, and phar-
maceuticals appeared in China in the 1990s.

In 1991, the Indian government established Software
Technology Parks of India (STPI) to broker broadband from the
country's satellite fleet. As they attracted IT companies, Bangalore
and Hyderabad quickly developed cybercity programs and
helped to make the call center into a globally popular spatial
product. In Hyderabad's HITEC City, buildings resembling
futuristic spacecraft rose up in an otherwise dusty landscape.[33] In
2007, India added Special Economic Zone incentives to the mix
of infrastructural offerings. Building on a long-standing cultural
link to Mauritius, STPI was even engaged to advise the island
country on Ebene Cybercity, which began construction in 2001.
Bolstered by broadband from international submarine cable and
offering EPZ status throughout the entire country, Mauritius has

---

30   See rtp.org; and Diamond and Diamond, *Tax-Free Trade Zones of the World*. In 1983, RTP applied for Foreign Trade Zone status and has headquarters and warehouses as well as sites of over 800 acres that qualify as tax-free zones. RTP now has a population of almost 3 million and covers a sixty-mile radius. See Chen, "The Evolution of Free Economic Zones," 605.

31   The USSR also built a number of top-secret science cities like Sverdlovsk-45 for developing Cold War technologies. More recent science cities, some of which are located in the old science cities, include: Tomsk, Dubna, Zelenograd, and St. Petersburg. See Chen, "The Evolution of Free Economic Zones," 605.

32   Starting in 1980, Taiwan eventually established three science parks (Hsinchu Science Industrial Park, followed by Southern Taiwan Science Park and Central Taiwan Science Park); and South Korea, Singapore, France, the UK, and Germany also established SIPs. See http://eweb.sipa.gov.tw/en; singaporesciencepark. com; Meng, "The Theory and Practice of Free Economic Zones," 35–6; and Chen, "The Evolution of Free Economic Zones," 605.

33   See stpi.in; and Keller Easterling, *Enduring Innocence: Global Architecture and Its Political Masquerades* (Cambridge, MA: MIT Press, 2005), 135–60.

deployed new zone formulas to become one of the most prosperous countries in the African continent.[34]

In 1996, Malaysia's Multimedia Super Corridor (MSC) used the special economic zone as part of a national information technology initiative with urban ambitions on a different scale. Based on a study by McKinsey, the initiative would allow the country to leapfrog into the twenty-first century armed with IT skills, facilities, and educational institutions. The MSC established a 750-square-kilometer zone of incentivized urbanism between the Petronas Towers and the Kuala Lumpur International Airport, offering, for instance, premium infrastructure, tax exemption for ten years, and duty-free import of multimedia equipment. The plan was to develop cybercities and cybercentres around the urban hub of Cyberjaya.[35]

Enjoying quasi-diplomatic immunities, global corporations provided nations with support or expertise as well as credentials when seeking funding from the IMF or World Bank. Construction companies and infrastructure specialists like Bouygues, Bin-laden Group, Mitsubishi, Kawasaki, and Siemens delivered technologies for high-speed rail, automated transit, airport, and skyscraper engineering. Conglomerates such as PSA (Port of Singapore Authority), P&O, Hutchison Port Holdings, and ECT (European Container Terminals) served as post-colonial counterparts of the old British or Dutch East India Company franchises. To container ports around the world, they delivered automated transshipment and warehousing technologies, "just-in-time" management techniques, and other materials-handling expertise for sorting and tracking all of the contents of all of the containers moving between zones on increasingly larger and larger ships.[36]

---

34 See e-cybercity.mu.

35 See mscmalaysia.my.

36 For a discussion of the development of global automated ports see Easterling, *Enduring Innocence*, 99–122. In the 1990s, Schiphol Group launched their plans to manage and build twenty-four-hour "airport cities" worldwide. With Schiphol Airport as a model, they hoped to create a formula or spatial product that synchronized layover times with shopping times and optimized tonnage of freight and numbers of passengers. See panix.com/~keller/wildcards/

In 1995, the sociologist and political scientist Xiangming Chen sketched an evolution of zones in three stages. The first, from the mid-1500s to the 1930s, he associated with the free port and early free trade zones. The second, from the late-1950s into the '70s, was characterized by the inclusion of manufacturing EPZs such as maquiladoras. The third stage, beginning in the 1980s, saw the rise of the Special Economic Zones (SEZs), Economic and Technological Development Zones (ETDs), and Science Industrial Parks (SIPs). Chen also drew attention to the development of cross-border conurbations of zone formations on, for instance, the Tumen River between Russia and Korea, as well as cross-national growth zones in the South China Sea. These zones were beginning to aggregate opportunistically to circulate products between jurisdictions, trading exemptions and filling quotas within the complex engineering of supply chains.[37]

Following the perfectly paradoxical scripts of liberalism or neoliberalism, private-enterprise boosters have argued that the zone's evolution has repaired its reputation and that labor unions may be responsible for any further failures. Labor unions presumably manipulate the market, thus spoiling the purity of an instrument for manipulating the market. The World Export Processing Zone Association (WEPZA) recently claimed that, "While the old free zone was often described as a static, labor-intensive, incentive driven, exploitive enclave, the new zone paradigm is a dynamic, investment-intensive, management-driven,

---

Index.html. This 1999 website collects research about a range of spatial products including the proposed airport cities of Schiphol Group.

37   Chen, "The Evolution of Free Economic Zones." Chen settled on the term "Free Economic Zone" for all of these forms and speculated on the ensuing phases of growth. Building on this analysis, Guangwen Meng identified seven generations of FEZ development that largely conformed to those described by Chen. A first generation associated with trade evolves to a second that includes manufacturing. The third generation includes service and the fourth includes science. Meng designates the fifth generation as comprehensive, inclusive of many business and industry functions. The sixth and seventh he designates as cross-border and cross-national types, noting, as does Chen, that these conurbations often now operate independently from the local state jurisdiction but in multiple extrastate networks. See Meng, "Evolutionary Model of Free Economic Zones," 103.

enabling, and integrated economic development tool."[38] In 1985, the tax and foreign trade experts Walter H. Diamond and Dorothy B. Diamond launched a quarterly newsletter for investors that tracked and mapped tax-free trade zones across the world, considering them to be "utilities" that exist "to serve the public."[39]

In his 1995 book *The End of the Nation State: The Rise of Regional Economies*, a former McKinseyite, Kenichi Ohmae, sketched a new neoliberal region state that bore a strong resemblance to zone urbanism—a conurbation of 5–20 million people with an international airport and a harbor capable of handling international freight, all servicing a lean, Japanese-style multinational corporation. He claimed that region states would be blessed with a new economic freedom from state governance, and with boundaries that could only be "drawn by the deft but invisible hand of the global market."[40]

The increasing complexity of the zone has further confused those economists attempting to classify it, even as it has continued to spread in waves across the world. In addition to "EPZ," the most popular designation, a 1998 World Bank report tracked nineteen different terms for the zone.[41] By the first decade of the twenty-first century there were sixty-six terms in circulation.[42] None of the modes of classification coincide.[43] As the OECD

---

38   Robert C. Haywood, "Free Zones in the Modern World," in *World Economic Processing Zones Association, Evergreen, Colorado, USA, CFATF Meeting* (Aruba, 2000).

39   Diamond and Diamond, *Tax-Free Trade Zones of the World*.

40   Kenichi Ohmae, "The Rise of the Region State," *Foreign Affairs* 72, no.2 (1993), reprinted in Patrick O'Meara, Howard D. Mehlinger, and Matthew Krain, eds., *Globalization and the Challenges of a New Century* (Bloomington: Indiana University Press, 2000), 93, 95.

41   The list included: free trade zone, foreign trade zone, industrial free zone, free zone, maquiladora, export free zone, duty free export processing zone, special economic zone, tax free zone, tax free trade zone, investment promotion zone, free economic zone, free export zone, free export processing zone, privileged export zone, and industrial export processing zone. See Kusago and Tzannatos, *Export Processing Zones*, Annex 1.

42   Meng, "Evolutionary Model of Free Economic Zones," 103.

43   See wepza.org. The World Export Processing Zone Association, has, like the ILO and the OECD, kept databases tracking zone growth. The WEPZA

notes, "The diversity of EPZs is matched only by the diversity of terminology used by analysts."[44]

The urban world that the sociologist Manuel Castells described in *The Informational City: Information Technology, Economic Restructuring, and the Urban Regional Process* (1989), and the world that he and Peter Hall described in *Technopoles of the World: The Making of Twenty-First-Century Industrial Complexes* (1994), was, in part, the world of zone urbanism— what Castells called a space of information "flows." The zone was not an accumulation of buildings, but urban space as the product of more formulaic drivers. Digital capital created the landscapes of logistics and IT within which, as Kevin Kelly has written, cars were "chips with wheels" and airplanes were "chips with wings."[45]

---

categorizes the various types as "wide area"—zones with a residential population that act as new cities, such as China's Special Economic Zones; "small area"— zones smaller than 1,000 hectares and surrounded by a fence; "industry specific"—which includes those zones related to a particular industry, such as an offshore banking zone that can attract investment from anywhere in the world; and "performance specific"—zones that conform to established criteria such as "degree of exports, level of technology, size of investment etc"; a maquiladora or research park would be an example of this type. Meng, for instance, indentifies a number of cross-border zones in an area around the confluence of national borders between the Netherlands, Brussels, and Germany. Yet, according to WEPZA, there are no EPZs in Brussels. WEPZA has a designation for industry specific zones that would include offshore banking facilities, and yet while Dubai is an offshore facility for the whole of its territory, the UAE is listed as a country without industry specific zones. See Meng, "The Theory and Practice of Free Economic Zones," 104. A World Bank publication from 2011 listed four types of zones: Free Trade Zone, Traditional EPZ, Free Enterprises, Hybrid EPZ, and SEZ/Freeport; see Farole and Akinci, eds., *Special Economic Zones: Progress, Emerging Challenges and Future Directions*, 2.

44   Engman, Onodera, and Pinali, "Export Processing Zones: Past and Future Role in Trade and Development," 6–7.

45   Kevin Kelly, *New Rules for the New Economy* (New York: Penguin Books, 1998), 76.

Dubai Internet City, 2012

The Zone is a City

The zone, in its next incarnations, began to call itself a "city"—an enthusiastic expression of advancement since its origins in ware-housing and shipping. Some nations used EPZs as a means of announcing their entry into a global market and their availability as contractors of outsourcing and offshoring. Countless zones were called "cyber cities," "technocities," or "logistics cities," where "city" might describe a small office park anchored by one or two buildings. Nevertheless, Malaysia's Multimedia Super Corridor as well as China's SEZs were beginning to deliver an entire skyline of buildings. While banishing many of the circumstantial frictions of urbanity, the zone transformed itself into a model for the metropolis that welcomes every conceivable residential, business, or cultural program.

Just across the water from Hong Kong, one of the oldest and most powerful of free ports, Shenzhen, once an experimental enclave sited in a former fishing village, has ballooned into a megacity sprouting stalk after stalk of generic concrete skyscrapers. With a transient population of around 14 million, the SEZ has expanded over the years to encompass all seven districts of the city spread across approximately 2,000 square kilometers.[46] The entire city offers free zone privileges, although there are also distinct EPZs within the SEZ, like the Shekou Industrial Zone (SKIZ), that allow businesses to negotiate with a zone authority rather than the Guangdong Provincial Administration that controls Shenzhen SEZ. The SEZ offers a number of tax reductions or tax holidays and exemptions, but the biggest attractions for business are the low rent and cheap labor. There are incentives to create joint ventures and to initiate the desired high-tech industries. Most of the city's investment comes from Hong Kong—a competitor that nevertheless finds advantage in Shenzhen's throbbing growth.[47]

After a quarter century of growth, Shenzhen has also become a crucible for its own forms of civic activism. A new middle class has, on occasion, acted to protect its new property interests, organized a boycott to protest increasing real estate prices, or agitated against the construction of a new highway. Others have formed a research group, Interhoo, to monitor development activities or run for government office at the municipal or district level.[48] As an industrial coal smog envelopes the skyline, lax environmental rules, together with a seemingly inexhaustible source of inexpensive labor migrating from the hinterland, have compounded both the corruption and the pollution. There are also thousands of labor strikes each year and petitions for higher

---

46 See english.sz.gov.cn/gi/; and "A Work in Progress," *Economist*, March 17, 2011.

47 Expansion was intended to ease real estate prices in downtown Shenzhen while also providing more citizens with the better health care and education now available in the zone. See Diamond and Diamond, *Tax-Free Trade Zones of the World*; and Jayawardena, "Free-Trade Zones," 438.

48 Howard W. French, "In Chinese Boomtown, Middle Class Pushes Back," *New York Times*, December 18, 2006; see interhoo.com.

wages, but these can be squelched by the state.[49] The sheer size of this city, the distance between the modern downtown, the factory, and the underworld, comprises a complex urbanity, a city in the shadow of a repressive regime that nevertheless grows out of control in ways both productive and dangerous.[50]

As Shenzhen is to Hong Kong, Pudong is to Shanghai. Pudong was established as an SEZ in 1993 on the east bank of the Huangpu River. At 1,200 square kilometers it is comparable to the size of Shanghai and home to over 5 million people. With a skyline aspiring to signature rather than generic outlines, the central skyscrapers and hotels—the Oriental Pearl Tower, the Jin Mao Building, and the Shanghai World Financial Center among them—signal luxury and world-class facilities.

Shenzhen and Shanghai are part of "city clusters" in the Pearl River Delta Economic Zone and the Yangtze River Delta Economic Zone that develop industrial synergies. Sometimes the term "cluster cities," or "supply chain cities," refers to backstage installations that optimize the logistics of manufacturing for one type of product. But "supply chain cities" or "super factories" can also refer to zones that concentrate all the phases of production from design to manufacturing into one area to minimize shipping costs and compress schedules. For instance, Chaozhou specializes in wedding dresses and evening gowns, Shengzhou in ties, Datang and Zhuji in socks, Jinjiang and Shenhu in underwear, and Xintang and Zengcheng in jeans.[51]

Perhaps even more so than China, the UAE has used the zone to its distinct advantage—to control foreign influence, elevate the status of privileged nationals, and leverage the region's oil and gas to create diversified industries. Shenzhen is a city as zone, but

---

49 The All China Federation of Trade Unions, of which the Guangdong Federation of Trade Unions is a part, permits only trade union activity organized from within the state hierarchy. Organizations of migrant workers who frequently work in abusive and dangerous situations are without much recourse. See clb.org.hk.

50 Howard W. French, "Chinese Success Story Chokes on Its Own Growth," *New York Times*, December 19, 2006.

51 Gereffi, "Development Models and Industrial Upgrading in China and Mexico," 46–7.

Dubai is a city-state as zone. For Dubai—an ancient entrepôt of trading and smuggling recently reawakened by oil—the zone may have seemed remarkably familiar while nationhood may have seemed a bit like a quaint custom necessary to join a global club.

Dubai's first free-trade zone, the Jebel Ali Free Zone, was established in 1985. Since then, Dubai has rehearsed the "park" or zone with almost every imaginable program, such that its urban fabric is now an aggregate of zones, each of which has often been named a "city." There is Dubai Internet City, which opened in 2000 (the first to mix the IT campus with the free-trade zone), Dubai Health Care City, Dubai Maritime City, Dubai Silicon Oasis, Dubai Knowledge Village, Dubai Techno Park, Dubai Media City, Dubai Outsourcing Zone, Dubai Industrial City, Dubai Textile Village, and Dubai International City, among many others. Each enclave offers a different set of incentives including streamlined customs, inexpensive labor from South Asia and Africa, foreign ownership of property, or rights to own real estate in special projects like the Palm Islands.[52] Dubai is an offshore financial center for the whole of its territory. Each zone may even have its own laws. For instance, Dubai Media City, the headquarters for major news outlets, allows some freedom of speech not technically permitted elsewhere in the state of Dubai.[53]

The resident population in the UAE is not offered as cheap labor, but rather is the beneficiary of free trade and other special bargains of extrastatecraft. Inexpensive labor is imported from South Asia and elsewhere like machinery or other equipment. After becoming ruler in 1966, Sheikh Zayed issued land grants to each national to ensure they would profit from development, and by 1976 he had also offered 5,000 units of "people's housing."[54]

---

52   See freezonesuae.com.

53   Keller Easterling, "Extrastatecraft," in Kanu Agrawal, Melanie Domino, and Brad Walters, eds., *Perspecta 39, Re_Urbanism: Transforming Capitals* (2007), 2–16.

54   Mohammed Al-Fahim, *From Rags to Riches: A Story of Abu Dhabi* (London: The London Center of Arab Studies, 1995), 140; Frauke Heard-Bey, *From Trucial States to United Arab Emirates: A Society in Transition* (Dubai and Abu Dhabi: Motivate Publishing, 2004, first published by Longman, 1982), 405.

The land grants were similar in principle to the many other laws stipulating that partnerships or enterprises must include UAE nationals as either associates or beneficiaries. The UAE government also established a program to channel foreign investment into industries that would support the country's long-term goals.[55] Since the number of nationals is small, the UAE has managed to convert the typically corrupt relationship between government and private-interest lobbies into a form of hyper-representation for a manageable handful of constituents.[56]

After many cycles of breeding around the world, some surprising traits have surfaced in the Middle Eastern zone city. Dubai Humanitarian City, for instance, is an outpost of relief agencies and NGOs.[57] Abu Dhabi's Masdar City, established by the Abu Dhabi Future Energy Company, is a free zone for green-energy enterprises. Masterminded by Norman Foster, the zone's square grid resembles that of an ideal town, while the sectional shape of the city is designed for shade and solar energy collection. An underground channel for automated rapid-transit vehicles transfers to urban transportation technologies first developed in transshipment landscapes.[58] Qatar Education City uses the campus/park/zone model to provide headquarters for the franchises of major universities around the world. Corporate sponsorship makes of the university a kind of incubator of intelligence and manpower for the corporation as well as the region. While none of these programmatic ideas of greening, humanitarianism, or education are redemptive, each demonstrates the extreme mutability of the zone form.

---

55   See tec.tawazun.ae. The UAE Offset Program Bureau, recently renamed The Tawazun Economic Program, was established in 1992 to diversify the UAE's economy by partnering with defense contractors. These offset projects have funded a variety of industries including fish farms, air-conditioning, health care, agriculture, shipbuilding, banking, and education.

56   uaestatistics.gov.ae; uaeinteract.com.

57   See ihc.ae.

58   See masdarcity.ae. It is in this way that the zone may be a peculiar form of intentional community like the repeatable urban formats of Spain's Laws of the Indies or the experiments of defecting religious groups in the New World of the Americas.

مدينة الملك عبدالله الاقتصادية
King Abdullah Economic City

Rendering of city center, King Abdullah Economic City

In King Abdullah Economic City (KAEC), on the Red Sea near Jedda, the zone is again an aggregate component of a full-blown city. Launched in 2006 by the Saudi government and the Dubai real estate developers Emaar, the city will eventually cover 168 square kilometers (about the size of Brussels). The Saudis also plan to build Knowledge Economic City in Medina, Jazan Economic City in Jazan, and Prince Abdul Aziz bin Mousaed Economic City in Hail, among others. In KAEC (pronounced "cake"), the first area to be developed will be an industrial zone covering a third of the city's entire area. The zone will house its own worker's dormitory, mosque, and prayer rooms, but it is not clear whether workers will have full access to the other "high-class" and "prosperous" securitized areas of the city.

The KAEC plans also envisage a manufacturing zone called "Plastics Valley" as a means to take advantage of auxiliary petrochemical resources as well as an international container seaport with logistics, warehousing, and transshipment facilities. As the city continues to grow over the next fifteen years, it hopes to incorporate resort functions, e-governance, home automation, and a connection on the Mecca-Medina rail line—part of a larger network of high-speed rail planned for Saudi Arabia. Incentives for foreign investment include ownership of property, low-cost financing, exemptions from import duties, no personal income tax, and a minimal 20 percent corporate income tax.[59] Digital fly-throughs render KAEC as a golden city with both modern skyscrapers and references to traditional Islamic buildings—all serving as a monument to the state and its "wise leadership."[60]

The Zone Is a Double

Shenzhen is a double of Hong Kong. Pudong doubles Shanghai. CIDCO, the City and Industrial Development Company of Maharashtra, operating under the motto "We make cities," is making Navi Mumbai the double of Mumbai.[61] Not only has the zone become a city, but major cities and even national capitals are now engineering their own zone doppelgängers— their own non-national territories in which to create newer, cleaner alter-egos, free of any incumbent bureaucracy. The zone embodies what political scientist Stephen D. Krasner

---

59   See kingabdullahcity.com and "Saudi Arabia to Allow Foreign Ownership in KAEC," at arabianbusiness.com.

60   Emaar press release, September 12, 2006, at emaar.com.

61   CIDCO is to deliver infrastructure that is the zone standard: an airport, mass rapid transit, railway stations, industrial compounds, a harbor, a central park, a golf course, and residential areas. A similar company, SKIL Infrastructure Ltd., will contract for some portion of the infrastructure as a private-sector endeavor. Navi Mumbai will be equipped with infrastructural and legal environments like those in Shenzhen and Pudong—city-states with not only commercial areas but also a full array of programs. See cidco.maharashtra.gov.in and skilgroup.co.in.

calls "hypocritical sovereignty"—where nations operate between multiple jurisdictions with potentially conflicting allegiances and laws—or what international relations professor Ronen Palan calls "sovereign bifurcation," where "states intentionally divide their sovereign space into heavily and lightly regulated realms."[62] The world capital and national capital can now shadow each other, alternately exhibiting a regional cultural ethos, national pride, or global ambition. State and non-state actors use each other as proxy or camouflage as they juggle and decouple from the law in order to create the most advantageous political or economic climate.[63]

Hong Kong and Shenzhen are like twins who can trick the world or trick each other. Hong Kong uses its sister city as a source of cheap labor and rent; Shenzhen competes with Hong Kong while accepting investment from its businessmen. Shenzhen also smothers its island sibling with symbiotic overachievement. *China Daily* projects the mainland's ambitions when it chirps that, given Shenzhen's spectacular success, Hong Kong will surely want to form a single metropolitan region.[64]

---

62   Krasner describes several forms of sovereignty that the nation must juggle: Westphalian, Interdependence, Domestic, and Legal. The zone sometimes eliminates conflicts between these different jurisdictions to streamline relations with foreign investment even as it creates yet another independent jurisdiction. Stephen Krasner, *Sovereignty: Organized Hypocrisy* (Princeton: Princeton University Press, 1999), 3–25; Ronen Palan, *The Offshore World: Sovereign Markets, Virtual Places, and Nomad Millionaires* (Ithaca, NY: Cornell University Press, 2003), 8, 182. See also Roy E. H. Mellor, *Nation, State, and Territory: A Political Geography* (London: Routledge, 1989), 59.

63   This argument joins those of other scholars who note that new incarnations of statehood, like those the zone sponsors, strengthen rather than diminish the power of the state. As professor of urban theory Neil Brenner writes, "the notion of state rescaling is intended to characterize the transformed form of (national) statehood under contemporary capitalism, not to imply its erosion, withering, or demise." Neil Brenner, *New State Spaces: Urban Governance and the Rescaling of Statehood* (New York: Oxford University Press, 2004), 4.

64   "Shenzhen SEZ Aims to Be 5 Times Bigger," *China Daily*, May 22, 2009.

New Songdo City under construction

Conforming to a global standard, the promotional video for New Songdo City in South Korea flies in from outer space and through a digital model, accompanied by a new-age soundtrack from the Icelandic band Sigur Rós. A complete international city designed by Kohn Pedersen Fox, Songdo is a double of Seoul in an expansion of the Incheon free-trade territories. It is the "city in a box" that developer Stanley Gale plans to reproduce elsewhere in the world. Aspiring to the cosmopolitan urbanity of New York, Venice, and Sydney, the city has a Central Park, a World Trade Center, and a Canal Street, as well as commercial, residential, cultural, and educational programs including an international convention center, a hospital, a Jack Nicklaus golf course, office buildings, luxury hotels, and shopping malls. There are also additional free-trade zone areas like a "Techno-park" and a "Bio

Complex."[65] Songdo will eventually cover only 15,000 acres and house a projected population of a quarter of a million.[66] Yet it already claims to be a major world city, a "smart city," a "green city," an "aerotropolis," and "a commercial epicenter of Northeast Asia" that provides access to one-third of the world's population in three-and-a-half hours.[67] The video's emotional soundtrack targets international business families looking for a home in the "world community."[68]

In some cases, surpassing all irony, the national capital and the zone have become the same entity, making the zone itself the seat of governance from which it is selectively exempt.[69] In 1997, the capital of Kazakhstan was simply moved from the old city of Almaty to the more strategic Astana, forming a central SEZ called "Astana-New City."[70] Even though Astana has a population of a little more than 600,000, it calls itself a "megacity."[71] President Nursultan Nazarbayev unabashedly created a twenty-three-square-mile (5,900 ha) area in which the nation could advertise its market enticements and display urban buildings saturated with national pride and regional imagery.[72] Astana is, in many ways, part of a campaign to position Central Asia as a paleo-Genghis corridor ready to compete with Dubai.

65   See songdo.com.

66   Chungjin Kim, "A Study on the Development Plan of Incheon Free Economic Zone, Korea: Based on a Comparison to a Free Economic Zone in Pudong, China" (master's thesis, University of Oregon, 2007), 13. Korea's four main Free Economic Zones are Incheon, Busan, Jinhae, and Gwangyang.

67   For a discussion of the Airport City see John D. Kasarda and Greg Lindsay, *Aerotropolis: The Way We'll Live Next* (New York: Farrar, Straus and Giroux, 2011).

68   "A Brand New City," at songdo.com.

69   In Hong Kong, Macau, Singapore, Mauritius, Fiji, Gibraltar, and Thailand, zone laws are permitted throughout the entire territory. See Diamond and Diamond, *Tax-Free Trade Zones of the World*, Far East, iii.

70   "Privileges for Participants in Special Economic Zones," at http://invest. gov.kz.

71   "Industrial Zones," at jordaninvestment.com.

72   In line with other world powers, Kazakhstan develops conurbations in business park units called "cities." Alatau IT City, one example outside of Almaty, follows the familiar template and features mirror-tiled buildings and towers with monumental but indeterminate reference.

Bayterek Tower, Astana

In 1997, Kisho Kurokawa, the late Japanese Metabolist architect, designed an axial master plan for Astana-New City anchored by Norman Foster's pyramidal Palace of Peace and Reconciliation. The religiously neutral icon offers, at the top of the pyramid, a place of retreat and summit for world leaders—the zone as a permanent version of an Olympic opening ceremony. Joining Foster's pyramid was the Khan Shatyr (roughly translated as the "tent of the Khan"), a 500-foot-tall, 140,000-square-meter ETFE tent creating an interior microclimate for recreation, shopping, restaurants, and green space.[73] Colored lights illuminate the buildings, the graphic flower beds, and the expressive Bayterek observation tower. Multicolored fountains and water shows, like those in Las Vegas or Macau, are

---

73   See fosterandpartners.com.

also recognized as necessary accoutrements of the new zone.[74] In 2010, three days of celebrations—coinciding with Nazarbayev's seventieth birthday—marked the opening of the indoor park with its monorail, tropical zone, wave machine, and beach. A performance by Andrea Bocelli, together with a circus and other spectacles, entertained the world leaders who gathered for the event.[75]

The Zone Prefers Non-State Violence

Administered by an authority independent from the state and able to grant a raft of legal exemptions, the zone would appear to be a quintessential example of a state of exception.[76] The zone aspires to lawlessness, but it is also distinct from the legal tradition of exception that applies to a nation. Zones cheat just as most maritime city-states have cheated for centuries, and in cross-national or cross-border growth zones products may circulate between a constellation of zones taking advantage of different laws, wage scales, or factory quotas.[77] Zones preside over a mongrel form of exception that is more resilient and potentially more insidious. The matrix of exceptions—between state and non-state jurisdictions—is harder to trace than the kind of exception associated with a single emergency of the state. While seeking out relaxed, tax free, extrastate spaces, businesses may also lobby for legislation in their home state, in order to promote, for instance, favorable trade agreements.

---

74   See astana.gov.kz/en/.

75   "Giant Indoor Park Opened for Kazakh President's Birthday," at telegraph. co.uk.

76   The state of exception, a legal concept deployed by the German jurist Carl Schmitt, granted the Third Reich an exemption from law during a moment of war or emergency—essentially legalizing the lawlessness of the concentration camps and other atrocities. Giorgio Agamben's recent analysis considers the state of exception in light of Roman law and as a spatial entity—the camp. He suggests that the idea of the camp is even naturalized in ordinary spaces—the *"zones d'attentes* of our airports and certain outskirts of our cities." Georgio Agamben, *Homo Sacer: Sovereignty, Power and Bare Life* (Stanford: Stanford University Press, 1995), 175.

77   Chen, "The Evolution of Free Economic Zones"; and Xiangming Chen, *As Borders Bend: Transnational Spaces on the Pacific Rim* (Lanham, MD: Rowman & Littlefield Publishers, 2005).

Rendering of residential villas, King Abdullah Economic City

In the zone, war is bad for business. The zone harbors not the violence of nations but the violence camouflaged by nations, and while some zones advertise their presence, others remain hidden. From its inception, the most overt and routine forms of violence have been aimed at workers. The zone has been a site for the fabled "3D" jobs (dirty, dangerous, and demeaning), as well as one of the chief instruments in the so-called race to the bottom—the competition between countries to provide the cheapest labor and the most deregulated conditions at the expense of workers and the environment. The 2013 Rana Plaza collapse in the Dhaka EPZ in Bangladesh revealed a list of retailers like Wal-Mart that had located production in Bangladesh because the wages were at the lowest end of the scale. Every player in that disaster had cheated the rules or chiseled the budgets to deliver inexpensive labor.[78]

---

78   Sarah Butler and Saad Hammadi, "Rana Plaza Factory Disaster: Victims Still Waiting for Compensation," *Guardian,* October 23, 2013.

Yet the zone is also capable of organizing a form of labor exploitation that is relatively stable within the law. Workers confront unsafe, strenuous, physically abusive, and psychologically intimidating situations. They have a job, but their wages fail to support a decent standard of living. Attempts to organize or form labor unions are squelched with lockouts, threats, and firings. Accusations of abuse or unsafe conditions may trigger an audit, but the audit will then be carried out after the accusers have been fired or during a temporary cleanup. Companies also dodge charges of abuse by simply disappearing or changing their name.

Since the zone's profits are quarantined and allowed to return directly to the multinational enterprise, there may be few lasting dividends for the host country. And if one country decides it is no longer proud to offer up its citizens as cheap labor, the zone will simply migrate to another poorer country, or will import the cheap labor like any other component of the industrial process.

In her discussion of "zoning technologies," the anthropologist Aihwa Ong notes that Carl Schmitt's definition of exception is a useful tool in analyzing the "variegated sovereignty" present in global trade. Yet, she argues, "The sovereign exception that I am interested in here is not the negative exception that suspends civil rights for some but rather positive kinds of exception that create opportunities, usually for a minority, who enjoy political accommodations and conditions not granted to the rest of the population."[79] In the altered landscape of neoliberalism, populated by new institutions of governance (e.g., NGOs, IGOs) and by states that have given up some of their power to proxies, she finds both new dangers and new opportunities.[80] Intermediary organizations may act as watchdogs, support groups, voluntary

---

79 Aihwa Ong, *Neoliberalism as Exception: Mutations in Citizenship and Sovereignty* (Durham, NC: Duke University Press, 2006), 103, 7.

80 Similarly, the philosopher Etienne Balibar considers the possible instrumentality of intermediary organizations outside of the state's limited palette of options for labor in a global market. See Etienne Balibar, *We, the People of Europe?: Reflections on Transnational Citizenship* (Princeton, NJ: Princeton University Press, 2004).

regulatory agencies, or, alternatively, as administrative shills for camouflaging, even perpetuating, abuses. Ong suggests that, rather than deliver laws and protections through citizenship (an offering that many workers do not even want), the cartography of this NGO constellation might render stronger and more salient forms of leverage.[81]

The ILO, the International Trade Union Confederation (ITUC), and the International Textile Garment and Leather Workers Federation are among the most prominent organizations in a much larger network of NGOs that have been monitoring the zone and advocating for worker's rights for over forty years. The ITUC has fought for a social clause in WTO agreements that will ensure minimum labor standards, including freedom of association, collective bargaining, and the abolition of forced labor, child labor, and labor discrimination.[82] The ILO has compiled a similar list of standards, but while many of the countries hosting the zones are signatories, the United States and most of the major Western powers are not.

In the absence of any other rights, often the only legal instrument that labor can use to redress grievances is a contract. In Dubai, workers can call a Ministry of Labor hotline to register a complaint. The Ministry of Labor can pressure a contractor to make restitution, or it can deport either the laborers or the contractors. In some cases, third parties that train, support, or contract workers in various locations have the power to create contractual pressures. There have also been riots and demonstrations that engaged both the Ministry of Labor and the police.[83]

The labor compounds in some of the more recent zones have become areas cordoned off *within* the global city. Many zones now have a new model village for labor, with sports fields

---

81   Ong, *Neoliberalism as Exception*, 12–13, 21.

82   The ITUC was formerly the International Confederation of Free Trade Unions or ICFTU. See Marhoz and Marcela, "Trade Union Campaign for a Social Clause, Behind the Wire: Anti-Union Repression in the Export Processing Zones", at http://actrav.itcilo.org.

83   See mol.gov.ae.

and air-conditioned dormitories. One such labor village forms part of Dubai Industrial City, located some distance from the center of Dubai. The workers in these villages often have insufficient funds to travel within the cities where they work, and thus have no choice but to board the bus that takes them back to the labor camp—far enough away from the city center to ensure they will not be seen. A Shenzhen worker, for example, asked if he ever visited the downtown skyscrapers and shopping malls, replied saying that he had never had the time: "I have to work every day."[84]

Countries claiming to have upgraded their zones have often portrayed them as essential tools for generating jobs and training. WEPZA advisor Richard Bolin continued to promote the zone in newsletters, once even quoting a 2001 letter from Peter Drucker claiming that "to create wealth, jobs and incomes in desperately poor countries, it [WEPZA] is the only poverty program that works."[85] The IT campuses in India and Malaysia insist on the presence of an educational institution to offer their citizens substantial training in software writing. Zones may also offer childcare and community or global contacts for young entrepreneurs. Some countries claim that the jobs outside the zone are far worse than those inside.[86]

Yet, despite the so-called upgrades, some of the zone's problems have simply been camouflaged. A clean, air-conditioned, high-tech firm like Foxconn in Shenzhen is a mega-mutation of the typical zone factory. As the world's biggest electronics maker, it is the Wal-Mart of zone suppliers, with 800,000 employees wearing crisp white overalls. Foxconn experienced a rash of worker suicides in 2010 that appeared to be a consequence of overwork in the highly regimented conditions as well as

---

84   French, "Chinese Success Story Chokes on Its Own Growth."

85   See wepza.org. Richard Bolin was an original advisor to WEPZA when it was established by UNIDO in 1978. In 2003, he was named "Director Emeritus" of WEPZA. The WEPZA website includes a number of his undated "editorials" promoting zone development.

86   Author interview with Tariq Yousef, Global Art Forum, Doha, Qatar, March 17, 2013. Yousef is a director of Silatech, an initiative promoting youth employment and entrepreneurship in the Arab world.

intimidation, stress, and isolation from family and friends. Most of the big brand names in electronics use components made by Foxconn, and claim to have reviewed the conditions at the factories. Steve Jobs was quoted as saying that the Foxconn facilities were "not a sweatshop."[87] The Fair Labor Association's relatively positive assessment of Foxconn has drawn further criticism since the NGO is partially funded by companies like Apple.[88]

While the zone often delivers the slow, debilitating, extrastate violence of denial, it can nevertheless exacerbate the larger military conflicts between states. For instance, in Khartoum, the capital of Sudan, development experts from Abu Dhabi and Dubai helped the Alsunut Development Company to plan Almogran, a project of 1,660 acres of skyscrapers and residential properties at the confluence of the White and Blue Nile. While the project may never go forward, the north's plans for overt expressions of oil wealth are the very things that intensify tensions between Sudan and the new country of South Sudan.[89] In the promotions for Al-Mogran—laced with persuasions about brotherhood and unity—the disconnect between rhetoric and disposition were all too apparent. Similarly, since 1967, Israel has been using zones as well as settlements to develop outposts in Palestinian territory in East Jerusalem and the West Bank. Offering wages to Palestinians workers that are difficult to refuse, zones have been characterized as a benefit. Still, those workers, in order to survive, must indirectly support the Israeli occupation.[90]

The Zone Is on Vacation

Operating in a frictionless realm of exemption, the zone quite naturally adopts the scripts of the resort and theme park, with

---

87   David Barboza, "Electronics Maker Promises Review after Suicides," *New York Times*, May 26, 2010; "After Suicides, Scrutiny of China's Grim Factories," *New York Times*, June 7, 2010.

88   "Fair Labor Association Finds Progress at Apple Supplier Foxconn," at fairlabor.org.

89   "Glittering Towers in a War Zone," *Economist*, December 7, 2006.

90   Jodi Rudoren, "In West Bank Settlements, Israeli Jobs Are Double-Edged Sword," *New York Times*, February 11, 2014.

their ethereal aura of fantasy. IT campuses in India and Malaysia sometimes even refer to themselves as *resorts*. Here, businesses are "members" in a special mixture of small-scale vernacular buildings and shiny offices set in lush vegetation. The transient workers, businessmen, and tourists create a temporary population that, like temporary agreements and shifting identities, is good for business. The tourists arrive to spend their vacation money at shopping festivals, golf tournaments, and theme parks, and leave without making any demands on government.

In keeping with its maritime history, the zone often gravitates to island retreats. In China, the largest SEZ, the island of Hainan, has some industrial facilities, but it largely attracts Japanese investment for beachside resort installations. Macau, which along with Hong Kong is a Special Administrative Region (SAR), remains a global tourist destination with special rules permitting gambling and other indulgences previously available on the Portuguese colony before independence in 1999. Since 1965, the United States Foreign Trade Zone Number Nine—a series of duty-free areas in Hawaii—has mixed free-trade business activity with tourism.[91] Dubai has marketed and expanded its waterfront resorts for expat businessmen, and is one of the top vacation destinations in the Middle East.

Jeju, off the coast of Korea, is a quintessential island retreat that, like many others, has sheltered all those programs or illicit activities that do not fit into the logics of the mainland. Yet today it has transformed itself from a penal colony and strategic military position into a "free economic city." Citing Dubai, Singapore, and Hong Kong as models, the Jeju island zone "guarantees the maximum convenience for the free flow of people, goods, and capital and for tax free business activities." A place of ecological purity, boasting casinos and a golfer's "amnesty" (a 50 percent reduction in green fees), this corporate retreat also hosts global sporting events and diplomatic summits.[92]

Already the perfect spatial instrument for externalizing

---

91 Diamond and Diamond, *Tax-Free Trade Zones of the World.*
92 See jeju.go.kr.

obstacles to profit, most zones also function as tax havens of some sort, and some merge the island resort with the offshore financial center. British territories like the Cayman Islands, the Turks and Caicos Islands, Anguilla, Bermuda, the British Virgin Islands, Gibraltar, Montserrat, and the Channel Islands are at the core of a global money-sheltering network that radiates from the City of London. Beyond the outposts of former colonial possessions, there are now many other such global networks tied to New York, as well as cities in the Middle East, Central Asia, and China. A company like Halliburton that receives US contracts paid by taxpayer dollars is perfectly free to move its headquarters from Houston to Dubai to take a break from taxes. The zone is also a natural interstice in the networks of transfer-pricing games in which corporations inflate the prices of items moved internally to hide profits or take advantage of currency differentials.[93] Investigative journalist Nicholas Shaxson has assembled evidence indicating that "over half of all bank assets, and a third of foreign direct investment by multinational corporations, are routed offshore." As offshore practices become more prevalent and as they collide with global lending and corrupt governments or individuals, the zone can become the vortex of an enormous drain of capital.[94]

No longer relying merely on a hidden address or a bit of server space, countries now deploy elaborate forms of high-profile urbanism to celebrate the vacation from taxes as a sound economic tool essential to the operation of global corporations. Such corporations are often only reservoirs for liberated money, and real estate operators will outfit the zone with the spatial environments and amenities that appeal to this kind of wealth. While corporate headquarters around the world once portrayed a sober atmosphere of

---

93   John Christensen, "Dirty Money: Inside the Secret World of Offshore Banking," in Steven Hiatt, ed., *A Game as Old as Empire: The Secret World of Economic Hit Men and the Web of Global Corruption* (San Francisco: Berrett-Koehler Publishers, 2007), 41–68.

94   Nicholas Shaxson, *Treasure Islands: Uncovering the Damage of Offshore Banking and Tax Havens* (Palgrave Macmillan, 2012), 11, 14, 16, 88, 140–1; James Henry, *Blood Bankers: Tales from the Underground Global Economy* (New York and London: Four Walls Eight Windows, 2003), xxiii–xxxii.

business-like competence, the new-style headquarters often project an image of kingdoms with unlimited wealth.

Dariush Grand Hotel, Kish

Harking back to its history as an ancient crossroads of traders and explorers like Marco Polo and Ibn Batuta, the island of Kish, off the coast of Iran, became a free-trade zone shortly after the revolution. The Kish Free Zone Organization provides spaces for warehousing and business as well as the regular menu of tax and duty exemptions to which corporations have grown accustomed. The island is also notorious for allowing a loosening of headscarves and greater opportunities for socializing between men and women. It is the third most popular tourist destination in the Middle East offering resorts, malls, and other leisure activities as extra incentives. Nearby fantasy hotels like the Dariush Grand Hotel recreate the grandeur of Persian palaces with peristyle halls, gigantic cast stone sphinxes, and ornate bas-reliefs depicting ancient scenes—a perfect place for petrodollars to get away and relax.[95]

The Zone Launders Identities

Yet the zone launders more than money. Countries just entering the global marketplace may use the zone as a front while maintaining the purity of state rhetoric. China's SEZs are the model of this phenomenon. In 1993, following the Chinese, North Korea's law on Free Economic and Trade Zones established the usual set of tax exemptions and options for foreign investment in Rajin-Sonbong, and the country has since established other economic free zones. Some of these contribute to the vast zone conurbations that continue to proliferate in the Tumen River Region between the DPRK and Russia. The Stalinist dynasty of DPRK understood the zone protocols so well they even characterized their Mount Kumgang resort near the Demilitarized Zone as a "special tourist zone."[96]

Announced in 2009, the newest Russian science city, Skolkovo, near Moscow, departs from the previous norms for secret science compounds while also distancing itself from the Russian state bureaucracy. Like many new sparkling cities, it has attempted to attract famous global architects and world-class businesses with its incentivized urbanism. Part of Skolkovo's laundered identity relies on its membership in the TECHNOPARK-Allianz. Founded in 2002, this global federation is a network of branded communities including Aargau, Luzern, Winterthur, Zürich, and now Skolkovo. Demonstrating that the city itself has become an *uber*-transnational spatial product, all members must adhere to the network's method for creating urbanism.[97]

---

95   See kish.ir.

96   For a discussion of the Mount Kumgang resort see Easterling, *Enduring Innocence*, 15–38.

97   Aleksander Vekselberg, "The Politics of Innovation: Skolkovo and its Impact on the Modernization of Russia," senior thesis, Yale University, 2011; see also

AllianceTexas, north of Ft. Worth, a classic corporate city as office park and distripark, redistributes many of the products made in Mexico under NAFTA agreements so that they can be sold in the United States for a profit. Designated in 1993 as the 196th Foreign Trade Zone in the United States, AllianceTexas is a planned city with a broad range of urban programs in a 17,000-acre site, approximately 10,000 acres of which is the actual Foreign Trade Zone with a freight airport and huge intermodal installation.[98] Subsuming the name of the state within its own name, AllianceTexas, as a global space dropped into a national space, wears "Texas" as a brand.[99] Pushing goods through AllianceTexas, the US auto industry now relies on a new Detroit composed of a constellation of manufacturing sites from Mexico to Canada.[100]

Some zones launder products in the name of diplomacy. Different from the industrial zones that Israel has established in the West Bank and East Jerusalem, Qualifying Industrial Zones (QIZs) are a special zone variant legislated by the United States in 1996. In the QIZ, Israel and either Jordan or Egypt are encouraged to collaborate in making a product. Those products are granted duty-free access to the United States as long as Israel has contributed a percentage of their value—8 percent for Israel-Jordan and 11.7 percent for Israel-Egypt.[101] Filling the remaining percentages, many companies from all over the world can operate in the QIZ and take advantage of the duty-free access to the US market. In Jordan in 1998, the Al-Hassan Industrial Estate in Irbid was designated as the first QIZ, and by 2010 six more

Natalia Kolenikova, "A Russian Silicon Valley Is Being Built from Scratch," *New York Times*, April 11, 2010.

98   Diamond and Diamond, *Tax-Free Trade Zones of the World*.

99   See alliancetexas.com.

100   Diamond and Diamond, *Tax-Free Trade Zones of the World*.

101   See qizegypt.gov.eg. Thirty-five percent of the entire value of the product must be derived from work in the actual zone in either Egypt or Jordan. Portions of each zone must be in both partnering countries, but they need not be contiguous. Although there are other sectors in play, in most cases the QIZ protocol applies to industries that import fabric from Israel, often at a relatively high price, and then export garments to the United States.

"specialized investment compounds" were established.[102] Egypt did not enter the QIZ program until 2005, but has since established fifteen QIZ sites.[103]

Many of the QIZ employ inexpensive workers, most of whom are women. In Jordan some of these workers even come from the nearby Palestinian refugee camps. Still, some Chinese, Sri Lankan, and Bangladeshi manufacturers have found that it is cheaper to import labor from southern Asia. The ILO alleges that forced labor and trafficking occur in the QIZs.[104] In her studies of the Al-Hassan Industrial Estate, filmmaker Ursula Biemann concludes that "the poorest and most marginalized segments of the population, the Palestinian refugees, find themselves ironically tied into an economic agreement that normalizes the very relations that segregate them." In Biemann's film, the young women in the factory, wearing work smocks and head scarves, smile because they are shy about being filmed. They hold up the finished product: a flesh-colored girdle for Victoria's Secret stamped "Made in Israel." [105]

In 2011, the Institute for Global Labour and Human Rights began reporting cases of serial rape and abuse that had been occurring since at least 2007 in the Classic Fashion Apparel factory in Jordan. The considerable amount of evidence they collected caught the attention of the global press and exposed clients of the factory like Wal-Mart, Target, Macy's, Lands' End, Hanes, and Kohl's. Better Work Jordan, an organization partnered with the ILO, claims that it has been unable to substantiate the allegations.

102   See "Qualifying Industrial Zones" at moital.gov.il. Recent QIZ include the Al-Hussein Ibn Abdullah II Industrial Estate in Al Karak, the Aqaba Industrial International Estate in Aqaba, Al-Tajamouat Industrial City in Amman, Ad-Dulayl Industrial Park near Zarqa, Cyber City in Irbid, and Al-Mushatta and Hallabat Industrial Park in Zarqa. See jordaninvestment.com.

103   See the FAQ at qizegypt.gov.eg.

104   See "Forced Labour and Trafficking In Jordan—A Pilot Programme on the Qualified Industrial Zones," at ilo.org.

105   Biemann and Oroub El-Abed, then a PhD at the Graduate Institute of International and Development Studies (IHEID) in Geneva, were among the first to research and film the QIZ in Jordan. Biemann's video research, *X-Mission*, features interviews with Oroub El-Abed. A web article, "The Refugee-Industrial Complex: The QIZ in Jordan," at arteeast.org, provides additional information.

Nevertheless, it acknowledges that "there may be a culture of quid pro quo sexual harassment at the factory in question," and notes that 25 percent of all "Jordanian garment workers feel that sexual harassment is a concern for workers in their factory." Meanwhile, to cleanse a tarnished image, the Classic Fashion Apparel website bristles with certifications and awards from ISO and other organizations. The site provides virtual tours of its bright, clean factories as well as photos of nearby dormitories. It congratulates itself on championing sustainability, corporate social responsibility, and progressive labor relations, all accompanied by images of smiling workers.[106]

The Zone Is Its Own Antidote

In some ways, the only reason for the universal appeal and continual proliferation of the zone has been the continual proliferation of the zone. Although rationalized by many experts, perhaps its popularity stems less from economic principles, and more from irrational social and cultural desires to conform to a global norm. Despite everything learned from the EPZs, thirty years after their most explosive growth spurt, there is a persistent belief that the form can continue to help the world's developing countries as a reliable economic instrument. Each uninitiated country angles for a new zone as their ticket into the global market. Each also anticipates the jobs that the zone may bring. Decades later, poorer countries like Kenya are eagerly awaiting fresh new SEZs, even as their own business and technical innovations may have outgrown the form.

Even as many projects fail, countries continue to play a confidence game with the global market, announcing fluid plans and gambling heavily, perhaps even recklessly, on the zone or on new cities supported by zones. Countries and companies with zone

---

106   See "Campaigns" at globallabourrights.org; "Sex Abuse Alleged at Apparel Maker," *Wall Street Journal*, June 30, 2011, B3; "Major American Brands Silent on Alleged Rights Abuses at Overseas Factories," *Huffington Post*, July 21, 2011; and "Response to Classic Fashion Apparel Industries Allegations," at http://betterwork.org; classicfashionapparel.com

expertise export the form as a heavy industry and a new foreign outpost. Lekki Free Zone—the largest free zone in West Africa and a double of Lagos—continues its expansion, with Chinese, not Nigerian, interests as the largest stakeholders.[107] India is building the $90 billion Delhi Mumbai Industrial Corridor with nine "mega-industrial zones," high-speed rail, three ports, six airports, and a superhighway funded in large part by Japanese loans.[108] On the other side of the world, Korean entrepreneurs have proposed a new science city called Yachay for the highlands of Imbabura north of Quito in Ecuador.[109] While the project has now been canceled, in April of 2012, Georgia announced plans for the new city of Lazika near the Black Sea. The customary promotional video scanned golf courses, fields of identical cartoon villas, and a cluster of skyscrapers that, sited on a swamp, would require foundations eighty feet deep.[110]

Fueling growth of the form, stories about the zone as a rational economic instrument join stories about the liberalism, freedom, and openness it promises to deliver. The zone is a quintessential apparatus of the neoliberal state, a mascot of "Washington Consensus" economics.[111] Yet paradoxically, state

---

107   See lfzdc.com and lekkizone.com.

108   See delhimumbaiindustrialcorridor.com. The author is indebted to Swarnabh Ghosh for sharing his research on DMIC.

109   See yachay.ec.

110   Ellen Barry, "On Black Sea Swamp, Big Plans for Instant City," *New York Times*, April 22, 2012. See also "New City Lazika" on YouTube. Giorgi Vashadze, a deputy minister of justice, "was browsing on the Internet when he came across the idea of a 'charter city,' with distinct regulatory and judicial systems that could attract foreign investors to build factories." A charter city is similar to a special economic region. Like a zone variant, it uses foreign investment to establish a new city with an autonomous government. Some exemptions from law may also be granted. See also "Lazika Construction to be Stopped in Georgia," *Black Sea News*, October 10, 2012. See blackseanews.net.

111   Referencing an argument of geographer Bae-Gyoon Park, urbanist Jonathan Bach describes the zone as a tool for selectively implementing neoliberal policies. Jonathan Bach, "Modernity and the Urban Imagination in Economic Zones," *Theory, Culture & Society*, 28, no. 5 (September 2011), 105. See also Bae-Gyoon Park, "Spatially Selective Liberalization and Graduated Sovereignty: Politics of Neo-liberalism and 'Special Economic Zones' in South Korea," *Political Geography* 24 (2005), 850–73.

将这个地区规划建设成为格鲁吉亚的经济特区
Georgian government is planning to develop Anaklia and making it
a special economic region in Georgia (hereinafter referred to as SER)

Promotional video, New City Lazika, Georgia

bureaucracy may be merely replaced with a more complex extra-state administration. The zone offers a clean, relaxed, air-conditioned, infrastructure-rich urbanism that is more familiar to the world than the context of its host country. Yet the masquerade of freedom and openness turns very easily to evasion, closure, and quarantine. Zones foster self-reflexive networks, and the same subset of corporations stick together in legal habitats that can be recreated anywhere in the world. The optimized, RFID-tagged zone promotes fluid, information rich, and error free environments. Yet because it only receives or recycles compatible information in closed loop, there is also the risk of what the industry calls "control error"—a potentially fatal denial of information to maintain the status quo.[112]

The story that the zone is a perfectly apolitical city is also decoupled from its reality on the ground. Not yet a site of intensified urbanity, the zone is often a place of secrets, hyper-control, and segregation. It oscillates constantly between closure and

112   For a discussion of "special stupidity" see Easterling, *Enduring Innocence*, 195.

reciprocity as a fortress of sorts that orchestrates a controlled form of cheating. Moreover, as the entrepôt of the world's resources, the zone, despite its attempts to be apolitical, invariably ends up in the crosshairs of pirates, terrorists, and traffickers of all kinds.

Yet all the paradoxical stories together with the mutability of the zone suggest that this, the MS-DOS of urban software, might be productively hacked. Despite its internal isomorphism, the global epidemic of zone building also means that it has become a powerful multiplier, one capable of carrying messages that unravel the zone formula itself. Its ubiquity represents at once a threat and opportunity. The first hack to the zone formula might deploy any number of active forms related to, for example, labor, the environment, building construction, telecommunications, or security—forms that might circulate within a population of zones with compounding effects. Reconditioning a transnational network already in place, these multipliers can encourage alternative urban dispositions and political goals.

Yet the most important manipulation of the zone software is even simpler. The wisest urban entrepreneurs will ask a question already posed by some of the earliest critics of the zone: Why create an enclave? Despite the infrastructure conditions that existed at the advent of the zone, and despite its antecedents in fenced compounds, how does incentivized urbanism benefit from being physically segregated from the urban space of existing cities? What are the economic and technical benefits that accrue from constructing a double of the city? The new zone entrepreneurs may find in the enclave not freedom but entrapment, just as do many of the transient populations who labor within them. Of the many irrationalities driving the development of the zone, the enclave may be the least productive component.

Zone incentives can be mapped onto existing cities instead of exurban enclaves, thus returning zone operations to the rule of law and bringing more financial benefits to the domestic economy. Different from an object form as master plan and more like an active form as contagion, this simple shift could have enormous impact on contemporary global urbanism. The most highly prized zone models—Singapore, Hong Kong, and Dubai—are already city-states. Given the zone's ambition to be a city, perhaps ironically, it is the carrier of its own reversal or antidote—an antidote that can be multiplied throughout the global population of zones.

Rather than giving away national assets in exchange for the zone, a more transparent bargain with foreign investment uses the existing city as a medium of information and intelligence— the other half of an interplay that leverages more infrastructure and resources. The next countries in line to adopt the zone might surprise the global consultancies and financial institutions that are pushing the form in its current state. They might proudly offer *selected* economic incentives as well as the symbolic capital that attends higher labor and environmental standards. A program to eliminate the expense of the old mirror-tiled skyline and to reinvest in the city itself would set these countries apart in the next negotiations of extrastatecraft.

CHAPTER 2

Disposition

Highways, first promoted with stories about freedom and uninterrupted movement, possessed an organizational logic that actually caused congestion. ARPAnet, first characterized as a stealth network for the military, lent itself to the kinds of exchanges that finally generated the internet. Promises of decentralization accompanied the first electrical utilities, just as promises of open access have accompanied contemporary broadband networks. Yet both networks, at certain junctures in their evolution, have sponsored constricting monopolies, whether scattered or centralized. The mass-produced suburbs sold unique country homes but delivered the virtually identical products of an assembly-line organization. Facebook, a platform created for social networking on a college campus, revealed another initially unrecognized potential when, in the Arab Spring, it was used as an instrument of dissent. Likewise the zone, created and promoted as a tool of free trade and economic liberalism, has often produced closed, exurban enclaves.

In all these cases, some of the most consequential political outcomes of infrastructure space remain undeclared in the dominant stories that portray them. Information resides in the technologies—from telecommunications to construction—as well as in the declared intent or story—from decentralization to stealth. Yet information also resides in a complex of countless other factors and activities. All these activities, taken together, lend the organization some other agency or capacity—a disposition—that often escapes detection or explanation.

Reading disposition in infrastructure space is like Twain's reading of the water's surface. The shiny new technology or the persuasive promotional story may command attention just like the pretty landscapes of the river, but in excess of that material, spatial organizations are always providing information about their inherent, if undeclared, activities. While beyond complete comprehension, disposition describes something of what the organization is doing—activities that may diverge from the stated intent. This misalignment with the story or rhetoric is one means of detecting disposition, but additional organizational attributes are also helpful in assessing it.

Perhaps the idea of disposition is not really so mysterious. A ball at the top of an inclined plane possesses a disposition.[1] The geometry of the ball and its relative position are the simple markers of potential agency. Even without rolling down the incline, the ball is actively doing something by occupying its position. Disposition, in common parlance, usually describes an unfolding relationship between potentials. It describes a tendency, activity, faculty, or property in either beings or objects—a propensity within a context.

Infrastructure space possesses disposition just as does the ball at the top of an incline. Few would look at a highway interchange, an electrical grid, or a suburb and perceive agency or activity in its static arrangement. Spaces and urban organizations are usually treated, not as actors, but as collections of objects or volumes. Activity might be assigned only to the moving cars, the electrical current, or the suburb's inhabitants. Yet the ball does not have to roll down the incline to have the capacity to do so, and physical objects in spatial arrangements, however static, also possess an agency that resides in relative position. Disposition is immanent, not in the moving parts, but in the relationships between the components.

When navigating the complex dispositions of a river, dimples or ripples on the water serve as markers; and when navigating or hacking the complex dispositions of infrastructure, some simple markers are equally useful. The infrastructural operating system is filled with well-rehearsed sequences of code—spatial products and repeatable formulas like zones, suburbs, highways, resorts, malls, or golf courses. Hacking into it requires forms that are also like

1   François Jullien, *The Propensity of Things: Toward a History of Efficacy in China* (New York: Zone Books, 1995), 29.

software. Different from the object forms of masterpiece buildings or master plans, these active forms operate in another gear or register, to act like bits of code in the system. Active forms are markers of disposition, and disposition is the character of an organization that results from the circulation of these active forms within it. Since these forms are always changing, as is the complexion of disposition, they cannot be catalogued as elemental building blocks or terms in a glossary. Rather, identifying just a few among the many active forms that might be manipulated, redesigned, or rewritten only begins to crack the code, making more palpable the dispositions they inflect and providing some instruments for adjusting political character in infrastructure space. Still, as signs of ongoing processes—like the ripples used for river navigation—the practicality of these forms relies on their indeterminacy.

An important diagnostic in the fluid politics of extrastate-craft, disposition uncovers accidental, covert, or stubborn forms of power—political chemistries and temperaments of aggression, submission, or violence—hiding in the folds of infrastructure space.

Active Forms

Multiplier

A field of mass-produced suburban houses is a common phenomenon in infrastructure space, and it is an organization with clear markers of disposition. In the case of the US suburb of Levittown, the developer did not set out to make 1,000 individual houses, but adopted a kind of agricultural method of house building—1,000 slabs, 1,000 frames, 1,000 roofs, and so on. The site was effectively an assembly line separating the tasks of house building into smaller activities each of which could be applied across the entire population of houses in sequence. Beyond the activity of the humans within it, the arrangement itself rendered some things significant and others insignificant. The organization was actively *doing something* when it directed urban routines. It made some things possible and some things impossible (e.g., the building of an individual house different from all the others).

There were different kinds of form involved: the object form of the house and the active forms that organized the components of the field. Levittown was simple software, and one obvious marker or active form in its organization was the multiplier. The house was not a singularly crafted object but a multiplier of activities. The developer, William Levitt, turned the site into an assembly line and the homes into a population of commodities, from their frames and roofs to their TVs and washing machines.

Redesigning a single house, or the object form of the house within the suburb, may not be as powerful as addressing the active form—in this case a multiplier. A designer who intervenes in the repetitive fields of suburban space with a single house will have little impact. But designing something to be multiplied within a population of houses has the potential to recondition the larger suburban field or hack the suburban software. For instance, when the car arrived in suburbia, it was a multiplier that required a garage to be attached to every house, and today recalibrating or reconceiving the car and its garage would multiply and spread spatial changes throughout a field of houses. More powerful than a single object form in these landscapes, multipliers piggyback on repetitive components.

The city grows or changes because of the multipliers that circulate within it—cars, elevators, mobile phones, laws, real estate formulas, structural innovations, and security technologies among them. Just as the car is a multiplier that determines the shape and design of highways and exurban development, the elevator is a simple example of a multiplier that has transformed urban morphology. In the late nineteenth century, the elevator, together with the stackable floors of structural steel skeletons, made vertical buildings possible. Those that first appeared in Chicago and New York have evolved into the modern skyscraper—a prevalent spatial product in cities around the world. The elevator's propagation, rather than its movement up and down, makes it an active form with a disposition to multiply in urban environments. Since the elevator carries the genetics of the skyscraper, altering its routines potentially has collateral effects. For instance, contemporary elevator technologies that experiment with horizontal as well as vertical movements are the germ of a very different urban morphology. The designer who deploys a new conveyance vehicle may not design the vehicle itself but the way in which it propagates in and rewrites the urban landscape.

The presence of a multiplier is not the only reason why a mass-produced suburb does not deliver on its promise of a leafy country home, just as the elevator, as multiplier, is not the only reason for the urbanity of a city like New York or the isomorphism of the zone skyline. The multiplier is only one active form, one factor in assessing or adjusting a disposition, but it is present in almost all of the software of infrastructure space.

Switch/remote

In addition to the multiplier, another common active form in infrastructure space is the switch. An interchange in a highway network acts like a switch. A dam in a hydrological network, a terminal in a transit network, an earth station in a satellite network, or an internet service provider in a broadband network are all switches. Like the ball on the inclined plane, they establish potentials. Like a valve, they may suppress or redirect. The switch may generate effects some distance down the road or the line. It is a remote control of sorts—activating a distant site to affect a local condition or vice versa. Exceeding the reach of a single object form, the switch modulates a flow of activities. However deliberate the activities of the switch, it cannot control all of its own consequences any more than one could account for every use of the water flowing through a dam.

Infrastructure space is filled with switches and remote controls, most of which are also multipliers repeated throughout the system, and tuning these active forms tunes the disposition of an organization. For example, at the end of the nineteenth century and in the first part of the twentieth, the electrical networks that spread across developed countries promising decentralized access to power were often actually composed of a patchwork of local utilities—powerful nodes or switches in the network that had controlling monopolies.[2] In the development of telegraph, telephone, and fiber-optic submarine cables, any landing point for the cable acted like a switch in the network that could similarly develop a monopoly and affect onward service and pricing. In both cases, generating redundant switches in the form of multiple cable landings and multiple service providers potentially gave the network a more competitive and more robust disposition.

A typical highway interchange offers only a change of direction at constant speed. It is a switch in the network, but not a very smart switch. In traffic engineering, it was believed that statistical evidence of larger and larger populations of cars warranted more and more lanes of traffic. Yet increasing capacity only increased congestion, in part because of inadequate switches. Tuning the switches in the network would be one way of addressing the fallacies of the traffic engineering interchange. Volumes of traffic, like those in rush hour, could best be handled by the larger capacities of mass transit. A smarter, more resilient transportation interchange or station might then offer an intermodal switch between highway, rail, air, and mass transit.

The character of the switches in electrical or highway networks is not the only reason why they can foster monopolies or congestion. But in each case the switch is one active form—one lever or dial in determining unanticipated dispositions in the networks.

Wiring/topology

The Königsberg Bridge Problem started with a bet in a pub. The challenge was to find a route through the eighteenth-century Prussian city of Königsberg that went from the city's central island and back again without crossing any of its seven bridges more than once. In 1735, the mathematician and physicist Leonhard Euler demonstrated that there was no possible route satisfying that criteria. In doing so, he developed a mode of

---

2   Thomas P. Hughes, *Networks of Power: Electrification in Western Society 1880–1930* (Baltimore: Johns Hopkins University Press, 1983), 14, 404–60; David E. Nye, *Electrifying America: Social Meanings of a New Technology* (Cambridge, MA: MIT Press, 1990), 182, 266, 349, 385–9.

analysis fundamental to contemporary thinking about network topologies—expressions of relative position and sequence in a network. Topologies model the "wiring" of an organization. It is perhaps telling that topological thinking originated with a game about circulating through urban space. Just as an electronic network is wired to support specific activities, so can space be "wired" to encourage some activities and routines over others.

Topologies are intuitive markers of disposition in an organization, and they can be considered to be assemblies of multipliers and switches. Just as we know the potential of the ball at the top of the incline, we are familiar with the potentials and capacities of networks that have, for example, linear, multi-centered, radial, serial, or parallel topologies. A linear network connects successive points along a line, as in the case of a bus, a train, or an elevator that connects sequential floors. The disposition of a linear rail system or a linear fiber-optic cable buried in the ground is different from the disposition of an atomized sea of mobile telephones. In a radial, or hub and spoke, network, like massmedia television or radio, a single central point controls the flow of information. Mainframe computing was a serial network that passed information sequentially, while a parallel network might be modeled as a more open mesh with information flowing simultaneously from many points.

Topologies are also markers of political disposition insofar as they highlight the ways in which the authorities circulate or concentrate information. In the United States, the patchwork of local electrical utilities that generated a scattering of monopolies and inefficiencies was eventually absorbed into larger centralized monopolies like General Electric and Westinghouse. The internet, often theorized as an open mesh in which every point in the network can reach every other point, may really be more like a multi-centered organization. Sites like Google or Facebook may either help to filter information, making the web more salient and less chaotic, or shape an internet that operates more like a utility network with monopoly control.[3] While portrayed as

---

3   Yochai Benkler, *The Wealth of Networks: How Social Production Transforms*

relaxed and open, the zone enclave often assumes the disposition of a closed loop that will only recirculate compatible information. Yet mapping some of the zone incentives onto the city potentially changes its wiring and disposition, inviting more channels of information, circumstance, and contradiction that are the hallmarks of open, public urban space.

Again, although a contributing factor, topology alone does not determine the disposition of an organization. The same topology can sponsor very different kinds of social and political activity. Disposition in infrastructure space almost always involves compound conditions, relying not just on multipliers, switches, or their topological arrangement. It can be modeled as a network or as an *interplay* of many different kinds of active forms to create increasingly complex spatial software.

Interplay/governor

In 1733, James Oglethorpe designed a scheme for the New World city of Savannah, Georgia. To control real estate speculation and damage from fire, he produced not a graphic master plan—a plat or a complete set of rectilinear blocks—but rather a growth protocol or governor that established relationships between different species of urban space. The town was to grow by wards, each of which was to contain a ratio of lots to green open space. A percentage of the lots around the green, called tythings, were reserved for residential and commercial properties, while another percentage was reserved for public or civic functions. For each ward that was developed, a quotient of agricultural space outside of town was automatically reserved. The ward was at once a multiplier and, like a calculus function, an expression of variability and interdependency where components balanced and offset each other. The Savannah protocol provided explicit geometrical instructions for each ward, but the pattern of accumulated wards could evolve without having to determine a fixed boundary or master plan of the town.

Markets and Freedom (New Haven: Yale University Press, 2006), 20, 7–16, 19–20, 278–85.

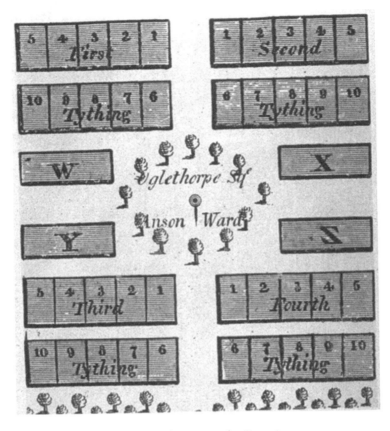

Typical ward, Savannah, Georgia

Savannah provides a vivid example of a suite of active forms, like multipliers and remotes, linked as interdependent variables in simple but sophisticated software that regulated an urban disposition. The growth protocol was like a governor in an engine or a thermostat that modulated the relative proportions of public, private, open, and agricultural space over time. It could direct not only additional development but also its cessation or contraction. Different from an object form, the Savannah software established the terms of an interplay between spatial variables.

The golf course community—another quintessential global spatial product—involves an interplay of active forms that, like the Savannah software, links interdependent spatial variables to perform as a governor. If the goal of Savannah was to control speculation, the goal of the golf course suburb or any spatial product is to maximize profit. Two crucial interdependent variables are the debt incurred from creating the golf course and the surface area of the course itself. The surface area determines the number of lots for course-side golf villas that can be sold to offset the debt incurred in constructing the course. The surface area governs the shape of the course and vice versa. Securing a celebrity endorsement from the likes of Jack Nicklaus or Arnold Palmer adds 15 percent to the value of each villa—just one of many variables in the game the developers play. While the appearance of the course is important, the object form is less important than its software—the powerful bits of code underlying millions of acres of development all around the world.

Many active forms circulating in the software that makes up infrastructure space can be used to hack that software. While not offering comprehensive control over an organization, active forms can nevertheless be inserted to counterbalance or redirect a disposition. They can multiply across a field, recondition a population, or generate a network. Like $\cos x$ or the mathematical *delta*, they can be part of an explicit expression for one way that the field changes. Active forms establish a set of parameters for what the organization will be doing over time. They have time-released powers and cascading effects. When the object of design is not an object form or a master plan but a set of instructions for an interplay between variables, design acquires some of the power and currency of software. This spatial software is not a thing but a means to craft a multitude of interdependent relationships and sequences—an updating platform for inflecting a stream of objects. Like the engine of interplay that philosophers Gilles Deleuze and Félix Guattari call a "diagram," an active form does not represent a single arrangement. It is an "abstract machine" generative of a "real that is yet to come."[4]

---

4 Gilles Deleuze, *Foucault*, trans. S. Hand. (Minneapolis: University of Minnesota Press, 1988), 37; Gilles Deleuze and Félix Guattari, "On Several Regimes of Signs," in *A Thousand Plateaus* (Minneapolis: University of Minnesota Press, 1987), 141, 142.

As the levers of disposition in infrastructure space, active forms, in different linkages and interplays, are tools of extrastatecraft.

Knowing That and Knowing How

Ascriptions of dispositions are actions.—Ludger Jansen[5]

Most urban and architectural designers—perhaps reflecting sentiments of the broader culture—are trained to work on object forms or master plans rather than active forms in interplay. When summoned to create an active form, designers naturally rely on what they are best trained to create—a formal object *representing* action or dynamic process. A more simple-minded confusion (made more powerful by being simple-minded) arises when action or activity is confused with movement or kineticism. A building is shaped to suggest a dynamic blur of motion, or the circulation of inhabitants is mapped with a blizzard of arrows. The more complex or agitated these tracings, the more "active" the form is seen to be. Or, reflecting a modernist faith in the succession of technologies, the form might be considered to be active only if it is coated with the newest responsive digital media.[6]

The distinction between form as object and form as action is something like philosopher Gilbert Ryle's distinction between

---

5   Ludger Jansen, "On Ascribing Dispositions," in Max Kistler and Brouno Gnassounou, eds. *Dispositions and Casual Powers* (London: Ashgate, 2007), 161.

6   Many contemporary architects use computer software and parametric thinking in the design of object forms. The discipline rarely applies parametric thinking to active forms—to the relationships *between* objects in the time and space of an expanded urban field. While digital software is not necessary to the contemplation of spatial software, Bruno Latour muses about digital software that not only manipulates geometry but also draws into interplay a web of other urban circumstances and consequences. See the interview with Bruno Latour by María J. Prieto and Elise S. Youn, "Debriefing the Collective Experiment," July 5, 2004, at academia.edu. Carlo Ratti and Joseph Grima's "Open Source Architecture" is a manifesto that imagines a more diverse role for digital media in architecture and urbanism. Digital media provides a common platform, like a wiki, to collect shared components, direct fabrication, and interface with the city—a city so embedded with digital devices that it has become an "internet of things." Carlo Ratti, Joseph Grima and additional contributors, "OSArc," *Domus Magazine,* no. 948 (June 15, 2011); Keller Easterling, "An Internet of Things," *E-flux,* (Spring 2012), at e-flux.com.

"knowing that" and "knowing how." With characteristic clarity and simplicity, Ryle once explained the difference between the two by using the example of a clown. The clown does not possess the correct answer to the question, "What is funny?" The clown's antics are not a single reasoned executive order. His knowledge and experience unfold in relation to the situation, from encounter to encounter, circumstance to circumstance. He has well-rehearsed knowledge of how to do a pratfall, exaggerate his facial expressions, modulate his voice, or introduce any other gag from his bag of tricks. What is funny involves a set of choices contingent on the audience's reactions, and the clown's performance relies on "knowing how" rather than "knowing that." For Ryle, the clown's skill represents "disposition, or a complex of dispositions."[7] "Knowing how" is, for Ryle, *dispositional*.[8]

Ryle's contemplation of disposition supports his broader critique of the mind-body split—a consequence of what he regarded to be the false logics of Cartesian dualism. He relished the fact that he often had to look no further than expressions in everyday speech to find the most withering challenges to these logics. Intelligence is often measured in terms of the amount of knowledge that can be acquired, identified, or named. Yet, as Ryle points out, a skill is not a logical proof that can be correctly or incorrectly reasoned. He argues for an intelligence or way of knowing that has to do with *knowing how* in mind and body. "A soldier does not become a shrewd general merely by endorsing the strategic principles of Clausewitz; he must also be competent to apply them. Knowing how to apply maxims cannot be reduced to, or derived from, the acceptance of those or any other maxims."[9] Addressing the designer, Ryle might have said that the object form of a master plan betrays a desire for *knowing that*, while a growth protocol like Savannah that unfolds over time exhibits a desire for *knowing how*. In infrastructure space, to ask "what is the master plan?" is like asking "what is funny?"

7 Gilbert Ryle, *The Concept of Mind* (Chicago: University of Chicago Press, 1949), 27–33.

8 Ibid., 27–32, 17–33.

9 Ibid., 31.

With simple examples Ryle demonstrates that disposition is something we already understand given that we use dispositional expressions to explain many common phenomena in everyday life. Ryle cites Jane Austen's changing perspective on the dispositions or temperaments of her characters as each novel unfolds. Only multiple observations of a person dealing with events over time can provide clues to their likely behaviors.[10] He also notes that non-human objects possess disposition. Only multiple deformations of rubber signal the material's disposition to elasticity, and only after time can one observe that it has lost its elasticity.[11] Just as the ball that does not need to roll down the incline, glass does not have to be shattered in order to be brittle. There is no need for movement or event. Disposition remains as a latent potential or tendency that is present even in the absence of an event. To "possess a dispositional property," Ryle writes, "is not to be in a particular state, or to undergo a particular change; it is to be bound or liable to be in a particular state, or to undergo a particular change, when a particular condition is realized."[12] It is a "hypothetical proposition" about the glass different from an event or "episode."[13]

To assess disposition is to assess how an organization deals with the variables over time—how it absorbs or deflects the active forms moving within it. Disposition does not describe a constant but rather a changing set of actions from which one might assess agency, potentiality, or capacity. Considering disposition to be determinate would be impractical. For Ryle, it is a subject of some mirth that dispositional attributes are sometimes regarded as fuzzy imponderables because they cannot be reified in an event or name. Ryle refutes those theories that associate disposition with "occult" agencies or regard things like the unshattered glass as temporal processes that are in "a sort of limbo world."[14]

Architecture and urbanism might have been a subject of Ryle's

---

10   Ibid., 42–4.
11   Ibid., 125.
12   Ibid., 43.
13   Ibid., 89, 116.
14   Ibid., 119–20.

sport. Treating active forms and dispositions as mysterious, unknowable conditions that cannot be legitimatized as objects or representations risks losing access to the enormous political power residing in infrastructure space.[15] The designer is left, for instance, trying to address a machine for making golf villas with a single house, or a volatile landscape with a master plan.

Active form is not a modernist proposition; it does not replace or succeed object form but rather augments it with additional powers and artistic pleasures. The potential for both kinds of form is always present in any design. Using either is an artistic choice. Active form may partner with and propel object form determining how it will align with power to travel through infrastructure space. A design idea for suburbia becomes more powerful when it is positioned as a multiplier that affects a population of houses. An urban scheme designed as a governor has a greater likelihood of remaining in place to influence growth.

Active forms, while perhaps under-rehearsed in the design disciplines, are quite ordinary in many others. A geneticist cannot represent all the gene sequences of DNA with an image of a double helix but can engage the ongoing development of an organism with an active form that alters one of those gene sequences. An environmentalist does not attempt to manage a

---

15   Artists and architects have, at various junctures, pursued design as software or an interplay of active components. For artists like Jack Burnham or Les Levine, software was at once a literal tool and a model or metaphor. The architect Cedric Price designed architecture as a performance of components rather than a single object, in projects like Fun House or Generator, among many others. Architect and mathematician Christopher Alexander used set theory to organize the relationships between components of urban and architectural design, arguing for the semi-lattice rather than the hierarchical tree as the underlying structure. Nicholas Negroponte's Architecture Machine Group attempted to use urban space as a physical test bed for an expanded field of computing. While the occasional desire for determinacy arguably weakened some of these experiments, they have, however anecdotally, nourished the project of active forms. See Jack Burnham, *Beyond Modern Sculpture: The Effects of Science and Technology on the Sculpture of This Century* (New York: G. Braziller, 1968); Cedric Price, *The Square Book* (London: Wiley-Academy, 2003), reprint of Cedric Price, *Works II* (London: Architectural Association, 1984); Christopher Alexander, "The City is not a Tree," *Architectural Forum* 122, nos. 1 and 2 (April–May 1965), 58–62; and Nicholas Negroponte, *The Architecture Machine* (Cambridge, MA: MIT Press, 1970), 70–93.

forest by wiring every bird in every tree or planting every sprig of undergrowth, but will send in instrumental players that inflect ecologies over time. Entrepreneurs design not only the product but also its passage through a market, perhaps using a mobile phone network or a repetitive suburb to multiply products and desires. A computer scientist would never attempt to fully represent the internet but would rather author active forms that ride the network with very explicit instructions. In all these examples, there is no desire for a singular, comprehensive or utopian solution. Power lies rather in the prospect of shaping a series of activities and relationships over time.

The extrastatecraft of infrastructure space is artistically and intellectually attracted to the idea of designing action and interplay as well as designing objects. Even though design orthodoxies may favor a training in *knowing that*, some of the real power players in the world, for whom infrastructure is a secret weapon, would never relinquish their faculties for designing both object and active form—for *knowing that* and *knowing how*.

Temperament

When the social scientist and cybernetician Gregory Bateson referred to a man, a tree, and an ax as an information system, he made self-evident the idea that the activities of infrastructure space can be a medium of information. For those like Bateson who foretold the digital revolution but were not yet completely surrounded by digital devices, it was perhaps easier to understand that anything—human or non-human, digital or non-digital— could be a carrier of information. Like Ryle, Bateson did not regard this activity to be "supernatural" or occult, but rather saw information as an ordinary currency for exchanges between humans and non-humans.[16] "Information is a difference that makes a difference," he famously wrote.[17] Objects do not need to be enhanced by

---

16   Gregory Bateson, *Steps to an Ecology of Mind* (Chicago: University of Chicago Press, 2000), 464, 472.

17   Ibid., 381, 462, 315, 272, 21.

digital technologies or coated with sensors. To the degree that they "make a difference" in the world, they create influences, intentions, and relationships that constitute information. The information manifests, not in text or code, but in activity.

Bateson's work also tutors an understanding of the active forms that manage information in infrastructure space. He wrote about "governors," like those found in a thermostat or a steam engine, as mechanisms for modulating information—the temperature or pressure in a system—just as Savannah was a governor for modulating real estate speculation. Of switches, he wrote that a switch is a thing that "is not." In other words, the switch controls a dispositional flow of changes—a flow of information. "It is related to the notion 'change' rather than to the notion 'object.'"[18]

While Bateson's more comprehensive cybernetic speculations about homeostasis in organizations are perhaps to be avoided, his work further deepens an understanding of disposition with its speculations on temperament or political bearing—the tension, violence, stability, or resilience immanent in organizations. Bateson's catholic intelligence ranged across mathematics, communication technology, neurophysiology, game theory, and logic and did not subdivide the world into the subjects of different sciences. Assessing any subject with this cybernetic epistemology—be it electronic circuits, nations, tribes from New Guinea, or Alcoholics Anonymous meetings—Bateson could also transpose sociological assessments of tension and violence to behaviors inherent in groups or to simple topologies and network relationships.

Bateson began by looking at a number of binary patterns in human behavior, whether between individuals or between groups, as in "Republican-Democrat, political Right-Left, sex differentiation, God and the devil, and so on." He noted that people even attempt to square off in binary oppositions over things that are "not dual in nature—youth versus age, labor versus capital, mind versus matter." So ingrained are these binary habits for group

---

18   Gregory Bateson, *Mind and Nature: A Necessary Unity* (New York: Hampton Press, 2000), 101.

behavior that they induce myopia in their proponents. Bateson was interested in ternary systems as an alternative to binaries. He suggested that the proponents of binary relationships "lack the organizational devices for handling triangular systems; the inception of a 'third party' is always regarded, for example, as a threat to our political organization." He was especially interested in how and why such binaries generate divisive situations.[19] Three models of binary relationships receive the most attention in Bateson's writings: symmetrical, complimentary, and reciprocal.

In symmetrical relationships both sides of the binary compete for same dominant position. They mirror each other, and their mimicry may escalate toward "extreme rivalry and ultimately to hostility and the breakdown of the whole system."[20] Imagine identical twins competing for parental affection. Some of these binaries he characterized as complementary motifs: "dominance-submission, succoring-dependence, and exhibitionism-spectatorship."[21]

In complementary behavior, one party provides an ingredient necessary for the other. Think of the beta dog consistently submitting to the alpha dog to maintain the stability of the pack hierarchy. While submission might be reinforcing and stabilizing in some instances, it can also lead to hostility if "submissiveness promotes further assertiveness which in turn will promote further submissiveness."[22]

In reciprocal relationships, individuals or groups oscillate between symmetrical and complementary relationships. There is an understanding that dominance might be shared, or that one group might be submissive in some encounters and dominant in others. Reciprocal relationships distribute power over time and allow for the trading of roles in a way that stabilizes the relationship. Imagine a group of poker players who take turns letting each other win so that no one member is wiped out and the entire group can continue playing.[23]

It may seem far-fetched to assign temperament to

---

19   Bateson, *Steps to an Ecology of Mind*, 95.
20   Ibid., 68.
21   Ibid., 95
22   Ibid., 68.
23   Ibid., 68–9.

infrastructure spaces, but concentrations of power, tension, competition, and submission are immanent in their arrangements. Applied to urban space, it is easy to see the latent violence in binaries of competition and submission such as East and West Jerusalem, San Diego and Tijuana, North and South Sudan, or the mirroring shores of Spain and North Africa.

Bateson also treats violence, tension, competition, and submission in terms of information flow. In competitive or destructive states, the flow of information collapses, whereas in balanced reciprocal organizations, information is more easily exchanged. Bateson considers the stabilizing effects of breaking binaries and increasing the possibility of exchange. His thinking highlights network arrangements that concentrate authority or constrict information, spatial relations that escalate violent situations, as well as organizations that are plural and robustly networked. Restrictions of information, like the closed loop of the zone or the monopolies in electrical or telecommunication networks, are—like the surface ripples on the river—markers of more complex and potentially dangerous dispositions.

Stories are Active Forms

Stories that a culture tells about infrastructure space can script the use of that space; yet in the case of highways, ARPAnet, electrical utilities, Facebook, or the zone, the organizations slipped away from the stories that were attached to them. The misalignment between the activity of an organization and its stated intent is often the first signal of an undeclared disposition. Yet beyond the declaration of intent, some social stories play an additional, powerful role in the ongoing process of shaping disposition.

The sociologist, anthropologist, and theorist Bruno Latour has long recognized that networks like infrastructure space are *active* and that they are composed of social and technical actors. Humans shape infrastructure space deciding, for instance, that electricity will be used for power, lighting, and telecommunications as a public utility accessed via sockets and plugs. But for Latour non-human technologies are also actors. Humans create computers, for example, but computers in turn act upon humans. They are shaped to human needs as devices that respond to hands and laps, but they also inspire further human uses and even the very mental structures that conceive of them. That altered way of thinking influences in turn the next iteration of the computer. In other words, technologies are non-human actors or "actants" influencing the desires and practices of the humans who reciprocally shape them. Indeed, beyond the human/non-human binary for Latour nothing is *merely* an object. Everything is "doing something" and cannot be separated from its actions.[24]

Latour uses this observation to destabilize the habits of his own discipline. He has been critical of those studies of social-technical networks that use evidence merely to confirm existing presumptions about social patterns or habits.[25] In response, he offers an analytic framework that he calls actor-network theory (ANT) to renovate and "[redefine] sociology not as the 'science of the social', but as the *tracing of associations*."[26] Rather than codifying or taxonomizing the social or cultural story, he describes a dialogue between humans and non-human technologies that is constantly unfolding and impossible to fix.

An active form can be organizational like a multiplier, a remote, a switch, or a governor, but since the social and technical interact with each other, an active form can also be a social

---

24 Latour, *Reassembling the Social*, 52.

25 STS scholars and theorists would include Bruno Latour, Wiebe E. Bijker, Trevor Pinch, Thomas P. Hughes, Thomas J. Misa, and David E. Nye among others.

26 Latour, *Reassembling the Social*, 8n11, 5. Latour criticizes Durkheimian practices and steps away from, for instance, Erving Goffman's or Pierre Bourdieu's work. Goffman and Bourdieu both use the term "disposition" in a way most pertinent to social studies. Bourdieu, who was also transposing his work to an active realm of practice, used the word to describe a repeatedly structured set of cultural activities or *habitus*. Latour perhaps extends this by suggesting that sociology might overcome its own *habitus* to further consider evolving practices. In this he departs from a branch of sociotechnical studies, arguing that it sometimes enshrines social forms as structured patterns and habits or reifies the structures of social "science." These are the very constructs he wishes to renovate by considering both humans and things, actors and non-human actants, in networks. He raises questions, for instance, about Wiebe Bijker's account in *Social Shaping of Technology* (1995), because "the social is kept stable all along and accounts for the shape of technological change."

story—not a vessel in which to fix meaning but a carrier to channel a flow of meanings. Form, Latour writes, is "simply something which allows something else to be transported from one site to another . . . To provide a piece of information is the action of putting something into a form."[27]

A story as an active form, however immaterial and non-spatial, can inflect disposition in infrastructure space and can be deployed with spatial intent. For example, the developer William Levitt associated his suburban housing with familial and patriotic narratives that were particularly infectious in the post-war period, and such stories accelerated the spatial effects of the house as multiplier. The house, its repetitive organization, and the story attached to it all constitute information that contributes to disposition. Similarly, cultural stories about the zone as a rational, apolitical instrument of economic liberalism are active forms that, however disconnected from the actual activities of the organization, drive the zone's popularity and shape its disposition. A new persuasion about the zone mapped back onto existing cities can be designed as a multiplier with both social and technological components— actors and actants that together alter urban space.

Latour, like Ryle, also uses theatrical performance as a model for the ways in which a string of social actions or stories can influence social-technical networks. Noting that it is "not by accident" that words like script and actor are used in social studies, Latour writes, "Play-acting puts us immediately into a thick imbroglio where the question of who is carrying out the action has become unfathomable." Actions are "dislocated . . . borrowed, distributed, suggested, influenced, dominated, betrayed, translated."[28] Social networks are "a conglomerate of many surprising sets of agencies that have to be slowly disentangled. It is this venerable source of uncertainty that we wish to render vivid again in the odd expression of actor-network."[29]

In some of his formulations of ANT, Latour even makes

27   Ibid., 39, 223.
28   Ibid., 46.
29   Ibid., 44.

passing reference to the sociologist Erving Goffman. While distancing himself from more conventional sociology, Latour uses Goffman to make palpable the activities that surround social interactions in excess of declared intentions. Goffman used the word "disposition" to refer to all the gestures, postures, facial expressions, and myriad subtexts deployed in an individual's almost theatrical presentation of self.[30] He marveled that while all these signals often overwhelm, or are "discrepant" from, what a person is actually saying, they are rarely "systematically examined."[31]

Discussions of performance, indeterminacy, and discrepancy in Ryle, Latour, and Goffman are suggestive of special aesthetic practices used to confront the politics of infrastructure space. With an artistic repertoire like that of a performer, the designer of active forms, comfortable with less control, works on an unfolding stream of objects rather than a single shape. For the designer of stories as active forms—social forms that are nevertheless intended to have spatial consequences—discrepancy presents additional opportunities. Just as the powers that be in infrastructure space are usually offering persuasive stories that are decoupled from what their organizations are actually doing, performers are accustomed to the idea that action is a carrier of information that may be discrepant from the stated text. Actors have a script (e.g., "come home son"), but their real work lies in crafting an action, usually with an infinitive expression (to grovel, to reject, to caress).[32] The action, not to be confused with movement or choreography, is the real carrier of information, meaning, and change, and it may be entirely disconnected from the text. Comfort with crafting discrepant, indeterminate action allows design to engage

---

30   Ibid., 46; Erving Goffman, *The Presentation of Self in Everyday Life* (New York: Anchor Books/Doubleday, 1959), 141–66.

31   Goffman, *The Presentation of Self in Everyday Life*, 254–5.

32   Sharing a sensibility for theater, Ryle, for instance, makes a distinction between active or "performance" verbs and verbs like "'know,' 'possess' and 'aspire.'" One would not say, for example, "'he is now engaged in possessing a bicycle.'" See Ryle, *The Concept of Mind*, 130, 116.

both the naturally occurring dislocations of meaning as well as the duplicitous politics of extrastatecraft.

Diagnostics

Neither deterministic nor wholly malleable, technology sets some parameters of individual and social action . . . Different technologies make different kinds of human action and interaction easier or harder to perform.—Yochai Benkler[33]

Disposition is an extra diagnostic tool for assessing undisclosed capacity or political bearing in infrastructure space. A multitude of active forms can be used to both detect and adjust a disposition. Like powerful bits of code that can hack the infrastructural operating system, these forms may be technological, organizational, or social. Indeterminate in order to be practical, such forms deliver not a plan but an interplay capable of adjusting different situations and managing a disposition over time.

A contemplation of disposition also summons Michel Foucault's theories about a social and political "apparatus" or "system of relations" that he called a *dispositif.* For Foucault a *dispositif* was "a thoroughly heterogeneous ensemble consisting of discourses, institutions, architectural forms, regulatory decisions, laws, administrative measures, scientific statements, philosophical, moral and philanthropic propositions—in short, the said as much as the unsaid."[34]

The designer of disposition in infrastructure space is a performer. Active form supplements the aesthetics of object form while addressing the politics of discrepancy in extrastatecraft.

---

33   Benkler, *The Wealth of Networks*, 16–17. Network theorist Yochai Benkler refers to what STS philosopher Langdon Winner called the "political properties" of technology, or what sociologist Barry Wellman called its "affordances," which describes some of the special capacities of social media and the internet; see also Jane Bennett, *Vibrant Matter: A Political Ecology of Things* (Durham, NC: Duke University Press, 2010).

34   Michel Foucault, "The Confession of the Flesh," a round table interview from 1977, in Foucault, *Power/Knowledge: Selected Interviews and Other Writings*, ed. Colin Gordon (New York: Vintage Books, 1980), 194.

Not limited to prescription, the designer can engage in improvisation—in the pleasures of *knowing how* as well as *knowing that*.

Finally, a reading of Latour also offers cautions that are further discussed in the chapter titled "Stories." The stories that humans attach to technologies like infrastructure space can become enshrined or ossified as ingrained expectations. Stories may evolve beyond fluid scripts for shaping a technology into ideologies that dictate the disposition of an organization. However immaterial, these ideological stories have the power to buckle concrete and bend steel, and they can often be difficult to escape.

CHAPTER 3

Broadband

The road between Nairobi and Mombasa is lined with, and virtually lit by, advertisements for the mobile phone companies that have entered the region—all promising new freedoms and economic opportunities. With their images of Masai tribesman in native dress phoning from a remote wilderness, the ads employ an essential trope of leapfrogging—the desire for a perfect collapse between technology and nature, tradition and modernity. The billboards express the enthusiasm of a world turned upside down, in which not the developed but the developing world has its hands around a majority of the world's cell phones.

Over the last 150 years, the ocean floor has been laid with thousands of miles of submarine cable of all types for telegraph, telephone, and fiber-optic infrastructure. In the nineteenth century, it took only thirty years for the British cable-laying companies to string the world with telegraph cable, and a little over a decade from the late-1980s to the late-1990s for most of the world to be connected to fiber-optic cable. Yet until recently, East Africa, one of the most populous areas of the world, had no fiber-optic submarine cable link and less than 1 percent of the world's broadband capacity. A country like Kenya had to rely for its broadband on expensive satellite technology acquired in the 1970s that cost twenty to forty times its equivalent in the developed world. Before 2009, one Mbps (megabit per second) of bandwidth could cost as much as 7,500 US dollars per month against the world average of $200. The monthly cost of putting twenty-five agents on the phone was $17,000 a month instead of the $600–900 that it would cost in other developed countries.[1]

---

1 Regional Communications Infrastructure Program (RCIP) videos, at worldbank.org/rcip; "Addressing Africa's 'Missing Link,'" at http://web.worldbank.org.

If telecommunications in East Africa has until recently been distinguished by deprivation, it is now often heralded for its explosive growth. In Kenya, the numbers have been skyrocketing. Between 2000 and 2008, the number of cell phone subscriptions increased over a hundredfold (from 127,404 in 2000 to 16,573,303 in 2008), and from 2008 to 2012 they nearly doubled again (30,731,745 in 2012).[2] After nearly fifteen years of planning, by the end of 2010 Kenya had gone from having no fiber-optic submarine cable to having three international cables and an expanding national fiber-optic system. The country needs broadband for mobile telephony,[3] but while many of its mobile phone users are now able to access the internet, Kenya is nevertheless still sorely lacking high-capacity premium fixed bandwidth for business and education.

The new power players of extrastatecraft are all present in Kenya—nations, kingdoms, global consultancies, and an array of international organizations and multinational enterprises. Broadband is now written into the policies of national governments and into the development goals of businesses as well as international organizations like the World Bank and the UN. The World Bank declares mobile telephony to be "the world's largest distribution platform."[4] A swarm of telecoms from all over the world compete for market share in underserved Africa. The expansion of new infrastructure capacities into densely populated, developing countries has also sponsored new business models and techniques of governance. Entrepreneurs identify

---

2   ITU, "World Telecommunications/ICT Indicators Database, 17th Edition." See also *The Little Data Book on Information and Communication Technology* (Washington, DC: World Bank, 2010). In 2000 there were 0.4 cell phone subscriptions per 100 people. By 2008 the number had risen to 42.1. See "Statistics Q1 2010–11," at cck.go.ke.

3   The World Bank defines broadband as requiring speeds of at least 256 kbps, while the ITU defines it in terms of capacity to carry voice, data, and video. See Mark D. J. Williams, "Advancing the Development of Backbone Network in Sub-Saharan Africa," in World Bank, ed., *Information and Communications for Development: Extending Reach and Increasing Impact* (Washington, DC: World Bank, 2009).

4   Mohsen Khalil, Philippe Dongier, and Christine Zhen Wei Qiang, "Overview," in World Bank, ed., *Information and Communications for Development*.

multipliers and borrow crowd-sourcing techniques to penetrate the market with a flurry of new apps. Kenya is now being characterized as a potential leader in developing information and communication technologies—a "silicon savannah" for the entire continent of Africa.[5]

Kenya is a good place from which to consider the spatial variables of broadband infrastructure. Plenty of analysts on the ground are trying to predict the effects of broadband on what they call "Development 2.0." Such analysis is undertaken in the languages of business, technology, informatics, and econometrics, but there is as yet little study of the interdependencies between broadband infrastructure and space. Urbanists frequently analyze the urban values and morphologies associated with physical infrastructure such as rail, highway, power and water utilities, yet the discipline is under-rehearsed in an analysis of the spatial dispositions attending broadband infrastructure.

The advent of satellite during the 1960s and '70s coincided with the emergence of many developing countries, and was seen as a means of leapfrogging the infrastructure monopolies and hierarchies of developed countries with an airborne network.[6] Yet some of these futuristic projections of a fully modernized world coexisting with an undisturbed pastoral landscape foundered at the so-called last mile—the position of fixed utilities like electricity that were necessary auxiliaries of the satellite signal. The device receiving the signals had to be plugged in, and where the auxiliary networks were inadequate, new networks for transportation, electricity, and broadband were bundled together and delivered to enclaves—self-contained office parks or zones that could attract foreign investment.

---

5 "Upwardly Mobile: Kenya's Technology Start-up Scene Is About to Take Off," *Economist*, August 25, 2012.

6 In his 1980 book, *The Third Wave*, Alvin Toffler was among those promoting satellites as a means by which developing countries might leapfrog over the infrastructural mistakes of the developed countries while maintaining their ties to a pastoral landscape. See Alvin Toffler, "Gandhi with Satellites," in *The Third Wave* (New York: William Morrow and Company, 1980), 362. See also Easterling, *Enduring Innocence*, 135–60.

Broadband capacity from the new fiber-optic cable is distributed in a three-part organization. Buried in the ground and extending from the landfall of the submarine cable, the terrestrial cable assumes a linear topology that physically territorializes like a railroad or highway. In Kenya, the fiber favors a well-worn path between Nairobi and Mombasa, but it will also contact remote villages. As it evolves, it is not clear whether the fiber will strengthen existing cities, generate zone-like enclaves, or encourage new approaches to development in rural areas. Relying on the same cable for bandwidth, mobile telephony forms a second atomized topology of microwave towers and handsets. While again promising a ubiquitous airborne medium, this time the device that receives the signals is battery powered and somewhat less reliant on last-mile contingencies. The service providers who sell and transfer broadband between these overlapping organizations add a third layer of organization—a cluster of switches or points of access. In the same way that any utility can harbor local monopolies, a bottleneck can develop anywhere within these linear, atomized, and clustered topologies.

Just as mobile telephony is an information network, infrastructure space itself is a carrier of information, and it reciprocally shapes the resilience and robustness of all the broadband networks. The road between Mombasa and Nairobi—two lanes for some of its length and poorly maintained—is a reminder that despite the ubiquity of the cell phone, major improvements are needed in the auxiliary infrastructure. Along the same road, a billboard cites the country's 40 percent unemployment rate. While mobile telephony is a development engine, reducing unemployment will heavily rely on universities and businesses with fixed high-capacity broadband in urban organizations. These urban organizations are important switches in the network.

For all the new digital software in play in Kenya, the outmoded zone is the only spatial software presently on offer, even as some of the new capacities of broadband begin to render it obsolete. The cell phone, like the new elevator, is a powerful multiplier that can be placed in a meaningful interplay with all of the other active forms in the broadband network to alter the design of the city, village, road, school, and market. Designing new interdependencies between all of these spatial and technical variables could maximize access to the information carried in telecommunication networks as well as the information carried in the space of the city. Just as Kenya and other populous countries are offering the world new business models, they might also offer an advanced lesson in broadband urbanism.

Broadband Is Extrastatecraft

Broadband infrastructure recalls the global industrial networks of the nineteenth century when Britain and the United States were the two most powerful developers of telegraph networks.[7] The first transcontinental telegraph line in the United States was completed in 1861, and by the end of the century Great Britain had deployed a fleet of cable-laying ships to wire its colonial empire with terrestrial and submarine telegraph cable. By the turn of the twentieth century, British telegraph companies vastly outnumbered those from other countries, and they controlled two-thirds of the cables in the water.[8] The capacities of the new technologies together with the territorial conquests of the private infrastructure industries lent extra powers to, and even inspired, the ambitions and policies of these states. By the end of the nineteenth century, the Americas and most of Europe, as well as Japan, India, Russia, China, Australia, and Africa, all had terrestrial telegraph networks linked to submarine cable.[9]

Since 1879, John Pender's Eastern & South African Telegraph Company had been laying telegraph cable in Africa, and soon after the Imperial British East Africa Company (IBEAC), established in 1885, began operating in what would become Kenya,

---

7 Paul Starr, *The Creation of the Media: Political Origins of Modern Communications* (New York: Basic Books, 2004) 153–89.

8 Armand Mattelart, *The Invention of Communication* (Minneapolis: University of Minnesota Press, 1996), 167.

9 Anton A. Huurdeman, *The Worldwide History of Telecommunications* (John Wiley & Sons, 2003), 91–145.

telegraph cable landed in Mombasa.[10] Telegraph lines eventually paralleled the IBEAC's railroad from Mombasa to Nairobi, a line that was intended to penetrate into Uganda and connect to Cecil Rhodes's projected Cape to Cairo railroad.

The heavy industries delivering telecommunications infrastructure fueled a global financial market and simultaneously created a need for international technical coordination and governance—a global exchange or extrastatecraft in a new form.[11] The International Telegraph Union (ITU) convened its first conference in 1865. With each succeeding conference, the organization developed new layers of governance for the next generations of telecommunication technologies. The ITU was soon coordinating not only telegraph and telephone networks but also radio and the new generations of coaxial cable. By 1963, the year Kenya gained independence from the British, the conference was allocating frequencies for satellite communication.[12] Across post-colonial Africa, however, most of the strands of submarine telegraph cable laid by the British and others in their frenzy of colonization were not replaced with the newest coaxial, telephone, and fiber-optic cable. In 1964, the ITU determined that Kenya had 50,842 phones. The figure in the United States for the same year was 88,787,000.[13]

While requiring or submitting to coordination from international or intergovernmental institutions, the big multinational industries continued to enjoy enormous extrastate independence and power on the seas and airwaves. Companies like AT&T,

---

10   See "Cable Timeline 1850–2012" at atlantic-cable.com; and Michael Tyler, Janice Hughes, and Helena Renfrew, "Kenya: Facing the Challenges of an Open Economy," in Eli Noam, ed., *Telecommunications in Africa* (New York: Oxford University Press, 1999), 81. These two sources disagree on the year of the cable landing. According to the Glover timeline, the landing date is 1890, but according the authors in the Noam volume, the landing date is 1888. John Pender's Eastern & South African Telegraph Company had been laying cable in East Africa since 1879. Huurdeman, *The Worldwide History of Telecommunications*, 137.

11   Huurdeman, *The Worldwide History of Telecommunications*, 217–21.

12   By the conference of 1927, the ITU had become a parliament of eighty countries and sixty-four private companies. See Huurdeman, *The Worldwide History of Telecommunications*, 358–9.

13   ITU, "General Telephone Statistics, 1964," at itu.int.

Siemens, Western Union, and Cable and Wireless survived wartime state co-option as well as various mergers to resurface as operators in the new world of coaxial and fiber-optic cable. The German electrical engineering company Siemens had aspired to become an international company from its inception.[14] It would work for or with any powerful player, state or corporation, that would further its ambitions, insinuating itself into different strata of the telecommunications business as manufacturer, heavy industry contractor, and inventor.[15]

The American Telegraph and Telephone Company, Bell Telephone Laboratories, and Siemens were all associated with TAT-1, the first transatlantic telephone cable launched in 1956. AT&T, France Télécom, and British Telecom collaborated on TAT-8, the first transatlantic fiber-optic cable that came on line in 1988. Alcatel-Lucent, a French firm with roots in late-nineteenth-century electrical and communication companies, has become a major player in contemporary fiber-optic cabling in Africa.[16]

Kenya, like many post-colonial African countries, merged colonial and private telecommunications entities into a parastate telecom with monopoly status. The British Cable and Wireless Company, another company with a history dating back to the cable-laying enterprises of the late nineteenth century, had already managed international communications in Kenya, and since 1933 the East African Posts and Telecommunications Corporation (EAP&TC) had administered telecommunications for Kenya, Uganda, and Tanzania (after the merger of Tanganyika and Zanzibar). In 1977, the Kenya Posts and Telecommunications Corporation (KP&TC) was established for Kenya alone, and by 1984 it had consolidated the administration of both domestic and international telecommunications into a single entity.[17]

---

14   Siemens was originally Siemens and Halske, then Siemens Brothers.

15   Wilfried Feldenkirchen, *Siemens, 1918–1945* (München: Piper, 1995).

16   See alcatel-lucent.com. The company was affiliated with Western Electric and AT&T in the United States and La Compagnie Générale d'Electricité (CGE) in France.

17   Tanzania was formed from the merger of Tanganyika and Zanzibar in

KP&TC would eventually administer relations with Intelsat, and after Kenya became a member of the satellite consortium in 1968, the country received its first earth station in 1970 on Mount Longonot just north of Nairobi.[18]

In addition to the established global telecommunications companies (some associated with colonialism), new players from developing countries approached telecommunications with new ambitions. Alcatel-Lucent and the Japanese company NEC joined with collaborators from the Middle East and South Asia to construct SEA-ME-WE 1, the first analog cable system in the Indian Ocean connecting Southeast Asia, the Middle East, and Western Europe.[19] Reliance Globalcom, a massive Indian communications company, acquired the FLAG or Fiber-optic Link Around the Globe, a cable system that circles the earth.

The Chinese companies Huawei and ZTE were established in Shenzhen in the 1980s. They have subsequently acquired expertise in partnership with some of the most prominent ICT firms and have developed research outposts in Stockholm and Bangalore. They provide everything from fiber-optic networks to switching, to handsets. Both companies operate all over Africa as ICT contractors.[20] Mixing innovation with low bids for contracts, they have strategized a global conquest of IT business. From the company's campus in Shenzhen, Huawei founder Ren Zhengfei speaks of using "the countryside to encircle and finally capture the cities," feeding its "wolf spirit" with each new acquisition of territory.[21] All of these players, old and new, are involved in supplying broadband to East Africa.

1964. After Kenyan independence in 1964, the British Cable and Wireless Company created an interim joint venture with the government called the East African External Telecommunications Company (EXTELCOMS). KP&TC eventually acquired the Cable and Wireless shares in 1974 within a company renamed KENEXTEL which fully merged with KP&TC in 1984.

18   Tyler, Hughes, and Renfrew, "Kenya: Facing the Challenges of an Open Economy," 81–84; Huurdeman, *The Worldwide History of Telecommunications*, 567.

19   Tyler et al., "Kenya: Facing the Challenges of an Open Economy," 90.

20   See huawei.com and en.zte.com.cn.

21   "The Long March of the Invisible Mr. Ren," *Economist*, June 4, 2011, 80–1.

Since independence, intergovernmental agencies and consultancies have joined the field of Kenyan extrastatecraft. The country's first World Bank funding came in 1960, for an agricultural project, and the bank has been active there ever since, organizing and lending to development projects.[22] The IMF has also offered assistance and credit since the 1980s.[23] The global management consultancy McKinsey & Company, operating in Africa since the 1970s, has consulted on a number of Kenya's broadband initiatives.[24]

Modeled after other intergovernmental agencies like the UN, the Organization for African Unity (OAU) was formed in 1963, just as many African nations were achieving independence from colonial powers. The OAU organized pan-African agencies for telecommunications, radio, and TV and established the African Development Bank. While the OAU came to be regarded as ineffectual, in the 1990s Muammar al-Gaddafi revived the idea. The African Union replaced the OAU but maintained its headquarters in Addis Ababa, Ethiopia.[25] One agency of the AU established in 2001, the New Partnership for Africa's Development (NEPAD), became a key player in the history of Kenya's fiber-optic submarine cables.[26]

Broadband Has Shadows

In 1982, nearly ten years after Martin Cooper of Motorola made his first fabled cell phone call (on a phone slightly larger than a brick), the ITU held one of its plenipotentiary conferences in Nairobi. It had begun in earnest to consider those not yet served by telecommunication infrastructure, and Nairobi was the capital of one of the most poorly served countries in

---

22 "World Bank Historical Chronology: 1960–1969," at http://web.worldbank.org.

23 See "Data and Statistics: Kenya" at imf.org.

24 Author interview with Dr. Bitange Ndemo, August 2007, Nairobi. See also mckinsey.com.

25 See african-union.org.

26 See nepad.org.

the world. The resulting report, *The Missing Link: Report of the Independent Commission for World Wide Telecommunications Development* (1984), assessed the significant lack of teledensity in developing countries and identified the organizations and banks that might make a concerted effort to upgrade the network. The report recommended that "all of mankind" have access to a telephone within the early part of the twenty-first century.[27]

By the 1980s, the EU was already setting aside frequencies for cell phones and the ITU had proposed a global cellular network, but Kenya was left out of the picture. In 1980 the country had only 74,000 direct telephone lines. Despite the ITU's attempts to increase teledensity, Kofi Annan observed in 1999 that "a quarter of all countries have not yet achieved even a basic level of access to telecommunications (at a teledensity of 1), and half the world's people have never made or received a telephone call."[28] A teledensity of 1 means 1 telephone per 100 people. That same year, IT analyst Eli Noam noted "Africa comprises 20 percent of the world's land mass and contains 12 percent of its population. But it accounts for only 2 percent of the world's telecommunications."[29]

In 1995, the Africa One project planned to circle Africa with a single fiber-optic cable linked to Europe, the Middle East, and beyond.[30] But before it could be fully negotiated, the privately funded SAT-3-WASC-SAFE cable came on line in 2002. It served the west coast of Africa and continued along well-worn routes of global trade and colonization with a connection to Mauritius,

27   Sir Donald Maitland, *The Missing Link: Report of the Independent Commission for World Wide Telecommunications Development* (Geneva: International Telecommunications Union, 1984).

28   Huurdeman, *The Worldwide History of Telecommunications*, 551, 529, 540.

29   Eli M. Noam, "Introduction," in Noam, ed., *Telecommunications in Africa*, 3. In 2000 Sub-Saharan Africa did achieve a teledensity of 1, and the ITU set a teledensity goal of 10 for 2010. See Huurdeman, *The Worldwide History of Telecommunications*, 551, 565, 540.

30   "Green Light for Major Undersea Fibre-Optic Cable System for Africa," *UN Chronicle* 35, no. 3 (1998).

India, and the Far East.[31] Nevertheless, on the west coast, whether as a result of parastate monopolies or lack of capacity, the new cable did not significantly relieve broadband pricing. Even by the late summer of 2009, 1 Mbps on the west coast of Africa still cost between \$4,500 and \$12,000 per month.[32] Meanwhile, the island country of Mauritius, flush with broadband from the SAFE cable landing and well-rehearsed in the techniques of export processing, was demonstrating that Africa could attract global business. Under the tutelage of Indian IT expertise, the country was even building its own IT industry with knowledge villages like Ebene CyberCity that are part of the history of zone development.[33]

Inspired to attract some of this business, in January 2003 a group at the East African Business Summit gathered to craft an independent cable project called EASSy, or the East Africa Submarine Cable System, running from Mtunzini in South Africa to Port Sudan in Sudan. A significant number of countries signed the EASSy memorandum of understanding in December 2003, but did not deliver all of the necessary investment money. It would take over five more years before EASSy came on line.

In 2010, on the 25th anniversary of the "Missing Link" report, the ITU Broadband Commission for Digital Development issued a report written in the breathless tone of a declaration of digital imperatives. The commission gathered public and private figures, government leaders, representatives of NGOs, UN affiliates, infrastructure consortiums (e.g., Intelsat), and entrepreneurs (including Carlos Slim Helu, Sir Richard Branson, Mo Ibrahim, Jeffrey Sachs, and Muhammed Yunnos) to model the kinds of partnerships necessary to implement broadband development.[34]

---

31   See "SAT-3-WASC-SAFE" at itu.int. The SAT-2 cable had already connected Portugal and South Africa since 1993.

32   Samuel Dowuona, "Africa: Fibre Optic Capacity Could Be Underutilized Due to Poverty and Illiteracy," *Public Agenda*, September 4, 2009.

33   See e-cybercity.mu.

34   "A 2010 Leadership Imperative: The Future Built on Broadband," ITU, Broadband Commission for Digital Development, 2010, see "Reports and Documents" at broadbandcommission.org. The ITU had previously formed the Partnership for Measuring ICT for Development in 2004 to determine fifty indicators

The group regarded broadband infrastructure as essential to the UN's 2010 Millennium Development Goals related to poverty, education, gender, health, and the environment.[35] In the "information age" broadband was more than a communication technology; it was now characterized as a "social asset"—"like water, electricity, and roads in the industrial age".[36]

Broadband Is Liberal

Kenya has been host to the economic liberalism or laissez-faire of the telecommunications industries as well as the free market liberalization or neoliberalism espoused by the so-called Washington Consensus—a global shorthand for the standard economic policies of the World Bank and the IMF. The ITU, the World Bank, and the IMF, among other international organizations, have pressed for the liberalization or privatization of state-run utilities like Africa's monopoly telecoms. In the 1990s, both the IMF and World Bank were concerned over mismanagement and corruption in Kenya. In 1997 the World Trade Organization (WTO) negotiated a major agreement that would break up the incumbent national telecommunications monopolies, allowing foreign companies to invest in and compete with them, while also taking a share of the market.[37] In 1998, KP&TC was separated into Telkom Kenya, Kenya Post, and the Communications Commission of Kenya or CCK.[38]

The role of the CCK, as the successor institution to Kenya's monopoly telecom company, is to manage, license, and regulate

for ICT development. See Partnership on Measuring ICT for Development, ITU, "Core ICT Indicators 2010," at itu.int.

35   The millennium development goals: 1) eradicate extreme poverty and hunger; 2) achieve universal primary education; 3) promote gender equality and empower women; 4) reduce child mortality; 5) improve maternal health; 6) combat HIV/AIDS, malaria, and other diseases; 7) ensure environmental stability; 8) develop a global partnership for development.

36   "A 2010 Leadership Imperative: The Future Built on Broadband," 55.

37   Richard Gerber and Robin Braun, *New Connections: Telecommunications in a Changing South Africa* (Cape Town: University of Cape Town Press, 1998).

38   The Kenya Communications Act, 1998, at cck.go.ke. See also Huurdeman, *The Worldwide History of Telecommunications*, 548.

private ICT industries in the country. It is the domestic institutional advocate leveraging solutions for some of the nation's problems regarding rural poverty, education, and employment. Private investment focuses on the large population centers, mostly along the corridor between Nairobi and Mombasa. The CCK is, in theory, devoted to providing universal access to the internet with projects such as school-based and community-based ICT centers that will penetrate rural areas in Kenya.[39]

As Telkom Kenya and KP&TC were privatized, the major global telecom players, some of them with ancestors from the early days of telecommunications, became shareholders. Commercial brands became the face of the former incumbents, although public interests still maintained shares and influence. Among the mobile telephone operators that obtained licenses were Safaricom, Zain Kenya (formerly Celtel, and now Airtel), and Econet Wireless. Since 2008, France Télécom has acquired 51 percent of Telkom Kenya, with the brand name Orange.[40] Launched in 1993, Safaricom is the private corporation that began as KP&TC. The government of Kenya previously held a majority of the shares, but Vodafone, the British-based global telecom, now owns a controlling stake in the company.[41]

Liberalization policies operating under the ethos of market freedom and deregulation are themselves forms of market manipulation and regulation. Ironically, as the state-run communication monopolies liberalized and shed state bureaucracy, they found themselves at the same table as another, now global, bureaucracy. The UN and agencies like the ITU, Intelsat, and the World Bank have been long-standing partners in the various attempts to deliver cable to the region, and their regulatory frameworks add layers of non-state governance into the loan conditions.[42]

---

39 It has also partnered with the Kenya Institute of Education to support digital learning in secondary schools.

40 See orange.co.ke.

41 See safaricom.co.ke.

42 Pierre Guislain, *Connecting Sub-Saharan Africa: A World Bank Group Strategy for Information and Communication Technology Sector Development*, World Bank Working Paper (Washington, DC: World Bank, 2005).

Masai tribesman with cell phone, Kenya

Infrastructure entrepreneurs also often find that the incumbent infrastructure network charged with opening, regulating, and stimulating the market has insufficient means to do so. An enormous gap remains between the economies of developed nations and those of Sub-Saharan countries, prompting the World Bank to concede that: "The model of market liberalization and regulation of access to the incumbent's network—which has been successful in the European Union, North America, and increasingly in Asia and Latin America—is not directly relevant in the region of Sub-Saharan Africa."[43]

Yet another strain of liberalism is present in Kenya—a

---

43 Williams, "Advancing the Development of Backbone Network in Sub-Saharan Africa," 63; Mark D. J. Williams, *Broadband for Africa: Developing Backbone Communications Networks* (Washington, DC: World Bank, 2010).

mixture of economic liberalism and a liberalism associated with the platforms of exchange made possible by new technologies. In countries like Kenya the low prices and large customer volumes of mobile telephony align with the new "trickle-up" business and management models emerging from populous countries in the global south. The idea is to sell a limited inexpensive service or product like the cell phone to a large number of people. Coimbatore Krishnarao Prahalad, author of *The Fortune at the Bottom of the Pyramid*, and Vijay Govindarajan, author of *10 Rules for Strategic Innovators*, are among the new gurus in this field. Companies like Tata, MTN, Safaricom, and Huawei have also been bypassing their Western counterparts with these new approaches.[44] In Kenya, cell phones are priced so low that everyone has one. Even before the country was flooded with broadband capacity, the cell phone provided access to the wider world and freedom from constraints of geography and time. Now, in line with these liberal sentiments, access to texting and the internet is also associated with the free sharing of information in non-market production and social networking.[45] The cell phone and access to information are regarded as individual rights or liberties.

Broadband Is a Game

Our first two years were really a study in project management. How do you implement a project that goes through thirteen different national waters, twenty-three different jurisdictions? —Brian Herlihy, President of Seacom[46]

---

44   C. K. Prahalad, *The Fortune at the Bottom of the Pyramid* (Upper Saddle River, NJ: Wharton School Publishing, 2005); Vijay Govindarajan and Chris Trimble, *10 Rules for Strategic Innovators: From Idea to Execution* (Boston, MA: Harvard Business School Press, 2005); "New Masters of Management: Pervasive Innovation Adds up to a New Management Paradigm," *Economist*, April 15, 2010.

45   Benkler, *The Wealth of Networks*, 7–16, 19–20, 278–85. See also *The Invisible Hand* podcast, episode 23, at theinvisiblehandpodcast.com; and the Creative Commons organization at http://creativecommons.org.

46   Brian Herlihy and Wang Jianzhou on "Mobility Driving Change," at The Global Forum 2010, June 26–28, Cape Town, South Africa, available on YouTube.

Confounding the master narratives that tend to organize histories and theories of globalism, Arjun Appadurai offered the model of "scapes." Stories of globalization do not necessarily follow familiar narrative arcs. They are lumpy, unfolding, variegated fields of interplay—ethnoscapes, mediascapes, technoscapes, financescapes, and ideoscapes.[47] With this framework, Kenya presents the quintessential "technoscape." "Cable Wars" was a typical newspaper headline that appeared during the period when the submarine cables were landing in East Africa, and yet this technological theater was not really like a military theater. Nor did the story reflect the default theories of free-market liberalization and competition as espoused by many. Instead, like the reciprocal dispositions that Bateson describes, both public and private players alternated between competitive and cooperative stances in order to leverage goals that benefited all parties—a complex poker game in which, on occasion, players strategically allowed other players to win.

EASSy

From 2003 to 2006, the EASSy project was still the only prospect for East African cable. The New Partnership for Africa's Development (NEPAD) helped to get World Bank funding for EASSy and developed a protocol to ensure that it would be an open-access system.[48] Unlike the cable situation in West Africa, new telecoms entering the system would not be charged more than the original members, and countries with access to the sea would not hold landlocked countries hostage. By fall 2006, NEPAD had managed to sign up only nine of the twenty-six countries with a potential stake in EASSy. It was nevertheless able to ratify the agreement and gain World Bank funding in

---

47 Arjun Appadurai, *Modernity at Large: Cultural Dimensions of Globalization* (Minneapolis: University of Minnesota Press, 1996), 33.

48 See africa-union.org. As the EASSy project was getting off the ground, African intergovernmental agencies also entered the governance picture. In order to fund the project, the leaders of EASSy joined forces with the newly formed NEPAD, which, like other agencies such as the African Development Bank, prioritizes infrastructure projects.

2007 while still affiliated with the original businessmen who formed the special-purpose vehicle overseeing the project.

In addition to its World Bank financing, EASSy is 90 percent African owned, with a raft of investors including many of the parastate telecoms as well as those investors and stakeholders drawn to Africa in the process of liberalization, including ISPs, cellular providers, and brokers of terrestrial fiber.[49] Alcatel-Lucent was awarded the supply contract, and, at the time, it was hoped that the cable would be operational by mid-to-late 2009.

TEAMS

While not officially withdrawn from the NEPAD protocol, by spring 2006 Kenya had raised the strongest objections about EASSy.[50] The cable delays, the result of efforts to ensure a free market with open access, were ironically having the same effect as had the very monopolies that NEPAD and others were trying to guard against. Dr. Bitange Ndemo, Kenya's Permanent Secretary in the Ministry for Information and Communications, positioned Kenya to remain a supporter of EASSy, but he also pursued alternatives to address the urgency of the situation and create healthy competition in the cable game. In 2006, the CCK proposed TEAMS, or The East African Marine System—a cable that would travel from Mombasa to Fujairah in the UAE at a cost of about $100 million (less than the approximately $250 million for EASSy). Etisalat, the UAE telecom, would own 15 percent, and 65 percent would be shared evenly between Telkom Kenya and Safaricom, two of the three entities created through liberalization. The remaining 20 percent would be available to local broadband providers and others. By October 2007, Alcatel-Lucent was awarded the supply contract for TEAMS as well. The cable was due to be the first to land in Mombasa in 2009, and was projected to reduce the price for connectivity by over 80 percent.[51]

---

49   Author interview with John Sihra, July 12, 2007.

50   "Country Has Not Pulled Out of EASSy, Says Government," *Africa News*, November 1, 2006.

51   Rebecca Wanjiku, "Teams Submarine Cable to Land First in East Africa,"

Submarine cables serving Sub-Saharan Africa, 2009

Submarine cables serving Africa, 2013

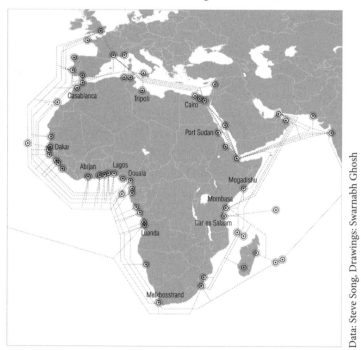

Data: Steve Song, Drawings: Swarnabh Ghosh

Seacom

Another project introduced during the confusion over EASSy was the Seacom cable, construction of which began in 2007 with private funding. Seacom was designed to connect South and East Africa directly to Marseilles and Mumbai. A Mauritian company, it is 75 percent African owned. Other investors included the Aga Khan Fund for Economic Development and Herakles Telecom, a US company based in New York City. Seacom claimed that the project would be the first to provide connectivity while meeting NEPAD's open access requirements, and it hoped to offer one Mbps at $100–$170 per month.[52]

Landings

Between the summer of 2009 and the summer of 2010, all three submarine cables landed in Kenya and East Africa. While the negotiations for the landings were highly technical, and the advances they made possible were quite sophisticated, in each case the cable itself was almost alarmingly small relative to the associated aspirations: a line only a few inches in diameter that was pulled ashore and attached to a substation. The landings for both Seacom and EASSy were delayed by piracy, adding millions to their cost.[53] Eventually, NEPAD itself pulled out of the EASSy project and started its own rival cable project.[54] A number of additional cables in the region have now landed or are scheduled

IDG news service, September 24, 2008, at networkworld.com; Terabit Consulting, "The Worldwide Submarine Cable Market and the State of African Submarine Communications," at terabitconsulting.com. Dr. Ndemo projected that the commercial price of connectivity would be reduced from $7,500 a month to $500.

52   See seacom.mu and http://manypossibilities.net.

53   The TEAMS cable landed in Mombasa on June 12, 2009, but did not go live until the following September. It was still testing when the Seacom cable went live on July 23, 2009. The EASSy cable landed on March 22, 2010, and went live on July 16, 2010. See Kui Kinyanjui, "Eassy Fibre Cable Finally Set for Landing," *Business Daily*, February 23, 2010. As the cables landed, the satellite broadband business, despite recent large investments, would be increasingly confined to a smaller share of the market. See Russell Southwood, "Satellite to Fibre—Continent's Big Change Is Really Under Way, Says New Report," at balancingact-africa.com.

54   NEPAD Broadband Infrastructure Network or NBIN (later Uhurunet). See http://mybroadband.co.za.

to land on the heels of these three landings.[55] Since 2003, when EASSy was first discussed, several more submarine cable projects—over ten by some counts—are in the works for the entire continent of Africa.[56] Many remain fluid, initially announced as independents only to merge with each other later, renaming themselves or disappearing altogether as other projects render them obsolete in terms of coverage or capacity.

Terrestrial cable: KDN

While all the cable operators were racing to get into the water, Kenya's most prominent terrestrial broadband provider, Kenya Data Networks or KDN (recently renamed Liquid Telecom Kenya), had become an especially agile partner of the government only because it had also been their competitor. KDN invested in Kenya at the time of liberalization and began building a terrestrial fiber-optic network years in advance of the submarine cable landings. The company planned to provide fixed broadband access to large institutions, banks, universities, and multinational corporations, and sell bandwidth to ISPs for their own resale. The initial route of the terrestrial cable was relatively

---

55   The privately funded MaIN OnE serves West Africa and came on line in July of 2010, linking Nigeria and Ghana to the world via Portugal and the UK. GLO-1 (Globalcom-1), sponsored by the Nigerian telecommunications company Globalcom, also came on line in 2010 and links sixteen West African Countries with Portugal, Spain, and the UK. LION, which links Madagascar with Réunion and Mauritius and is funded by France Télécom, Orange Madagascar, and Mauritius Telecom, came on line the same year. It was soon joined by LION2, linking these countries to Mayotte and Mombasa via Madagascar. The West African Cable System (WACS), linking the entire western seaboard of Africa with London, came on line in 2012. It is funded by a large consortium of telecommunications players including some with long histories in colonial cabling, like Cable and Wireless Worldwide, as well as some of the newest multinationals from the developing world, like Tata Communications. The Africa Coast to Europe Cable (ACE), which also came on line in 2012, is largely redundant with WACS and is funded by another consortium of telecommunications players including many of the West African France Télécom entities such as Orange Mali, Orange Cameroon, and Orange Niger. SAex cable, connecting South America, Angola, and South Africa, is projected to be operational in the second quarter of 2014. See mainonecable.com; gloworld.com; http://lion. orange.com; eafricacommission.org; http://wacscable.com; ace-submarinecable. com; and "African Undersea Cables," at http://manypossibilities.net.

56   See "African Undersea Cables," at http://manypossibilities.net.

KDN (Liquid Telecom Kenya) Terrestrial Fiber Network

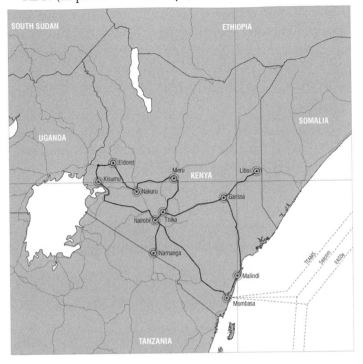

National Optical Fiber Backbone Infrastructure (NOFBI)

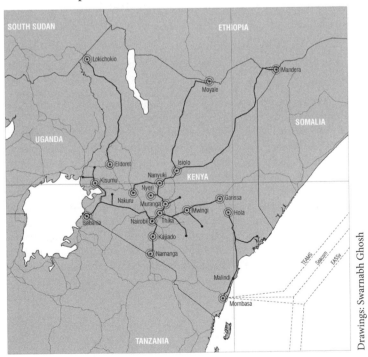

easy to determine in relation to return on investment. It connected the major population centers, again following the line of the old IBEAC railway and running alongside the roads between Mombasa, Nairobi, and Kisumu. By December 2007, the French company Sagem, together with Huawei and ZTN, had contracted to lay the cable.[57]

Originally accused of attempting to secure a terrestrial monopoly at odds with the national interest, KDN has also negotiated alongside the Kenyan government. The company owns 10 percent of the TEAMS cable, and raised essential questions about the project and its onward capacity—the price Fujairah would charge to connect to the rest of the world.[58] KDN's occasional pushback, together with their investment, gave the government extra power at the global bargaining table.

In addition to the commercial backbone, through the CCK, the country has plans for a larger branching network that would extend to remote villages and regions of the country to foster e-governance, health care, and distance learning.[59] Illustrating again a form of cooperation between competitors, the speed with which KDN was able to implement the first fiber corridor in their plan provided an extra incentive for the CCK to implement parallel networks. As CCK has announced its plans for a regional fiber network that will reach rural areas (the National Optical Fibre Backbone Infrastructure or NOFBI), KDN has announced

---

57   Author interview with Kai Wulff, August 2007. See kdn.co.ke. See also "Kenya Date Networks, Africa," at wimax-industry.com.

58   See "African Undersea Cables," at http://manypossibilities.net; ictvillage. com. See also Okuttah Mark, "KDN Begins Rollout of Digital Village in Slums," *Business Daily*, July 24, 2008; and see also kdn.co.ke. A South African company, Altech, bought a 51 percent stake in KDN in March 2008. KDN perhaps also finds some public relations projects good for business as well as political relations. In collaboration with ictvillage.com, "a business lobby for ICT innovation," KDN has set up a digital village in the Korogocho slum in Nairobi. Al-Taawon, a youth organization in Korogocho, manages the network, pursuing its goal of providing e-governance, education, access to employment, and a base for business ventures. The project is part of a larger $2.5 million scheme to create a number of ICT villages around the country. KDN has also supplied broadband to Kenya's Red Cross Society.

59   See cck.go.ke. The initial plan was for a 4,300 kilometer national fiber-optic network with the acronym FONN.

similar plans, raising its game as a friendly competitor and potentially placing a check on bureaucratic delays.[60]

Broadband pricing

Once the three cables had landed in Kenya, the complex recali-
bration of bandwidth cost and speed began. As speeds increased,
and demand for satellite broadband fell off sharply, the prices for
broadband did not miraculously drop. Instead of the predicted
50 to 90 percent reductions, some cable companies were suggesting that the drop would be closer to 20 or 30 percent, with prices
sometimes still remaining 300 times what were in Europe. In
August 2009, after Seacom had gone on line and TEAMS was
still testing, KDN shrewdly dropped its price by 90 percent,
calculating that the first company to offer lower prices had a
better chance at gaining a larger market share.[61]

Yet ISPs down the line encountered other problems. For
instance, Safaricom invested millions in both TEAMS and
Seacom, investments which it claimed it must first recoup before
lowering prices. Also, until terrestrial cable could be laid to hard-
wire remote villages, the satellite service had to be retained.[62]
Some ISPs were still paying long-term contracts at a different
rate.[63] Some had also agreed to buy capacity before having

---

60   On an even broader regional scale, the World Bank's Africa Regional
Communications Infrastructure Program (RCIP) will provide "catalytic funding" to
organize and leverage private money for ICT development in Africa. The first three
East African countries to enter the program were Kenya, Burundi, and Madagascar.
By the end of the program, it is expected that all capitals and major cities in East and
Southern Africa will be linked to competitively priced high-bandwidth connectivity.
RCIP has also developed a policy supporting clusters of growth that crystallize
around existing resources and talents, like Kenya's flower industry in the Rift Valley.
See "Addressing Africa's 'Missing Link,'" at http://web.worldbank.org; and Douglas
Zhihua Zeng and World Bank, *Knowledge, Technology, and Cluster-Based Growth in
Africa* (Washington, DC: World Bank, 2008).

61   Kui Kinyanjui, "KDN Dial up Rates Slashed as Internet Pricing Wars
Intensify," *Business Daily*, August 5, 2009. Still, the ISPs who bought services from
KDN's fiber backbone did not decrease prices, claiming that they needed to recoup
investment or that their contracts would first have to expire before they could offer
reductions. They also claimed that cable maintenance would be costly.

62   Ibid.

63   Stanford's PingER project tests transmission speeds on sites around the

acquired a sufficient share of the market to be able to use it.[64] Piracy, spam, corruption, and vandalism also triggered extra security costs.[65] There were even claims of too much competition, as well as insufficient demand due to poverty, illiteracy, and problems with the electrical grid.[66] Predictably, telecom business representatives called for bigger tax incentives and more public funding for infrastructure to bring down their costs, citing the need for much larger investments in developing countries.[67]

While slow to thaw, prices have nevertheless been drifting downward as speeds increase, and cell phone subscriptions continue to rise dramatically. Safaricom initially estimated that they might have 3 million subscribers by 2020, but they already had 14 million by 2009, over 17 million by 2011, and over 20 million by 2013. Zain and Orange both achieved a growth rate of over 50 percent in 2011.[68] In 2013, the total number of cell phone

---

world. See "New E. Coast of Africa Fibre," at https://confluence.slac.stanford.edu; and Rachel Pollock, "Fiber Optics in Sub-Saharan Africa Improve Infrastructure," at mediaglobal.org.

64 Catherine Riungu, "No Hope of Cheap Internet with Providers Locked into 25 Year Deals," *The East African*, October 5, 2009.

65 The cable is sometimes excavated because it is mistakenly assumed to be copper that can be resold. Other cases of vandalism are the result of deliberate sabotage among ISPs fighting for first contact with the market.

66 "Operators Claim Too Much Competition in Fibre," *Middle East and Africa Telecommunications Insight* 46 (2010); Dowuona, "Africa: Fibre Optic Capacity Could Be Underutilized Due to Poverty and Illiteracy."

67 Dr. Ndemo has been a leader throughout, agitating against price fixing in every possible public forum. At the East African Fiber Summit, in December 2009, Ndemo noted that many internet service providers promised to reduce the price of one megabyte of bandwidth from $4000–$6000 to $600, but Ndemo had wanted the price reduced to $200. He once advocated that disrupting the cable should be punished with a life sentence. Speaking for the EASSy project, John Sihra claimed that the shorter-term contracts with EASSy would be the real stimulus to competition since the twenty-year contracts with TEAMS and Seacom were helping to maintain the status quo. See Ander Comstedt, "East African Fiber Optic Summit: Submarine Cables on the Beach, Now What?," at aitecafrica.com; Abdirahman O. Sheikh, "Building Networks for Life," at the East African Fiber Summit, Nairobi, 2009; Jonathan Fildes, "Broadband World: Connecting Africa," at bbc.co.uk; and Kui Kinyanjui, "Eassy Fibre Link Brews Fresh Internet Price War," *Business Daily*, December 2, 2009.

68 CCK, "Quarterly Sector Statistics Report" (July 2010–September 2011). Safaricom, which has a 22.5 percent stake in TEAMS, experienced a 53 percent

subscriptions in Kenya was over 31 million, or over 76 percent of the population.[69] While there are ephemeral barriers related to prices and speeds, the major global telecoms like Huawei, Nokia, Samsung, Google, and RIM are competing to get their handsets or tablets into the hands of a ready market.[70] In 2011, the *Economist* noted that "All manner of services, from independent television stations to one of the region's biggest call-centres, are flourishing" as a result of increased broadband capacity.[71]

Broadband Makes an Internet of Things

A device that was a yuppie toy not so long ago has now become a potent force for economic development in the world's poorest countries.—Economist, May 29, 2008

In the ITU's 2010 Broadband Commission for Digital Development, prescient global entrepreneurs predicted that the increasing numbers of cell phones in countries like Kenya would create an "internet of things."[72] The phrase is usually used to describe a world embedded with digital devices—not only mobile phones but also smart vehicles, RFID tags, transit systems, sensors, or smart architectural elements. Having escaped the box of the computer, this distributed set of "circuits" interfaces with the internet but also creates its own network of intelligence.

---

growth in subscribers in 2009. See Safaricom, "Annual Report," 2010 and Safaricom, "Annual Report", 2013.

69   The population of Kenya is approximately 40 million. CCK, "Quarterly Sector Statistics Report (July–September 2013)," 9-10, at cck.go.ke; Jenny C. Aker and Isaac M. Mbiti, "Mobile Phones and Economic Development in Africa," Center for Global Development, 2010. Some users may have multiple subscriptions, but some phones may also be shared, so the number of people with access to cell phones may be much larger than the studies reflect.

70   "Digital Revolution," *Economist*, April 9, 2011.

71   "Revving Up the Pace," *Economist*, May 21, 2011, 80–1.

72   "A 2010 Leadership Imperative: The Future Built on Broadband," 55.

Cell tower, Kenya

Kenya's broadband space is indeed an "internet of things"—a world where the cell phone is a chip, sensor, switch, circuit, or processor that has escaped the computer to become embedded in physical space. The phone, a device that without changing its shape can become, among other things, a computer, a flashlight, a clock, a camera, or a musical instrument, is seen as an essential piece of equipment for both the young professional and the farmer. Whether or not phones are able to access the internet, text messaging generates an information network parallel to the internet and, with the aid of apps, that network sometimes intersects with and draws on internet resources. The phone call and handset are often secondary to the content platforms the device is able to carry. Just as with the internet, the more cell phone users, the more robust is the network of information. The trickle-up paradigm not only establishes a large customer base but also uses the cell phone as a multiplier in any number of new business schemes.

For instance, with Safaricom's M-PESA, a platform developed in Kenya, the mobile phone became a global banking tool. All around the world, M-PESA users can send remittances home, pay bills, or repay loans on their mobile phones.[73] Perhaps because it is less expensive to use M-PESA than a formal or informal bank in Kenya, and because most Kenyan citizens do not have access to banks, Safaricom quickly reached nearly a quarter of the country's population, capturing a larger share of the banking business than any other financial institution in Kenya, and making the company millions of dollars in profit.[74]

M-PESA is not just for the poor paying off microfinance loans; it is also being used in urban areas as an alternative to traditional banking. Long before the rest of the world was using a platform like Google Wallet, Kenyans were paying for taxis and other services with their cell phones.[75] In 2009, Safaricom transferred funds worth 10 percent of the country's GDP.[76] Brian Herlihy, the president of Seacom, forecasts that the communication business will begin to rely less and less on delivering access and more and more on partnerships that combine infrastructural assets with content.[77]

---

73   Claudia McKay and Mark Pickens, "Branchless Banking Pricing Analysis," Consultative Group to Assist the Poor (CGAP) 2010. M-PESA is offered by Safaricom (since 2007) or Zap on the Zain network. Zain offers the cheapest of these services in the world, and Safaricom is also among the least expensive.

74   See mobilemoneyexchange.org; and "Notes on Regulation of Branchless Banking in Kenya," CGAP, 2007. Questions remain about how the country should regulate this financial activity. Because Safaricom does not retain interest from funds, it is not technically a banking business and cannot be regulated as such. Maximum account balances and transfers, together with a fund held in trust, will hopefully either prevent or cover abuses such as money laundering.

75   Nathan Eagle, "TEDx Boulder Colorado, November 9, 2010," video available on YouTube.

76   Aker and Mbiti, "Mobile Phones and Economic Development in Africa," 19, 4.

77   Brian Herlihy and Wang Jianzhou on "Mobility Driving Change" at The Global Forum 2010, available on YouTube; Author Interview Brian Herlihy, January 16, 2013.

M-PESA is only one of many new business ventures related to mobile telephony.[78] Google is developing additional mobile phone services for Africa such as Google SMS, in collaboration with the carrier MTN in Uganda and the Grameen Foundation. Google Trader and Farmer's Friend in Uganda let farmers access market information without making a long journey. Entrepreneurs can communicate with suppliers and coordinate supply chains more efficiently. HIV and AIDS patients can receive text message reminders to take medication. To fight counterfeit drug distribution, another mobile service allows users to check whether or not a drug is genuine by texting a code printed on the drug packaging. Esoko, a mobile stock market of sorts founded in Ghana, allows users from fifteen African countries to share market data of all kinds. Mobile trading platforms like KenyaBUZZ sell tickets for sports and other events over the phone.[79] Safaricom's iCow helps dairy farmers track their cows while providing best practice advice on how to improve milk yield.[80]

The technology itself provides job opportunities for those entrepreneurs selling access to services in remote villages or selling phone cards. The Dabba network in South Africa buys wireless capacity from carriers that continue to charge large connectivity fees, and then resells it to local networks at a more affordable rate. Dabba has developed its business model as one that can be emulated by other micro-operators.[81]

With the Ushahidi platform, imaging capability together with crowd-sourcing software turned the mobile phone into an

---

78   "New Masters of Management: Pervasive Innovation Adds Up to a New Management Paradigm," *Economist*, April 15, 2010.

79   "Not Just Talk: Mobile Services in Poor Countries," *Economist,* January 27, 2011; esoko.com.

80   See safaricom.co.ke.

81   See http://allafrica.com; shuttleworthfoundation.org and villagetelco.org. Dabba worked with the Shuttleworth Foundation to develop a project called "Village Telco." Steve Song, a fellow of the Shuttleworth Foundation, is working on similar telecommunications solutions and maintaining a blog about these issues that features a graphic chronology of the various African cable landings. See "African Undersea Cables," at http://manypossibilities.net.

instrument of political oversight. Ushahidi, which means "testimony" or "witness" in Swahili, was launched in Kenya after the 2008 elections to allow observers to map evidence of violence or deliver assistance using GPS-enabled phones. Having received its first trial in Kenya, Ushahidi is now an open-source platform run as a non-profit, and has been used to track violence in Gaza, monitor elections in India, gather information about wildlife in Kenya, help organize the clean up of the Deepwater Horizon oil spill, and assist in the aftermath of the earthquake in Haiti.[82]

Another crowd-sourcing platform, also first tested in Kenya, uses a similar technological apparatus but often toward very different ends. While in Kenya teaching classes in software development for mobile phones, Nathan Eagle, a data analyst and software developer, was able to develop platforms for information gathering that compensated users with airtime in exchange for data. A nurse could text information about blood supplies. A Masai herdsman could help develop speech-recognition software for his dialect. A homemaker could transcribe audio into text. Eagle's platform, launched in 2009 and originally named txteagle, was characterized as a tool of empowerment and new source of income. "What," he asked, "could we do with the world's largest work force?"[83]

The platform, renamed Jana (meaning "people" in Sanskrit), now has the ability to communicate with and "incentivize" around 3.5 billion cell phone users—or more than half of the people in the world. Jana gains access to this massive population through service providers seeking revenues from data collection. Its clients include the UN, hoping to gather information more efficiently and cheaply than it could with face-to-face surveys, but also many multinationals (e.g., Unilever, Ponds, Wrangler, Danone) planning to market a product or service to populous emerging markets in, for instance, China, South America, or Africa. Such companies need to build "relationships with the

---

82   See ushahidi.com.
83   Nathan Eagle, "Txteagle: Mobile Crowdsourcing," at http://realitymining. com; Nathan Eagle, "TEDx Boulder Colorado, November 9, 2010."

world's 'next billion' consumers"—the emerging middle class that will no longer be located in developed countries.[84]

The adoption of the cell phone and its social media platforms brings with it both broad opportunities and particular dangers. The staggering growth of mobile telephony in the broadband landscape delivers information to many, but it also returns information to the cell phone operators who suddenly have data from, and direct access to, a huge population of consumers and informants. While billed as a way to reverse the exploitative use of personal data by providing compensation, Jana is nevertheless an instant conduit for market contact, one that raises immediate questions about how access will be deployed and compensation calibrated.[85] Jana may offer compensation as well as communication, but it may also have unintended consequences—especially as billions of subscribers in the developing world are increasingly used in market research. A platform celebrating its broad reach, open access, and free circulation of information within an internet of things may also become a network concentrating authority in an organization with a highly centralized disposition.

Broadband Space Is Information

The "internet of things" relies on telecommunications devices to convey information, but in broadband urbanism, information is also immanent in the disposition of the space itself with or without telecommunication. Space is much more than just a source of friction in discussions of the "last mile." Broadband networks present compound dispositions—the linear topologies of terrestrial fiber-optic cable buried in the ground, the atomized airborne topology of mobile telephony, and the switches between the two. Each has the power to territorialize, alter settlement patterns, and redistribute resources. Broadband and ICT infrastructure are socio-technical networks. Just as the technology prompts

---

84   See jana.com.

85   See http://txteagle.com; "Txteagle has 2.1 Billion Numbers on Speed Dial," at http://online.wsj.com; and "A Chat with Serial Entrepreneur Nathan Eagle," Txteagle: Mobile Research Conference 2011, available on YouTube.

many new uses and social structures, the social structures and physical organizations of urban space in turn influence the development of the technology.

While slower, cheaper mobile internet access in Kenya has begun to grow, the high-end broadband on which the country is staking its economic viability has not yet found a comparable growth market. It is cheaper for ISPs to provide wireless broadband for mobile rather than fixed devices because mobile allows them to more quickly calibrate capacity and investment to market needs.[86] Yet mobile phone entrepreneurialism sometimes raises questions about its real beneficiaries and draws attention away from the larger health, education, and employment issues that rely on high-capacity fixed broadband. The proportion of people accessing the internet in Kenya in 2013 was estimated to be about 47 percent, and while there are over 11 million mobile internet subscriptions, only about 62,000 subscriptions were using high-speed fixed links.[87]

Despite the heavy promotion of open, universal access, the default spatial vessel for fixed premium broadband is the enclave—a switch in the broadband network that is the

---

86   Williams, "Advancing the Development of Backbone Network in Sub-Saharan Africa."

87   CCK, "Quarterly Sector Statistics Report (July–Sept. 2013)," 21–2 at cck.go.ke. In 2012, the percentage of the population with access to the internet stood at around 32 percent with only 43,000 fixed high-speed subscriptions. ITU, World Telecommunications/ICT Indicators Database, 17th Edition, June 17, 2013. Convergence—when a single network develops the capacity to carry multiple different services that used to require separate networks—has contributed to Kenya's resourceful entrepreneurialism. The word is also used in relation to the corporate merger of different ICT industries. When Google buys YouTube or Netflix, it expands beyond a search engine enterprise to include new allied enterprises and content to establish the internet as the new movie or TV screen. While these convergence strategies can intensify monopolies, they can also lower prices, increase competition, and broaden markets. See Rajendra Singh and Siddhartha Raja, "Nothing Endures But Change: Thinking Strategically About ICT Convergence," in World Bank, ed., *Information and Communications for Development*. Prices for international calls in Kenya dropped by nearly 80 percent after Voice Over Internet Protocol (VOIP) was legalized as a service. CCK, "Sector Statistic Report" (Q2, 2009–2010). While the chief convergence format is internet over telephone, digital television was also launched in Kenya in 2009–2010.

equivalent of a closed loop. ISPs laying underground cable favor existing linear infrastructure like highway and rail lines. For residential services, many locate redundantly in the less populous wealthy areas of Western Nairobi like Karen just north of the superdense Kibera slum.[88] They prefer an urban pattern of gated communities that provide security and simplify the laying of terrestrial lines.[89]

The Kenyan government and its collaborators are even promoting the default zone formula as a development goal. In 2008, in the aftermath of the violent elections of the previous year, the coalition government of President Mwai Kibaki and Prime Minister Raila Odinga introduced Vision 2030, a plan for developing Kenya into a "middle income economy."[90] The plan remains in effect under the current president, Uhuru Kenyatta, son of Jomo Kenyatta. With its upbeat projections and organizational diagrams, Vision 2030 promises to address and exceed the UN's Millennium Development Goals with a broad spectrum of changes to infrastructure, security, health, education, and employment. The program also hopes to grow business in tourism, agriculture, offshore processing, and financial services. Crucial to all these plans is a fiber-optic network running throughout the country, serving transportation infrastructure, zone development, and "digital villages" in remote areas.[91]

As part of the plan, the Athi River EPZ is slated for upgrade, as is the Jomo Kenyatta Airport and the Mombasa port.[92] Athi River was the first export processing zone created after an Export Development Program was introduced in 1990, and it has been struggling.[93] For instance, most of the inexpensive textiles in Kenya are made in China. In one Athi River factory, Kenyan cotton is processed into thread, shipped to China, and then

88   Waita, Sheikh, and Fildes, East African Fiber Summit, Nairobi 2009.

89   Comstedt, "Submarine Cables on the Beach, Now What?"

90   "Reforms to Improve Service Delivery in Public Sector," at planning.go.ke.

91   "Kenya Vision 2030: A Globally Competitive and Prosperous Kenya, First Medium Term Plan, 2008–2012," Government of the Republic of Kenya, 2008, at vision2030.go.ke.

92   Ibid.

93   See epzakenya.com.

Keller Easterling

Athi River EPZ, 2007

returned as cloth to a garment factory next door to the first. Kenyan businesses thus forfeit a large slice of the profit from the blue jeans that are eventually manufactured.[94] The zone is a global habit that is hard to break, and Kenya's zones have been waiting for the broadband capacity that will make them viable job creators in the global network of export processing.

Vision 2030 also calls for new zone-style cities like Konza Technology City, planned as a 5,000 acre incubator for Kenya's role as "silicon savannah." Dr. Ndemo is promoting and coordinating investment for Konza Technology City and its projected 200,000 new jobs. As announced at an investor's conference in August of 2012, the city "offers all the benefits of a greenfield,

94   Author visit to Athi River EPZ, August 2007.

'clean sheet' site [that] is nevertheless right at the centre of things: 60km from the heart of Nairobi; 50km from Jomo Kenyatta international airport; 500km from Mombasa and its ports; the railway within 4km." The strain of zone formulas that has finally arrived in Kenya and informs Konza Technology City at least includes not only civic and cultural functions but also some intelligent approaches to landscaping. The enclave's central park and 10km surrounding buffer zone are designed to control development and preserve wilderness. The rest of the promotional literature is, however, familiar. The Konza master plan "is based on successful 'new town' projects around the world—put together by an international team of experts. It is a model in line with best practice from countries all over the world to ensure global competitiveness." Near Konza, two more Dubai-style cities have been proposed—Machakos New City and the Kenya-China Economic Zone.[95]

The most startling political, economic, and infrastructural proposal in Vision 2030 is one that would create an entirely new transportation corridor—a double of the Mombasa–Nairobi corridor from the coastal city of Lamu, through eastern Kenya, to Juba in Southern Sudan. The Lamu Port–Southern Sudan–Ethiopia Transport Corridor (LAPSSET), would begin with a new deep-water port in Lamu. Despite dredging, the port of Mombasa is still not deep enough to handle the large Panamax container ships. The corridor, a bundle of superhighway, oil pipeline, rail, electrical, and fiber infrastructure will travel to Isiolo, which will become a new tourist center. A branch traveling toward Moyale on the Kenya–Ethiopia border will eventually connect with Addis Ababa and Djibouti. Lamu, a World Heritage site that preserves an ancient and delicate Swahili settlement, would also see the development of an oil refinery, an

---

95 See konzacity.co.ke. In 2012, the World Bank's International Finance Corporation working with the Kenyan government hired a design and development team that includes HR&A Advisors, Inc., SHoP Architects, Dalberg Global Development Advisors, Center for Urban and Regional Planning, OZ Architecture, and Tetra Tech. See "Konza City Status Update," at scribd.com; *Daily Nation*, "China to Put Up Sh65bn 'Dubai' in Machakos," April 5, 2014, at nation.co.ke.

international airport, and a tourist city. Japan Port Consultants—a firm capable of delivering the global standard in twenty-first-century port and zone infrastructure—was hired in 2010 to begin carrying out the plan.[96]

Despite progressive talk about openness, new business, and political brotherhood, LAPSSET is perhaps laced with other dispositions: particularly the isomorphism of the zone enclave and the binary political aggression between Northern and Southern Sudan. While the plan rescues South Sudan from its landlocked position adjacent to a hostile neighbor, it nonetheless becomes reliant on the success of the new country as an independent state. With significantly superior infrastructure and powerful global partners, the arrangement may encourage a reciprocal, cooperative disposition between all of the players. But it may also be a point of contention, irritating those cultural differences between Ethiopia, Sudan, and Kenya that were previously buffered by largely undeveloped areas. Kenya risks becoming embroiled in the Sudanese conflict—another African country gripped by ethnic conflict and oil wars.

Although received urban formulas related to zones and heavy resource extraction currently prevail—encouraged by politicians, global consultancies, and international contractors embedded in the bureaucracies of extrastatecraft—Kenya is nevertheless poised to harness communication technologies in a way that may shift expectations about the need for roads, zones, and highways. The coexistence of fixed linear broadband and a large population of mobile phones should inspire new urban experiments from spatial entrepreneurs that may be as consequential as those of the new telecom entrepreneurs.

---

96   See "LAPSSET" at vision2030.go.ke and Jeffrey Gettleman, "Future Kenya Port Could Mar Pristine Land," *New York Times*, January 12, 2010.

Broadband Is ICT4D

In the absence of more sophisticated innovations from spatial practitioners, economists and informatics specialists are shaping the experiments in broadband development. A number of new branches of research involving information/communication technology and development have been roughly assembled under the rubric of "ICT4D," or ICT for development. The World Bank and the ITU as well as private consultancies continue to develop increasingly sophisticated econometrics that appear in the annual reports of the CCK.[97] The World Bank has researched links between broadband penetration and GDP, as well as correlations between broadband and gender, education, and governance.[98] McKinsey has gathered data about African economies and developed tools such as the LRI or "Location Readiness Index" in an attempt to shape them as attractive eligible objects for foreign investment.[99] The consultancy has also developed theories and metrics for what it calls ITES—"information technology enterprise solutions"—the entrepreneurial use of IT in so-called "more than mobile" or "more than voice" uses.[100]

Richard Heeks, director of the Centre of Development Informatics at the University of Manchester, is an expert in development, working between economics, the social sciences, and IT technologies. He is among those scientists who have suggested that econometric indicators alone are insufficient in assessing

97   "Annual Report," CCK, 2007–2008 at cct.go ke.

98   Christine Zhen-Wei Qiang, *Telecommunications and Economic Growth* (Washington, DC: World Bank, 2009); World Bank Development Data Group and World Bank Global Information & Communication Technologies Dept., *Information and Communications for Development Extending Reach and Increasing Impact* (Washington, DC: World Bank, 2009); Khalil, Dongier, and Qiang, "Overview," 5.

99   Randeep Sudan et al., *The Global Opportunity in IT-Based Services: Assessing and Enhancing Country Competitiveness* (Washington, DC: World Bank, 2010).

100   Ibid.; "Not Just Talk: Mobile Services in Poor Countries," *Economist*, January 29, 2001. The International Federation for Information Processing, a secretariat outside of Vienna, also established a working group to study ICT and development. See Working Group 9.4, "Social Implication of Computers in Developing Countries," International Federation for Information Processing, 2001, at ifip.org.

policy. He argues that it is important to look at economic, socio-cultural, and legal ramifications as well as "winners and losers" in the equation to have a real sense of economic impact.[101] When treated as a "silver bullet," ICT sometimes does not deliver on its projected promises.[102] Increasingly called into question are metrics that fail to sufficiently account for complexity or context in their economic predictions. In response to the failure of several theories on the ground, Heeks has found it fruitful to consider actor-network models such as those theorized by Bruno Latour.[103]

Heeks speculates that the powerful drivers of "Development 2.0" will not be utopian prescriptions but processes that will have to be continually reevaluated, and he catalogs a number of qualitative markers of ICT performance that are already in place as potential building blocks. He claims that technologies are most successful when, like Google Trader, they manage to "connect the excluded" or remove the middleman. ICT also becomes a platform for "digital production" in sites that compensate information gathering with phone time. The improvisational use of media is a kind of "digital innovation" (e.g., using the beeps or rings of cell phones as free coded messaging). Not only crowd-sourcing but also "crowd-voicing" may provide collective power in the contexts of government or the market. And a "social enterprise" business that links IT with social or cultural concerns is beginning to emerge to coordinate all of these phenomena.[104]

---

101   Richard Boateng, Richard Heeks et al., "E-Commerce and Socio-Economic Development: Conceptualizing the Link," *Internet Research* 18, no. 5 (2008).

102   Richard Heeks, "Do Information and Communication Technologies (ICTs) Contribute to Development?," *Journal of International Development* 22 (2010), 625–40.

103   Richard Heeks and Carolyne Stanforth, "Understanding E-Government Project Trajectories from an Actor-Network Perspective," *European Journal of Information Systems* 16 (2007).

104   Heeks, "Do Information and Communication Technologies Contribute to Development?"; Richard Heeks, "Development 2.0: The IT-Enabled Transformation of International Development," *Communications of the ACM* 53, no. 4 (2010). Heeks and others have suggested that since grassroots entrepreneurs and fair-trade policies use some of the same ICT tools and techniques, they might together begin to shape a self-regulating mechanism by which business, global NGOs, and IGOs can track labor and trade figures in an information-rich network. See Richard Ducombe and

Just as Heeks positions informatics in a more complex test bed, the economists Abhijit Vinayak Banerjee and Esther Duflo, in their studies of poverty and aid in countries like Kenya, are finding new ways to test the presumptions of economic theory. Observing that aid is often not effective in reducing poverty, they decided to "step out of the office and look more carefully at the world." Using randomized trials like those employed in medical testing, they have devised a number of more finely grained tests to identify pivotal variables. Are mosquito nets more effective if sold or if given away? What factors related to distance, timing, or compensation most effectively encourage vaccinations? Under what conditions is the use of fertilizer most successful and economically sustaining? While such questions have often been answered in terms of broad economic theory or ideological pref-erence, Banerjee and Duflo want better data, and they want to redefine what constitutes data. They find quantification tech-niques more productive when their projects surround a set of small but consequential choices that their subjects must make in a specific context.[105]

Designing active forms for broadband space is not a matter of data-gathering or arriving at the correct answer, but the spatial counterparts to these experiments in informatics and economics might identify spatial variables and relationships that enhance both fixed and mobile broadband networks. Does it make a difference if users can access fixed broadband by foot, bicycle, car, or public transport? Is the urban composition of assets—the topology or urban wiring—as important as the arrangement of the technological network itself? What urban arrangements will best leverage resources from all the non-state players—from global telecoms to NGOs and IGOs—involved in Kenya's broad-band technoscape? These spatial variables might, in turn, become part of innovative structures in finance and informatics.

Richard Heeks, "An Information Systems Perspective on Ethical Trade and Self-Regulation," *Information Technology for Development* 10 (2003).

105   Abhijit V. Banerjee, *Making Aid Work* (Cambridge, MA: MIT Press, 2007); Abhijit V. Banerjee and Esther Duflo, *Poor Economics: A Radical Rethinking of the Way to Fight Global Poverty* (New York: Public Affairs, 2011), 13.

Broadband Space Is Interplay

Designers can overwrite the default spatial software that is currently organizing broadband urbanism. When master plans and formulas like zones or highways become mere containers for the current crop of spatial products they may be as bankrupt as a failed economic theory. Joining others in questioning disciplinary assumptions, broadband urbanists might offer an alternative organ of design—not an object form like a master plan, but an active form or an *interplay* of spatial variables. Savannah established not a master plan but a set of counterbalancing interdependencies. Spatial variables were linked in ratios. Public space was in a ratio with private space, and each ward generated a green space as well as an agricultural space. Broadband space can similarly be redesigned as a kind of software or a machine of interdependencies.

While in Savannah the intent was to control speculation, for broadband urbanism the object of interplay is to maximize access to information—the information carried in telecommunication devices as well as that carried in the physical spaces of the city. A number of markers or active forms might become variables in this interplay. A road, village, factory, farm, market, school, or wilderness ceases to be merely an object form when it is treated as an interdependent variable in spatial software. The mobile phone is clearly a powerful multiplier in shaping urban morphology. Important switches lie at the interstices between linear and atomized topologies of the broadband and microwave infrastructure. A switch might be an internet service provider, an earth station, a cell tower, or any village, university, school, or business with a fixed broadband connection. Any of these can function as a remote control. A school, or a market is now not just a single building but a network that might have global reach.

The simple zone antidote that maps incentives back into cities like Nairobi or Mombasa is one place to start. Urban space is the extended medium of trickle-up economics. Messiness and multiplicity in digital communication, like complexity in urban space, makes more robust networks. Nothing about broadband technology demands enclaves, and the zone antidote replaces the isomorphic disposition of the exurban enclave with a more resilient, heterogeneous urban "wiring." Rather than stigmatizing the existing city, with its slums or other urban problems, a smarter entrepreneur might see in it powerful multipliers—decreased travel times for workers in denser populations, a crossroads of international business, and fertile ground for the innovative work of universities.

A city like Nairobi demonstrates how zone incentives in the city can become part of an interplay like a switch or a governor. A simple but potentially powerful governor could link broadband capacity and public transportation as interdependent variables. In lieu of investing in a newly minted zone enclave, investments in high-capacity broadband in Nairobi invite business into the city. Special revenues from the use of that broadband, when linked to the funding of transportation, might begin to have mutually beneficial effects. Nairobi is sorely in need of transit, and that transit would also more efficiently deliver labor to the new businesses that invest in it. In this new urban software, the components of the zone have been productively hacked— disassembled and recombined to create a new bit of code or a generative spatial engine. Not only telecommunications technologies but also spatial technologies generate information through new software of relationships.

Outside the city, software for the "digital villages" proposed in Kenya's Vision 2030 might offer another interplay between, for instance, broadband capacity, remote educational or tourist institutions, transportation networks, and wilderness. The urbanist's newest challenge is to deliver world-class infrastructure to villages with minimal disturbance to wilderness landscapes, animal habitats, and indigenous populations, all of which may be valuable to remote institutions or businesses related to education or tourism. The village, if served with fixed broadband, could deliver the premium capacity necessary to sponsor a school, a research station, or a tourist destination, with remote connections to universities and cities abroad. While access to the digital information available via broadband is crucial, access to the information stored in the space of the village and the landscape is equally important. Like a switch in the larger broadband network, spatial variables in the village can form a governor that modulates access to all kinds of information.

The counterbalancing linkage between fixed broadband and transportation networks may form a counterintuitive governor. Contrary to many notions of progress, some of which are espoused by the LAPSSET project, when dialing up broadband in the village it may be best to dial down roads. Roads are often considered essential for access to schools and other community provisions, and since broadband is usually located along their length, roads and broadband are often bundled together. Yet roads can also reduce access to the information stored in urban space. If sized to accommodate cars and trucks, they may unnecessarily inflate spaces and walking distances for a village population that travels largely on foot or bicycle. A road can also reduce the information stored in wilderness landscapes if, along its length, it attracts unplanned development that destroys forest or jungle and encroaches on animal habitats and indigenous territories. In certain contexts then, reducing road capacity can increase access to remote global educational resources, revenues, and personnel. Designing roads with landscape buffers discourages new roads, intersections, and potentially destructive developments, and since cable is usually buried next to roads, buffers also add an extra degree of security. Reducing roadway widths to privilege pedestrians and cyclists concentrates development and shrinks travel distances. The information stored in urban space—the exchange among scholars, citizens, tourists, and the global assets of village cultures and landscapes—is then potentially enriched.

Another kind of software for the digital village might consider interdependencies between agriculture or manufacturing and remote global markets. The smartphone has already changed the relationship between farm and market, eliminating the need for travel until prices are sufficiently attractive. The infrastructure for the rural market may also now be directed toward selling to a global market, requiring access to airports or seaports rather than simply local or regional trucking. Replacing expensive trucking and highways with airport and rail infrastructure may increase access to these ports and the markets beyond.

The content of this spatial software—which could be limit-less—is perhaps less important than the idea of interplay itself. Interplay encourages the politics of balance rather than control. Unlike the phased master plan for a free zone filled with any number of default or generic amenities believed to conform to global expectations, active forms in interplay might link evolving local needs to specially tailored foreign investment. The econo-metric and informatic expertise that currently organizes investment in free zones and highway projects might develop innovative banking products as well as more resilient informa-tion technologies. These more finely grained levers, tied to physical spaces, do not offer a single planimetric pattern but a weighted engine of development. They can modulate rather than control development in ways that can be visibly assessed. The resources—that both foreign investment and local players need— can be built into the very particular public urban space of the city or the village rather than a space cordoned off solely for generic foreign investment. The Kenyan citizen's access to information is then balanced against the world's access to Kenya's resources.

Kenya can be among those countries telling innovative new stories about emerging forms of development. An interplay of spatial variables is a check on the rhetoric of liberalization and individual liberty—one that shifts the story away from discus-sions of freedom to discussions of obligation, cooperation, and interdependence. Recalling the political temperaments outlined by Bateson, a spatial interplay brokers a more reciprocal disposi-tion—a backflow of information from institutions halfway around the world. Rather than the bold new skyline or the poster-tribesman with a cell phone—images that only measure the penetration of multinationals or global telecoms—Kenya may display its own conquest of global territory in a network of commercial and educational institutions. It may present images of its own urban inventions as sites of mutually beneficial global exchange. The last group of countries in the world to receive premium international broadband could also be the first to bene-fit from new urban models born in their own context.

CHAPTER 4

Stories

For many historians, the first meeting of the International Telegraph Union (ITU) in Paris in 1865 may be worthy of no more than an obscure technical footnote. Telegraph networks had been growing throughout Europe, prompting the need for international protocols regarding, among other things, currency, tariffs, the Morse telegraph platform, and use of the French language. The tedious proceedings lasted from March 1 to May 17, but the chairman, French Minister of Foreign Affairs M. Drouyn de Lhuys, was nevertheless excited. He likened the convention to a "Peace Conference" intended to prevent the misunderstandings that are often the cause of war. Telecommunications historian Anton Huurdeman has noted that it "was the first international agreement concerning most of Europe since the Peace of Westphalia in 1648."[1] The ITU, recognizing national rather than private entities as members, only convened representatives of European nations. Even though the transatlantic cable had been in the water since 1856, the United States, then in the final stages of Civil War, did not attend the conference because its telegraph operations were commercially organized.

The delegates at the convention posed for a stiff group photograph that was considerably drier than the history painting commemorating the Peace of Westphalia at the end of the Thirty Years' War. The ITU had actually come together not so much as diplomats to sign a peace treaty, but as delegates sorting out a number of seemingly innocuous technical expediencies. Still, the members arguably represented a new sort of power emerging at the end of the nineteenth century—a period of growth for international infrastructure, international

---

1   Huurdeman, *The Worldwide History of Telecommunications*, 219.

organizations, and modern management techniques for large organizations of capital.

The group portrait is suggestive of several master narratives that each claim infrastructure as a mascot. Infrastructure is often portrayed as an apparatus of nation-building that is closely tied to the state and its military. Yet it is also often advanced as a standard-bearer of economic liberalism. Or, drifting toward yet another ideological vortex, it is treated as a universal platform for rationalizing global exchange.

These stories, histrionic forms of the narratives that always attend a dialogue between humans and technologies, are often decoupled from what the infrastructure space is actually doing in its more complex context on the ground.[2] They deliver the predetermined expectations concerning social and cultural behavior about which Latour cautions. However exhausted these stories may be, Enlightenment or modernist tautologies continue to revive them. They may even drift and oscillate between contradictory meanings as both the left and the right deploy them in different ways. Still, they can assemble political arias with fixed tableaus and ready audiences. These are the stories that, however immaterial, are powerful enough to buckle concrete or bend steel, and they can maintain an inescapable grip on the disposition of infrastructure space.

However, considered together, ideological stories about the military, the liberal, and the universal jostle each other, and it becomes easier to stroll out of their dominant ideological theaters to access the histories they obscure—the less sensational or less totalizing histories of extrastatecraft.

---

2   See also David E. Nye's discussion of narratives that attend spaces and infrastructure networks in his *Narratives and Spaces: Technology and the Construction of American Culture* (New York: Columbia University Press, 1997).

1865 Meeting of the International Telegraph Union

Military

I am read seriously by the French military.—Paul Virilio[3]

The ITU group photo, with only national representatives seated as members, seems to support the idea that international endeavors are a matter of nation-states coming together as they did for the Peace of Westphalia. Costumed in the accoutrements of Westphalian sovereignty, the Grand Strategists of realpolitik continue to enshrine and embellish this fabled moment when states recognized each other's rights to self-determination and non-intervention. Nations and wars go hand in glove, they claim, and the nation-state must remain the undisputed agent of historical continuity, managing the necessity of war and a peace that is the corollary of that war. Following the dictum of Prussian general Carl von Clausewitz, "war is the continuation of politics by other means." Within this view, infrastructure is cast as a primary military asset of warring

---

3   Paul Virilio and Sylvère Lotringer, *Pure War* (New York: Semiotext(e), 1983 and 1997), 14.

states that also provides the technology and direction for civilian infrastructure and urban development. Historical evidence that does not fit within this story can be ignored.

The Grand Strategists of the twentieth and twenty-first centuries have continued to regard realpolitik as the most durable framework. In the United States, Henry Kissinger, an advocate of realpolitik for a good portion of the twentieth century, has loaned his expertise to the political right. Clausewitz has influenced military thinking in the United States since the Vietnam War, and during the Gulf Wars, a so-called cult of Clausewitz was influential at the Pentagon.[4]

Yet the political left also has its own "cult of Clausewitz," and regards the Napoleonic Wars as formative in infrastructure history. When Armand Mattelart, a leftist sociologist and scholar of communication media, writes that "Communication serves first of all to make *war*," he refers to the Chappe graphic telegraph that Napoleon used almost exclusively for military purposes.[5] Like Mattelart, the leftist urbanist Paul Virilio points to Antoine-Henri de Jomini, a contemporary of Clausewitz, to mark the advent of logistics—the delivery of supplies and services to troops and an important test of the administrative and organizational skills necessary to develop infrastructure.[6] Virilio argues

---

4 Joel Achenbach, "War and the Cult of Clausewitz: How a Long-Dead Prussian Shaped US Thinking on the Persian Gulf," *Washington Post*, December 6, 1990. For instance, the grand strategies of realpolitik undergirded the Project for the New American Century, a neoconservative think tank that supported President Bush. Yale University even offers a popular course titled "Studies in Grand Strategy" that claims to maintain intact the principles of realpolitik for the next generation of leaders facing new security challenges. Charles Hill, a signatory of the Project for the New American Century and something of a cult figure at Yale, teaches the course with Paul Kennedy and John Gaddis. See Molly Worthen, *The Man on Whom Nothing Was Lost: The Grand Strategy of Charles Hill* (Boston: Houghton Mifflin, 2005); Mark Binks, "A Yale Class Seeks to Change the World . . . Before Graduation" (2004), at jrn.columbia.edu; and Bruce Fellman, "Training the Next Leaders," *Yale Alumni Magazine*, March 2003.

5 Armand Mattelart, *Mapping World Communication: War, Progress, Culture* (Minneapolis: University of Minnesota Press, 1994), xiii. The only civilian use was to broadcast the result of the lottery.

6 Armand Mattelart, *The Invention of Communication* (Minneapolis: University of Minnesota Press, 1996), 200; and John Shy, "Jomini," in Peter Paret, ed.,

that not mercantile, but rather military urges are at the heart of urbanism and infrastructure. For Virilio, "Total War" is indistinct from civil society, replacing political economy and almost every aspect of culture and industry.[7] The philosopher and theorist Sylvère Lotringer, in conversation with Virilio, has claimed great things for the latter's position, describing it as "a Copernican revolution in the relations of strategy to politics."[8]

The left has also been drawn to the famous Clausewitzian dictum as if it were a riddle to be continually unpacked, reassembled or eventually solved. Foucault inverted the phrase as well ("Politics is the continuation of war by other means.") arguing that power maintains itself through its military victories.[9] Virilio too has joined the great men who have inverted or rephrased the nostrum, in one instance recasting the phrase thusly: "the Total Peace of deterrence is Total War by other means."[10]

Rehearsing arguments that link infrastructure and the military has become routine. During the World Wars, the ITU itself suspended all meetings, and many multinational infrastructure enterprises that had been acting independently and in service of

---

Makers of Modern Strategy: From Machiavelli to the Nuclear Age (Princeton: Princeton University Press, 1986), 184–5.

7   Virilio and Lotringer, *Pure War*, 12, 14, 17. Virilio was also referencing the total war espoused by German general Erich Friedrich Wilhelm Ludendorff.

8   Ibid., 17.

9   Michel Foucault, *Society Must Be Defended* (New York: St. Martin's Press, 2003). Lenin's analysts and contemporaries claimed that his policies inverted the dictum that politics is the continuation of war by other means. See William E. Odom, *The Collapse of the Soviet Military* (New Haven: Yale University Press, 1998), 11. Odom quotes Lenin's contemporary Viktor Chernov writing in *Foreign Affairs* in 1924 after Lenin's death: "It has been said that war is a continuation of politics by other means. Lenin would have undoubtedly reversed this dictum, and said that politics is the continuation of war by another guise." Viktor Chernov, "Lenin," in James F. Hodge, Jr. and Fareed Zakaria, eds., *The American Encounter: The United States and the Making of the Modern World* (New York: Basic Books, 1997), 50.

10   Virilio and Lotringer, *Pure War*, 31. He also proffered, "it will no longer be war that is the continuation of politics by other means, it will be what I have dubbed 'the integral accident' that is the continuation of politics by other means." CTheory interview with Paul Virilio, "The Kosovo War Took Place In Orbital Space: Paul Virilio in Conversation with John Armitage," at ctheory.net.

multiple governments were deputized by their state, put in the service of the military, and drawn into the rhythms of war and peace. Infrastructure enterprises built highways, fortifications, and railroads and developed airplane flight, radar, encryption, and computing among many technologies used in the military. Ever since Eisenhower uttered the words "military-industrial complex," infrastructure and militarization have been increasingly entangled. Sophisticated critique (from, e.g., James Der Derian or Manuel DeLanda) has demonstrated the ways in which war has infiltrated every aspect of society from consumer materials and commodities to communication and security devices, robotics, and even computer games.

Some of the most nuanced contemporary arguments about militarization clearly demonstrate that space itself is a military apparatus. The architect and theorist Eyal Weizman argues that urbanism is often not merely a trophy of war or a development in its aftermath but is itself deployed in military strategies.[11] He points to the settlements in the West Bank and Gaza as tools of military aggression and human rights abuse.[12] Going further, scholars like Stephen Graham see in the securitization of everything from suburbs to free zones to world cities a militarization that blurs the boundaries between the civil and the military as each borrows techniques from the other.[13]

The insights of these scholars, analysts, theorists, and designers make clear the crucial connections between military and civilian infrastructure. Nevertheless, historians and theorists

---

11   The conception of urbanism as a target or a military adversary joins other theories of "urbicide" (the coinage of Marshall Berman). Consider General Curtis LeMay's napalm bombing of Vietnamese cities, the gradual destruction of Sarajevo, or terrorist attacks on the civilian spaces of cities. Theorists including Mike Davis, Stephen Graham, Ryan Bishop, Gregory Clancey, and Daniel Bertrand Monk have done exceptional research on this phenomenon. A remarkable collection that includes contributions by many of these authors is Stephen Graham, ed., *Cities, War, and Terrorism: Towards an Urban Geopolitics* (London: Wiley-Blackwell, 2004).

12   Eyal Weizman, *Hollow Land: Israel's Architecture of Occupation* (New York: Verso, 2007).

13   Stephen Graham, *Cities Under Siege: The New Military Urbanism* (New York: Verso, 2009).

have also argued that military intent is insufficient to describe many infrastructure developments. Mattelart has called for a "critical history" of global infrastructure, contending that "historical research is manifested mainly in the form of a return to national histories, while the international is still left by the wayside."[14] Thomas P. Hughes, a historian of socio-technical networks, has argued that "History is often popularly imaged as the story of such obvious events as wars, revolutions, and shifting alignments of political power."[15] Similarly Paul Starr, professor of sociology and public affairs, has written, "The idea that war is the mother of the state is a staple of comparative history," yet, as he demonstrates, it is hardly the only determining factor in infrastructure decisions.[16]

Technologies do not have predestined uses, military or otherwise. They are constantly reassigned to different tasks, just as ARPAnet, a military technology, was reborn as a social network. In the early days, when ARPAnet's twin, USENET, relied on the same technology, it often became a repository of "lists of people's favorite movies, and recipes for goulash, and arguments about metaphysics and so on."[17] At CERN, when redesigned as the World Wide Web, the same technology generated a still more open disposition. As Bruce Sterling writes, "ARPA's network, designed to assure control of a ravaged society after a nuclear holocaust, has been superseded by its mutant child the Internet."[18]

Nevertheless, theories about the internet, emerging in the

---

14   Mattelart, *Mapping World Communication*, 243.

15   Hughes, *Networks of Power*, 407.

16   Starr, *The Creation of the Media*, 164. Infrastructure historians, among them Hughes, Starr, David E. Nye, Wolfgang Schivelbusch, and others, have developed narrative forms that simply follow a technology (e.g., rail, electricity, communications) as one thread around which many stories crystallize. See Wolfgang Schivelbusch, *Disenchanted Night: The Industrialization of Light in the Nineteenth Century* (Berkeley: University of California Press, 1995 reprint), 79–114; and Nye, *Narratives and Spaces*.

17   See "Chapter Three: History of Electronic Mail," let.leidenuniv.nl.

18   Bruce Sterling, "Short History of the Internet," *Magazine of Fantasy and Science Fiction*, February 1993.

1990s from the RAND Corporation, demonstrate the difficulty of detaching infrastructure space from even the most conventional military narratives. Not surprisingly, the Defense Research Institute at RAND—the quintessential think tank of the military-industrial complex—has long been busy identifying new security threats linked to information and communication networks. But the story of RAND researchers John Arquilla and David Ronfeldt is striking in that it (perhaps accidentally) exposes the persistent power and attraction of military and binary dispositions in the rhetoric of both the left and the right—even in infrastructure analysis that attempts to establish a new or divergent paradigm.

In a number of books published in 1990s, Arquilla and Ronfeldt offered an alternative to the familiar grand strategies of political histories. They argued that in addition to "America's two main schools of grand strategy: realpolitik and liberal internationalism," there was a third strategy: noopolitik. In the midst of an "information revolution," "non-state actors" were acquiring new powers and "global interconnectivity" was "generating a new fabric for world order"—an entirely new security environment in which non-state actors, whether NGOs or terrorists, were as powerful as state actors deploying the "soft power" of ideas and persuasions in resilient networks.[19]

In their book *Networks and Netwars* (2001) Arquilla and Ronfeldt modeled patterns of "netwar" activities with network diagrams like those that appeared in RAND predecessor Paul Baran's 1964 memorandum "On Distributed Communications" (1964)—seminal diagrams of centralized, decentralized, and distributed network topologies that essentially modeled the

---

19   The French philosopher Pierre Teilhard de Chardin's conception of the noosphere remained unacknowledged as the authors hastened to stake out a new global paradigm. John Arquilla and David Ronfeldt, *The Emergence of Noopolitik: Toward an American Information Strategy* (Santa Monica, CA: RAND, 1999), 28. See also John Arquilla, David F. Ronfeldt, and Rand Corporation, *Cyberwar Is Coming!* (Santa Monica, CA: RAND, 1992); John Arquilla et al., *The Advent of Netwar* (Santa Monica, CA: RAND 1996); John Arquilla and David F. Ronfeldt, eds., *In Athena's Camp: Preparing for Conflict in the Information Age* (Santa Monica, CA: RAND, 1997).

intent of ARPAnet. Using network diagrams captioned as "chain," "hub," "all-channel," or "full-matrix," Arquilla and Ronfeldt attached a new security threat to topologies similar to those originally used to model precursors of the internet.[20] The "Zapatistas," the "Battle for Seattle," and "hacktivism" were offered as examples of these "acephalous" or "polycephalous" networks. The authors reported that the stealth networks previously proposed by the United States in the Cold War were now even being used to target the United States in elusive ways. Netwar had replaced Cold War.[21]

While congratulating themselves on the originality of their new paradigm, Arquilla and Ronfeldt unwittingly mirror a similar struggle with military stories in leftist political theory—theory with which they presumably share few other sentiments. Just as Virilio swaggered about the relevance of his own revolutionary ideas, Arquilla and Ronfeldt claim that their first speculations about cyberwar in 1993, and netwar in 1996, seem to have even influenced the likes of Manuel Castells or Subcomandante Marcos of the Zapatista movement.[22] Yet acknowledging nourishment from other thinkers, a stray footnote in *The Emergence of Noopolitik* references the writings of Michel Foucault and Jacques Derrida concerning "narrative and discourse in the exercise of power."[23] Arquilla and Ronfeldt also suggest in the opening pages of *Networks and Netwars* that contemporary war is fought not like a chess game of national strategies, but rather, as they put it, like the "Oriental game of Go." With this reference, they perhaps unwittingly share a similar argument with leftist thinkers Gilles Deleuze and Félix Guattari as expressed in their work *Nomadology: The War Machine* (1986).[24]

---

20   John Arquilla and David F. Ronfeldt, "The Advent of Netwar (Revisited)" in *Networks and Netwars: The Future of Terror, Crime, and Militancy* (Santa Monica, CA: RAND, 2001), 8.

21   Ibid., 2–3, 7.

22   Ibid., 3, 192. The authors write, "For its part, the high command of the Mexican military also espoused admiration for the concept during 2000."

23   Arquilla and Ronfeldt, *The Emergence of Noopolitik: Toward an American Information Strategy 53*, note 27.

24   Arquilla and Ronfeldt, "The Advent of Netwar (Revisited)," 2. "Treatise on

In "Treatise on Nomadology: The War Machine," Deleuze and Guattari use the model of Go to describe the dispositions of the "war machine"—a source of conflict that is "exterior to the state." The violence dispensed by nomadic bands of non-state players, like Genghis Khan, is not officially war, in their argument, unless it engages a state.[25] Yet a state may temporarily appropriate non-state actors, as in the case of military proxies or privateers. Such a band of non-state actors is a war machine when it *induces* war from the state.[26] For Deleuze and Guattari, the war machine conquests operate in the "smooth" space of Go, instead of the "striated" space of chess. Like official agents of the state, chess offers each game piece established hierarchical routines for movement and strategy. The "smooth" space of Go, like the extrastate war machine, allows non-hierarchical black or white stones to move fluidly on a grid as each tries to capture ever-changing territories.[27] Arguing that "commercial organization is also a band of pillage, or piracy for part of its course and in many of its activities," Deleuze and Guattari use Go and the war machine to model the powers of Capital.[28]

Arquilla and Ronfeldt, like Deleuze and Guattari, also reach for Go to model a new paradigm—this time, not the violence of Capital but the security threat of terrorism—and yet they

---

Nomadology" was published as a segment of Deleuze and Guattari's *Mille Plateaux* in 1980 (translated into English in 1987), but it was first published separately in English as *Nomadology: The War Machine* (New York: Semiotext(e), 1986). The texts of Arquilla and Ronfeldt join those of other security specialists who use complexity theory as a fresh tool for theorizing about defense. For just two examples from different quarters, see Joshua Cooper Ramo, *The Age of the Unthinkable: Why the New World Disorder Constantly Surprises Us and What We Can Do About It* (New York: Little, Brown and Co., 2009) (Ramo was managing director of Kissinger Associates); and a book referenced by Eyal Weizman in several of his articles: Shimon Naveh, *In Pursuit of Military Excellence: The Evolution of Operational Theory* (London: Frank Cass, 1997).

25   Deleuze and Guattari, "Treatise on Nomadology," in *A Thousand Plateaus*, 351, 354.

26   Ibid., 417.

27   Ibid., 352–3, 356.

28   Ibid., 360.

quickly transform it into a familiar binary. In the afterword to *Networks and Netwars* (quickly added after September 11, 2001), they write: "Theory has struck home with a vengeance . . . This book is suddenly much more pertinent than we expected." Al Qaeda—the apotheosis of netwar—had been predicted in chapter after chapter of the book.[29] In retaliation, the authors first consider a state-to-state war, suggesting (with still more prescience) that Iraq might be targeted as the rogue sponsor of Al Qaeda. They also consider a Samuel Huntington-style "clash of civilizations." Both are set aside to foreground new netwar strategies, but these seem merely to diversify techniques for gathering information about the targeted enemy. All the previous discussions of complexity return to a binary duel, as if the Cold War face-off had only been updated with a new opponent and a new map.[30] The Go versus chess trope has even become a favorite of Henry Kissinger and other security consultants belonging to Clausewitzian cults.[31]

Yet Deleuze and Guattari themselves also arguably have difficulty escaping the tautological grip of Clausewitz or the competitive disposition of binaries, even as they try to dismantle them. They argue that states have become the tool of a worldwide, "postfascist" war machine that "assumes increasingly wider political functions." As if to win philosophical arguments, they declare that only now "total war itself, is surpassed." Only now "Clausewitz's formula is effectively reversed; to be entitled to say that politics is the continuation of war by other means, it is not enough to invert the order of the words as if they could be spoken in either direction." The war machine produces a "terrifying peace."[32] The machine is, after all, still associated with war, and there must be a new characterization for peace, as its opposite. The argument names an opponent—an "Unspecified

29   *Networks and Netwars*, 363–4.

30   That new map perhaps resembles the one in Thomas P. M. Barnett's *The Pentagon's New Map: War and Peace in the Twenty-First Century* (New York: Putnam, 2004).

31   "No Go," *Economist*, May 19, 2011.

32   Deleuze and Guattari, "Treatise on Nomadology," 421, note 110.

Enemy"—facilitated by the state and Capital. It is suggested that alternative forces can assume command of the machine to redirect and remold the state to "blaze their way for a new earth."[33] Michael Hardt and Antonio Negri's *Empire*, in dialogue with Deleuze and Guattari, is structurally very similar in its Empire/counter-Empire opposition.[34] With dramatic narratives, both pairs of authors declare an enemy in rhetoric that assumes a binary structure.

This story of mirroring theories and inescapable habits of mind only nourishes a curiosity for what lies beyond it. At the very least, the thorough attentions and energies expended on the military story, whether direct or residual, perhaps allow attention to drift to other questions. Is there evidence in infrastructure space that resists or exceeds automatic links between infrastructure and the military, despite its virtuosity and prominence? Moreover, is even the rhetorical identification of a single enemy (e.g. Capital, terrorism, or an "unspecified" entity) useful when it is neither sufficiently complex nor vigilant to address the compound dispositions immanent in infrastructure space?

Given the security apparatus of gates and fences necessary for its political quarantine, the zone has been characterized as an example of securitized space that is virtually indistinguishable from military space. Yet with aggressions that are different from those associated with the grand strategies of realpolitik or the binaries of military aggression, the zone embodies bifurcated or multiple forms of sovereignty that leverage the state to relinquish its resources in exchange for forms of global competition.[35] Never bothering with war, it embodies other violent dispositions marked by isomorphism and denial. More disturbing than a binary competitive stance is its cooperative reciprocal stance. It is not a means by which nations attack each other, but a means by which both state and non-state actors cooperate at someone else's expense—usually the expense of labor.

---

33   Ibid., 422–3.

34   Michael Hardt and Antonio Negri, *Empire* (Cambridge, MA: Harvard University Press, 2000), 42–66.

35   Palan, *The Offshore World*; Krasner, *Sovereignty: Organized Hypocrisy*, 3–25.

The violence within the zone is often stranger or more insidious than that of war. The 2013 Rana Plaza collapse in the Dhaka EPZ in Bangladesh was the deadliest accidental structural collapse in human history, killing over 1,127 people and injuring approximately 2,500 more. It was not an epic, chest-beating, symbol-laden story of conflict. It was the registration of the final straw, of a slowly unfolding form of violence that only really grabbed attention when the scene—the mutilation of bodies—resembled that of warfare. Just as glass does not have to shatter to possess a brittle disposition, the collapse was not the only marker of violence. Rana Plaza was a tragic example of the undeclared, even hidden, but potentially violent dispositions immanent in infrastructure space.

The binaries of war are also not especially useful in analyzing a broadband technoscape like that found in Kenya. The story does not assume the dramatic arc that usually accompanies military conflict. There are too many players engaged in reciprocal exchanges or the complex bargains of poker games rather than simple face-offs or duels. Aggressions that are temporary and fluid best support the survival of each player, and these competitions are often strategically deployed to further not only the self-interest but also the mutual benefit of multiple players.

Reaching for military stories in the hope of presenting an acute and penetrating portrayal or to fulfill a historical quest for relevance can lead to imprecise analyses. The aggressions within infrastructure space often occur with no defining moments and no satisfying declaration of an enemy. The consequential evidence may be found in the innocuous details—an invisible buildup of neglect or a silent form of attrition. Avoiding binary dispositions, this field of activity calls for experiments with ongoing forms of leverage, reciprocity, and vigilance to counter the violence immanent in the space of extrastatecraft.

Liberal

It is a basic error to search for the essence of something as heterogeneous and discontinuous as the liberal tradition. Liberalism is not the kind of thing that has an essence. —John Gray[36]

The ITU convention of 1865 might be likened, not to a commemoration of the Peace of Westphalia at end of the Thirty Years' War, but to a mid-century "Peace Conference" in what the economic historian Karl Polanyi called the "Hundred Years' Peace." In his 1944 book *The Great Transformation: The Political and Economic Origins of Our Time*, Polanyi identified the Hundred Years' Peace as the period between 1815 and 1914, an era filled with many small wars, civil wars, and colonial aggressions but no sustained general war. During this period, infrastructure was a protagonist in histories where, not wartime, but the intervals between wars were marked with the red-letter dates.[37]

The Hundred Years' Peace was also coincident with the growth of large private organizations, the largest of which were often associated with infrastructure building, and the 1865 ITU group photo bears some resemblance to countless other period photographs of sober, starched characters—not representatives of member nations, but members of the corporate board. Those who most fascinated Polanyi were the representatives of *haute finance*—another species of civilian administration and emergent transnational agency at the end of the nineteenth century, and one that often came to prominence thanks to infrastructure projects. Polanyi described finance as an "undisclosed social instrumentality at work in

---

36   In political philosophy, liberal thought—as it interrogates the individual's relationship to governance—percolates through traditions of different cultures (e.g., French and Anglo-Saxon) with many antecedents and many ongoing branches of inquiry. While these inquiries share "family resemblances," as John Gray has suggested, the very spirit of the tradition is at odds with a prescription about polity or "a partisan claim for the universal authority of a particular morality." Rather, it pursues "the search for terms of coexistence between different moralities." John Gray, *The Two Faces of Liberalism* (Cambridge: Polity, 2000), 27, 138.

37   Karl Polanyi, *The Great Transformation: The Political and Economic Origins of Our Time* (Boston: Beacon Press, 1944, 1957, 2001), 5.

the new setting, which could play the role of dynasties and episcopacies under the old."[38]

Infrastructure building when not characterized as a military project is often treated as an economic instrument—the spearhead of Capital's unstoppable march. The successes of business in the late nineteenth century emboldened a belief in *homo economicus*, laissez-faire, and the utopian liberal state. Polanyi returned to this period to track the development of a "market society" and the myth of the market as free, natural, self-balancing, and necessarily independent of state regulation. From the late nineteenth century to today, these platforms of economic liberalism—even though multiplied, inverted, and adopted by diametrically opposed political parties on the left and the right—have been consistently used to promote infrastructure.

For Polanyi, the Hundred Years' Peace that "rested upon economic organization" was different from the peace that is a corollary of war.[39] Prior to this period, he argued, peace was something obtained through war or through the threat of war.[40] But from 1815 to 1914, not only the "heavy industries" but also trade "was now dependent upon an international monetary system which could not function in a general war. It demanded peace."[41] Indeed many of the financiers, like the Rothschilds, gambled with war, but they used it like a valve that could be turned on and off to create profits from currency differentials. As Polanyi wrote, "Every war, almost, was organized by financiers; but peace also was organized by them."[42]

---

38   Ibid., 15–16.

39   Ibid., 10, 18. Polanyi even adopts Otto von Bismarck, a favorite mascot of realpolitik Grand Strategists, as a character in his historical scan, arguing that Bismarck traded in his state-on-state aggressions for a shrewd calculation that Germany's interests would increasingly rely on a powerful non-state entity—the international monetary system.

40   Ibid., 18.

41   Ibid., 15–16.

42   Ibid., 16. Polanyi writes: "business and finance were responsible for many colonial wars, but also for the fact that a general conflagration was avoided . . . For every one interest that was furthered by war, there were a dozen that would be adversely affected."

The "heavy industries"—arguably a war machine, alter-ego, and occasional partner of the military—were often organizations so vast that they worked for many different nations and claimed parity with their host state.[43] Some of the most common infrastructure of transportation and communication were initially developed not as public works but as huge private international enterprises. Still they were largely engaged in constructing the terms of civilian life—laying the cable, providing the rolling stock, building the canal or the dam. They amassed significant capital and developed a management apparatus designed to administer large numbers of people. They often shaped legislation and determined the values that were worth defending militarily. Infrastructure building often required titanic physical and political movement. In its scale and power, and with its frequent use of explosives and armies of construction workers moving around the world, it perhaps often satisfied a country's epic energies.

Rail was the Wal-Mart of the late nineteenth century. The historian Marc Linder writes that the "development of the world railway network approximately mirrored the geographic penetration of capital." Between 1840 and 1870, a "handful of bankers and contractors controlled nearly all railway building in the world, outside the USA."[44] Nineteenth-century British construction firms like Brassy and Peto & Betts built a significant portion of British rail at home and abroad. Brassy, with its army of 100,000 laborers, was considered to be a "European power."

By the end of the nineteenth century, the United States had laid over 200,000 miles of railroad across the continent. Business historian Alfred D. Chandler noted that "for several decades the consolidated US railroad systems remained the largest business enterprise in the world."[45] It was "the most powerful institution in the American economy and its managers the most influential group of economic decision makers." It even "provided a basic

---

43   Ibid., 16.

44   Marc Linder, *Projecting Capitalism: A History of the Internationalization of the Construction Industry* (London: Greenwood Press, 1994), 75, 15, 37.

45   Alfred D. Chandler, Jr., *The Visible Hand: The Managerial Revolution in American Business* (Cambridge, MA: Harvard University Press, 1977), 88.

impetus to the rise of the large-scale construction firm and the modern investment banking house."[46] Chandler argued that, for such American organizations, the "visible hand of management replaced what Adam Smith referred to as the invisible hand of market forces."[47]

Chandler famously used the example of the US railroad to make a case for the supremacy of private over public enterprises, including the military, in providing administrative training and developing managerial paradigms for the emerging multinational enterprises. While the mid-century rail companies initially deployed military models of management, by the end of the century their scale of operation required another degree of innovation that now exceeded that of the military.[48] As Chandler writes, in a passage worth quoting in full:

------

46   Ibid., 1, 94.

47   Ibid., 1.

48   Chandler, *The Visible Hand*, 95. A small historical feud—one of interest in this context—has developed around Chandler's rejection of sustained military influences on railway administration in the United States. Chandler contends that while the military may have had an "indirect impact on the beginning of modern business management," "there is little evidence that railroad managers copied military procedures." In contrast to Chandler, Robert Angevine and Charles O'Connell have argued that the US military, not unlike the French, provided not only the engineering expertise for railroad infrastructure but also the organizational models for "modern management." O'Connell argues that the army's "management model provided a conceptual and procedural framework that the officers advanced when there were not other equally suitable models available in the business community." Charles F. O'Connell, Jr., "The Corps of Engineers and the Rise of Modern Management 1827–1856," in M. R. Smith, ed., *Military Enterprise and Technological Change* (Cambridge, MA: MIT Press, 1985), 90, 116. The dispute itself is interesting since, working backward, as Angevine does, from a conceptual framework that begins with "the military-industrial establishment," it is somehow more difficult to argue that the military could be rejected as an influence or that business historians could be correct in their assessment that military procedures proved inadequate in a rapidly evolving industry. More interesting still is the way in which the various arguments largely concur. All three locate the moment of military influence in the incipient phases of US railroad development. They praise some of the same early railroad directors for developing procedures that learned from the military, but acknowledge that business management developed new techniques to meet the considerable demands of large-scale infrastructure like the US railway network. See Robert G. Angevine, *The Railroad and the State: War, Politics and Technology in Nineteenth-Century America* (Stanford: Stanford University Press, 2004), xvii.

No public enterprise, either, came close to the railroad in size and complexity of operation. In the 1890s a single railroad system managed more men and handled more funds and transactions and used more capital than the most complex of American governmental or military organizations. In 1891 the Pennsylvania Railroad employed over 110,000 workers. In the same year the total number of soldiers, sailors, and marines in the United States armed services was 39,492. The permanent managerial staff . . . [of the Post Office] . . . was smaller than that of the major railroad system. Two years later when the expenditures of the federal government were 387.5 million and its receipts 385.8 million, those of the Pennsylvania Railroad were 96.5 million and 135.1 million. That year the total gross national debt of 997 million was only 155 million more than the Pennsylvania's capitalization of 842 million. In the United States, the railroad, not the government or the military, provided training in modern large-scale administration.[49]

Even though the hierarchical administration of business developed its own governance—or its own visible hand—this structured authority paradoxically also mythologized the invisible hand of the market as a powerful political persuasion. In this perennial conundrum of economic liberalism, business fought against government regulation even as it created its own heavy administration and manipulated government toward its own ends. Infrastructure was one pawn in this supposedly unmanipulated free market that had to be manipulated to optimize its freedom.

Theories of liberalism generated still more paradoxes as the liberal *label* became affiliated with very different political sentiments in British and US contexts. In the early nineteenth-century British Parliament, the Whigs had adopted the term "liberal" and the Tories the label "conservative." Liberal ideology evolved in England over the course of the century, from "classical" liberalism to new liberalism. Migrating from Jeremy Bentham toward John Stuart Mill, new liberalism advocated for freedom from the

---

49   Chandler, *The Visible Hand*, 204–5.

tyrannies of big business that shaped the market to its own advantage and promoted curbs on the freedom of *homo economicus* in order to secure more freedoms for more people.[50] In 1908, Churchill defended the new liberalism against claims of socialism by saying, among other things, "Socialism exalts the rule; Liberalism exalts the man. Socialism attacks capital; Liberalism attacks monopoly."[51] By the 1920s and '30s, John Maynard Keynes was one of many who regarded liberalism as a means to moderate economic systems.[52]

On the American scene, during the 1930s the liberal label underwent similar transformations, even inversions, in meaning. It did not become an important term in American politics until the New Deal. Herbert Hoover had used the label to signal economic liberalism or laissez-faire.[53] As a gambit to attract Republican Party support for his Democratic policies, Franklin Delano Roosevelt adopted the label to indicate something closer to social liberalism or progressive capitalism that was nevertheless not socialism.[54] Rexford Guy Tugwell, who advised FDR on policy and served as the director of the Resettlement Administration, recalled once talking to Roosevelt about the origin of his use of "liberal." Roosevelt, well aware of the political power of the discrepancy, did not answer him, but rather "laughed and asked if it mattered."[55]

Writing *The Great Transformation* in the United States as World War II was ending, Polanyi, a Viennese émigré, argued that the management, cooperation, and voluntary regulation

---

50   Ronald D. Rotunda, *The Politics of Language: Liberalism as Word and Symbol* (Iowa City: University of Iowa Press, 1986).

51   Ibid., 27–30. "Old classical liberalism was poured out of the bottle and welfare liberalism was poured in; but although the contents were new, the label 'liberalism' was not changed. Since welfare liberalism grew out of basic elements of classical liberalism, it seemed reasonable to many that the same label would be used to describe both philosophies."

52   Ibid., 30.

53   Ibid., 52–3. Hoover would characterize the New Deal as the opposite of what he regarded as authentic liberalism, as a loss of individual freedom that was closer to "fascism or communism."

54   Ibid., 18–31, 32, 52–63.

55   Ibid., 59.

necessary to administer large projects like infrastructure demonstrated the impossibility of the market's magical freedom. How, he wondered, do both "giant trusts and princely monopolies" at one end of the spectrum and trade unions at the other fight to increase their freedom?[56] While he rejected the authoritarianism of Communism, he highlighted the role that regulation had played in creating the so-called free market: "Laissez-faire was planned; planning was not."[57] Polanyi continued to question who exactly was liberated in a liberal utopian world. Economic liberalism seemed to mean "the fullness of freedom for those whose income, leisure, and security need no enhancing and a mere pittance of liberty for the people, who may in vain attempt to make use of their democratic rights to gain shelter from the power of the owners of property."[58] Finally, Polanyi claimed that liberal philosophy "leaves no alternative but to either remain faithful to an illusionary idea of freedom and deny the reality of society, or to accept that reality and reject the idea of freedom. The first is the liberal's conclusion; the latter the fascist's."[59]

A contrasting strain of thought from two other Austrian émigrés, Ludwig von Mises and Frederick A. Hayek, attempted to establish a proper lineage of thought about liberalism in order to oppose fascism. They wished to reset the meaning of liberalism since, in the post–New Deal United States, the liberal label had become associated with the left and linked by its opponents to a longer tradition of "big government" and support for social programs.[60] Inspired by von Mises, Hayek published *The Road to*

---

56   Polanyi, *The Great Transformation*, 265.
57   Ibid., 147.
58   Ibid., 265.
59   Ibid.
60   For von Mises, liberalism meant simply "private ownership of the means of production." Ludwig von Mises, *Liberalism: the Classical Tradition* (Indianapolis: The Liberty Fund, 2006), xiii, 158. When translated into English in 1962, von Mises's 1927 book, *Liberalism*, was titled *Free and Prosperous Commonwealth: An Exposition of the Ideas of Classical Liberalism*, to avoid confusion over the ideological migration of the term in the post-war period. The anti-statist liberal tradition of nineteenth-century America was and continues to be variously associated with both conservatives

Serfdom in 1944. He traced a lineage of Anglo-Saxon thought from John Locke to Adam Smith to fashion a defense of liberalism against central government and state intervention.[61] Years later, Hayek served as a touchstone for both Margaret Thatcher and Ronald Reagan in their efforts to effect a global sea change in economic policy.

The Marxist geographer David Harvey returns to Hayek in order to trace the outlines of the contemporary neoliberal state— one with widening class separation, increasing deregulation, concentrations of wealth, susceptibility to financial crisis, uneven global development as directed by the "Washington Consensus," and a new association between private global actors and nationalist sentiment.[62] While liberalism, in most of its incarnations, has traditionally been proposed as a bulwark against either socialism or fascism, Harvey finds in contemporary neoliberal policies a new kind of authoritarianism.[63]

Yet it is not only those on the left who see in the liberal tradition the same dangers of authoritarianism. Indeed, the most formidable critic of the philosophical tradition of liberalism, Carl Schmitt, theorized fascism as its inevitable outcome. Political

---

and libertarians. See Alan Brinkley, *Liberalism and its Discontents* (Cambridge, MA: Harvard University Press, 1998), 282–4.

61   The book argued against central government control but nevertheless outlined a role for government in economic planning. Keynes read the book on the way to the Bretton Woods Conference and wrote to Hayek to compliment him on "a grand book," although it was not clear to him precisely how government planning, as Hayek described it, would be advocated or assessed. See F. A. Hayek, *The Road to Serfdom: Text and Documents, The Definitive Edition*, ed. Bruce Caldwell (Chicago: University of Chicago Press, 2007), xxxvi.

62   David Harvey, *A Brief History of Neoliberalism* (Oxford: Oxford University Press, 2005). Looking for the origins of neoliberalism in a contemporary context, Harvey returns to the 1947 meeting of the Mount Pelerin Society, a group that included von Mises, Hayek, and the economist Milton Friedman. Dealing selectively with the larger philosophical tradition as well as the history of party politics, they attempted to reconstruct a proper tradition of "classical" liberalism. Harvey argues that while analysts questioned the rigor of Hayek's argument, it garnered political support among private wealth, think tanks, and corporate organizations. It gained academic legitimacy when Hayek and Friedman were awarded the Nobel Prize in 1974 and 1976 respectively.

63   Gray, *The Two Faces of Liberalism*; Harvey, *A Brief History of Neoliberalism*.

scientist and Carl Schmitt–scholar John P. McCormick traces relationships between Schmitt and the major components of contemporary American conservatism, especially those strains associated with Hayek.[64] McCormick discusses fascism as a "radicalization of liberalism," claiming that there is even "a certain fluidity between liberalism, with its apparently insurmountable categorical contradictions, on the one hand, and the phenomenon of fascism, on the other, which may not be an altogether distinct alternative to liberalism, but which itself appears to be a product of, and solution to, liberalism's theoretical-practical impasses."[65]

Surveying a number of incarnations of liberal thought—from classical liberalism to new liberalism, New Deal liberalism, and neoliberalism—is perhaps sufficient to expose the volatility inherent in the term. Arguing that instability and paradox are built into the tradition, the historian Jerrold Seigel suggests that "Liberal politics thus vacillates between exalting the state and defending against it, while simultaneously alternating between idealized and demonized visions of society and human nature."[66]

For Aihwa Ong, the liberal label in itself offers little information. She challenges the characterization of "neoliberalism as a tidal wave of market-driven phenomena that sweeps from dominant countries to smaller ones" and wants to track more precisely how "*Homo economicus* . . . becomes translated, technologized

---

64   John P. McCormick, *Carl Schmitt's Critique of Liberalism: Against Politics as Technology* (Cambridge: Cambridge University Press, 1997).

65   Ibid., 14, 13. Neoliberalism in the United States is synonymous with neoconservative positions and a reaction against the political liberalism of the "nanny state" that impinges on the freedom of the individual. The Tea Party movement, emerging during the 2008 election season and flourishing during the first years of the Obama presidency, has rediscovered Hayek. Conservative broadcasters like Glenn Beck cite Hayek's *The Road to Serfdom* and *Constitution of Liberty* as foundational theory, cautioning against the potential despotism that can result from big government. Additional strains of contemporary liberal thought, such as those associated with libertarianism or anarchism, swing between left and right and between radical and conservative camps. See http://hayekcenter.org and "The Glenn Beck Effect: Hayek Has a Hit," at http://blogs.wsj.com.

66   Jerrold E. Seigel in the foreword to Pierre Manent, *An Intellectual History of Liberalism* (Princeton, NJ: Princeton University Press, 1994).

and operationalized in diverse, contemporary situations."[67] Ong aims to address "a dynamic process of sovereignty often ignored in studies that assess sovereignty in terms of broad 'liberal', 'democratic', or 'authoritarian' labels."[68]

Despite the long-standing vagaries of the liberal label as well as its refractions through various disciplines, it continues to attract hopeful attention and utopian energies. Exploiting its multiple associations, some may shrewdly deploy the term precisely because it sponsors controversial debate about political freedom. Or it may be—like Clausewitz for defense strategists— a mountain that economic thinkers return to again and again in the hope of an ultimate conquest.

Yochai Benkler, a scholar and analyst of information technology, theorizes a use of liberal thought in what he calls "commons-based peer production." In *The Wealth of Networks: How Social Production Transforms Markets and Freedom*, Benkler considers forms of freedom in the non-market economies where information is freely shared outside of the conventional licenses and copyrights for intellectual property—wikis, social media networks, and other means of exchanging goods or services like those developed in Kenya's broadband networks. Going beyond the notions of property or market that often feature in liberal thought, Benkler's liberalism considers other values of trade and production—parallel markets that, perhaps ironically, produce freedom through cooperation rather than self-interest.[69]

Bruno Latour and Antonin Lépinay reach for the liberal label when considering the work of the nineteenth-century sociologist Gabriel Tarde. Tarde questions the terms of economics itself, the existence of *homo economicus*, the visible or invisible hand, and the assumed "providence" that accompanies these beliefs. He chooses instead to observe the values and passions generated in social networks, marked by irrational exchanges and contagions that spread through a culture.[70] In *The Science of Passionate*

---

67 Ong, *Neoliberalism as Exception*, 12, 13.
68 Ibid., 102.
69 Benkler, *The Wealth of Networks*, 20, 7–16, 19–20, 278–85.
70 Bruno Latour and Vincent Antonin Lépinay, *The Science of Passionate*

Interests: An Introduction to Gabriel Tarde's Economic Anthropology, Latour and Lépinay show how Tarde's work prefigures theories, like those of Benkler, about the viral social networks that currently model new economies in market and web exchanges. Imagining that Tarde rather than Karl Marx had left the most influential legacy, the authors speculate about multiple or alternative conceptions of the market operating outside the dominant logics of Capital. They find in Tarde's refreshing lack of an economic belief system a "politics of *liberty*." "Liberalism then?" they ask tentatively, quickly adding that the label must be dissociated from any predestined or providential utopia. In their artful spin on the term, liberalism is freedom from ideology itself.[71]

In the infrastructure space of zone urbanism, economic liberalism in its various incarnations agitates for the freedom of selected actors. By insisting that unions or laws protective of workers should not curtail the freedoms of the market, the zone has virtually enslaved the labor that supports it. The zone defends the freedom of money to escape to tax havens, but does not defend the freedom of taxpayers whose increased burdens result from a loss of tax revenues. In zone logic, the worker or the taxpayer are free to accept whatever jobs or benefits eventually result from the liberty of multinational corporations. Ironically, however, the zone will accept some self-imposed bureaucracy and barriers to profit in order to conform to global management styles or purchase expensive symbolic capital in the form of a shiny skyline.

The broadband landscape in Kenya has cultivated multiple, often contradictory ideologies of economic liberalism—from the laissez-faire liberalism of the nineteenth-century telegraph cable contractors, to the liberalizing free market of the "Washington

---

Interests: An Introduction to Gabriel Tarde's Economic Anthropology (Chicago: Prickly Paradigm Press, 2009). Concerning the notion of liberalism Tarde wrote, "I am well aware that the liberal school of economists advocates the non-intervention of the state, but advising the state to withdraw when its presence is indiscreet and harmful to its own ends is nonetheless speaking as a statesman and positing rules for an intelligent policy." Gabriel Tarde, *On Communication and Social Influence, Selected Papers* (Chicago: University of Chicago Press, 1969), 4–5, 67.

71 Latour and Lépinay, *The Science of Passionate Interests*, 5.

Consensus," to the new liberalism sometimes associated with shared digital production. In the case of the cable landings, the agents of "Washington Consensus" liberalization ironically created the most stubborn bureaucratic obstacles. In the case of market data-gathering, a crowd-sourcing program like Jana purports to provide access to communication, while positioning half the world's population as consumers.

Despite the conundrums that accompany the liberal label. Remarkably the word continues to be used as casual jargon or even revived in attempts to change the game and herald a radical new paradigm shift. Is freedom the pivotal value in "free market" economic exchange? What kind of infrastructure space might initiate a real paradigm shift, campaigning not on promises of freedom but on promises of interdependence, balances of freedom, or even obligation? The experiments of extrastatecraft might simply continue to assess, with every decision made in infrastructure space, whose freedom it is that is being protected.

Universal

An "international third space" (as in Third Estate) . . . might find a place between intermarket logics and interstate logics that mediate respectively the pragmatism of the merchant and the Realpolitik of the prince fettered by the reason of state. —Armand Mattelart[72]

The ITU group portrait of 1865 captured one of the first appearances of an international organization—a significant event in the cultural story of infrastructure technologies as rationalized universal platforms of exchange. As was reflected in chairman de Lhuys's enthusiasm at that first ITU meeting, broadly adopted infrastructure technologies—from telegraphy and electricity to contemporary telematic networks and standards—have sometimes been treated as emergent, redemptive, or utopian tools. The international organizations designed to coordinate this infrastructure have also been regarded as the first growth of a

72   Mattelart, *Mapping World Communication*, 233–4, note 26, 282.

burgeoning sphere of global governance able to maintain independent continuities despite the actions of either states or markets.

From 1865 up to World War I, the ITU operated as a third party negotiating between states and multinational enterprises—enterprises led by giant organizations as well as entrepreneurial inventors like Thomas Alva Edison, Guglielmo Marconi, or Alexander Graham Bell.[73] The ITU hoped to preempt disagreements between nations while preventing dangers and deaths that often had nothing to do with national aggressions. Early conferences worked on international telephone, radio, and wireless protocols and established a global SOS signal to address incidents on the high seas like the sinking of the Titanic in 1912. At the International Radio Conference in 1927 in Washington, DC, the ITU, by then a parliament of eighty countries and sixty-four private companies, began allocating radio frequencies. An international organization of nations and commercial interests had begun to format an airborne medium, an atmospheric condition that did not conform to the typical boundaries of sovereignty or property.[74]

The destruction of infrastructure such as phone lines and submarine cables during the world wars only strengthened the ITU's administrative presence as it orchestrated reconstruction, technical coordination, and international agreements. In 1932, the ITU, renamed the International Telecommunications Union, officially merged telegraph, telephone, and radio communications under one authority, and in 1947, the organization became part of the UN.[75]

Moments of planetary integration through infrastructure development inspire universal dreams. For the Saint-Simonians

---

73   There would be a million telephones installed around the world by 1896. See Huurdeman, *The Worldwide History of Telecommunications*, 603.

74   Ibid., 358–9. At the 1903 conference major global powers signed a protocol agreeing that "coast stations should be bound to receive and transmit telegrams originating from or destined for ships at sea without distinction as to the system of radio used by the latter." The 1906 conference officially incorporated radio and wireless within the purview of the organization and established SOS as a distress signal.

75   Ibid., 597.

of the early nineteenth century, science and industry formed a new religion. Railways and canals were contributing to a new planetary order.[76] In 1869 the transcontinental rail road joined both coasts of the United States, and the Suez Canal was completed, thus shrinking global travel times. In 1945 Arthur C. Clarke predicted that satellite fleets and television might govern a global village, and by 1963, from its global capital in Geneva, the ITU had begun allocating frequencies for satellite communication.[77] Japan broadcast the 1964 Olympics via Intelsat satellite, and that same year launched the high-speed Shinkansen rail line. In July 1969, a year before Kenya got its first earth station, satellites broadcast the Apollo II moonwalk.

Universal stories have also accompanied aspirations for shared, rationalized infrastructure platforms. By the late nineteenth century, the electric light was being promoted in international expositions and anointed as a panacea for many urban ills. US regionalist planners from Gifford Pinchot in the 1920s to New Deal advocates in 1930s argued that hydroelectricity would help to rationalize settlement patterns. The concurrent technocracy movement proposed that a global parliament of engineers should replace monetary values with energy values which would be used to tabulate and redistribute the world's resources. Modernist architects and urban planners like Le Corbusier and others in the International Congresses of Modern Architecture (CIAM 1928–1959) proposed international principles for designing urban space.[78] Today, mobile telephony and digital media are the latest technology believed to engender global democracy and a creative commons of shared information that transcends conventional market motives.

Yet these one-world aspirations for infrastructure have often also sponsored some of the most profound inversions or

---

76   Albert Leon Guerard, *French Prophets of Yesterday: A Study of Religious Thought Under the Second Empire* (London: T. F. Unwin, 1913), 167–8.

77   Arthur C. Clarke, "Extra-Terrestrial Relays—Can Rocket Stations Give Worldwide Radio Coverage?" *Wireless World*, October 1945.

78   Eric Mumford, *The CIAM Discourse on Urbanism, 1928–1960* (Cambridge, MA: MIT Press, 2002).

irrationalities. Each spawned their own new science or profession with its own self-reflexive theories—traffic engineering, information science, marketing science, social or managerial science among them. The global satellite village that Clarke projected became multiple global villages—satellite systems that served more Balkanized political regions. The false logics of traffic engineering—based largely on statistical traffic volumes—generated congestion rather than speed. Political scientist and anthropologist James C. Scott argues that modernist planning schemes around the world failed in part because the engineering of a universal system often rejected or omitted the practical flexible systems of knowledge and practice—the *mētis*—on which urbanism thrives.[79] Similarly Evgeny Morozov argues that "cyber-utopianism" and "internet-centrism"—the sense that the internet is the answer to everything—is delusional. As long as it can be controlled by authoritarian power with a kill switch, counting on the web to deliver freedom and salvation is too risky.[80]

International organizations themselves, like the ITU, were initially linked to utopian or activist attempts to establish universal networks for the exchange of information. Paul Otlet, dubbed the father of information science and inventor of the Universal Decimal Classification System, and Henri La Fontaine, a Belgian bibliographer and lawyer, established the Union of International Associations in 1910. The UIA hoped to create an information database and retrieval system for a global society. Otlet's prescient proposals included a mechanical/electrical desk that would flip through index cards, and, connected by telephone and/or "electric telescope," project "links" and images onto a screen. The UIA was also part of various world congresses and helped to bring about the League of Nations of which La Fontaine was a

---

79   James C. Scott, *Seeing Like a State: How Certain Schemes to Improve the Human Condition Have Failed* (New Haven: Yale University Press, 1998), 6–7, 340.

80   Evgeny Morozov, *The Net Delusion: The Dark Side of Internet Freedom* (New York: Perseus, 2011), Introduction. See also Evgeny Morozov, *Click Here to Save Everything: The Folly of Technological Solutionism* (New York: Public Affairs, 2013).

member; and in the aftermath of war, the UIA's *Yearbook of International Organizations* began to chronicle the phenomenon of international organizations of which it was a part.[81]

Global organizations of all types have been growing explosively since World War II.[82] Just a few years before the ITU joined the UN, a significant group of intergovernmental organizations (IGOs) emerged: the World Bank, the IMF, and GATT (later WTO) at the 1944 Bretton Woods Conference; the OEEC (precursor to the OECD) in 1948 as part of the Marshall Plan; and NATO in 1949. The number of international NGOs, hovering around 1,000 in the middle of the twentieth century, had risen to 6,000 by its end—addressing everything from environment, labor, animals, and peacekeeping to professional association, among many other things.[83] As the sociologist John W. Meyer and his colleagues have pointed out, "organization" is, for some, a useful word to describe the increasing number of formalized associations in the world that sidestep the state, the customary corporation, the family, or other highly structured forms.[84]

The universal stories accompanying international organizations

---

81   See uia.be. The UIA now partners with UNESCO.

82   Many who projected that this sphere of association would provide a means to rationalize economies and subdue conflicts wanted a means of tracking its growth. In 1947, the same year that ISO was founded, Harvey H. Bundy, President of the World Peace Foundation, introduced *International Organization*, a journal established for just that purpose. See Harvey H. Bundy, "Introduction," *International Organization* 1, no. 1 (1947).

83   Gunnar Folke Schuppert, ed., *Global Governance and the Role of Non-State Actors* (Berlin: Wissenschaftszentrum Berlin für Sozialforschung, 2006), 235–7; and Kenneth W. Abbott and Duncan Snidal, "The Governance Triangle: Regulatory Standards Institutions and the Shadow of the State," in Walter Mattli and Ngaire Woods, eds., *The Politics of Global Regulation* (Princeton: Princeton University Press, 2009), 44–88. There is even an International Union of Architects, founded in Lausanne in 1948. See uia-architectes.org.

84   Meyer, Drori, and Hwang, "Introduction," in *Globalization and Organization*, 2, 1. Meyer and his colleagues consider organizations as entities that are "distinct from, and in partial opposition to such traditional structures as bureaucracy, professional association, family or family firm, and perhaps other structures." See also Alfred Dupont Chandler and Bruce Mazlish, *Leviathans: Multinational Corporations and the New Global History* (Cambridge: Cambridge University Press, 2005).

also harbor their own contradictions and paradoxes.[85] In 1977, Meyer and fellow sociologist Brian Rowan argued, in a pivotal article titled "Institutional Organizations: Formal Structure as Myth and Ceremony," that organizations deploy ceremony and ritual to demonstrate that they are rationalizing and optimizing their stated goals. Yet they often protect those very goals by "decoupling" from them when close scrutiny might uncover evidence of failure or contradiction. "Hospitals try to ignore unfavorable information on cure rates, public services avoid data about effectiveness, and schools deemphasize measures of achievement." Often an organization "cannot formally coordinate activities because its formal rules, if applied, would generate inconsistencies." In these cases, the ability of individuals to "coordinate things in violation of the rules—that is, to get along with other people—is highly valued." This decoupling or looking the other way becomes part of the professional repertoire of "organizational elites" as they develop more elaborate ways to manage "public image and status."[86]

Demonstrating some paradoxes of the universal, the

---

85   The narratives of universal rationalization collide with those concerning militarism and nationalism in that they attempt to create an authority above that of the nation. Arquilla and Ronfeldt might have associated these ideas with the grand strategy of "liberal internationalism." The same narratives of universal rationalization associate with yet more strains of social liberalism that collide with ideas of economic liberalism. Meyer and his colleagues must repeatedly make the distinction between the liberal tradition they claim and the notion of "'neo-liberal' with its raw economistic meanings." Even though the distinction between economic and social liberalism does not produce a durable clarification or separation, the separation is nevertheless attempted again thusly: "In many analyses (particularly those focused on the extremes of a revanchist neo-liberalism), the liberal system is about markets, markets are about exploitation, and the subjective freedom of market participants is reactive false consciousness. In the view put forward here, global liberalism has spread as a political, cultural, legal and quasi-religious model of collective action and organization." John W. Meyer, "World Society, the Welfare State, and the Life Course: An Institutionalist Perspective," in *World Society: The Writings of John W. Meyer* (London: Oxford University Press, 2010), 292.

86   John W. Meyer and Brian Rowan, "Institutionalized Organizations: Formal Structure as Myth And Ceremony," *American Journal of Sociology* 83, no. 2 (1977), reprinted in Walter W. Powell and Paul DiMaggio, eds., *The New Institutionalism in Organizational Analysis* (Chicago: University of Chicago Press, 1991), 57–58, 61. Meyer's work prompted Krasner to theorize about what he calls "problematic sovereignty" or "hypocritical sovereignty."

zone—regarded by UNIDO as an instrument to rationalize economic exchange and organize member nations in a "federation of free trade zones"—was promoted despite early recognition that it delivered suboptimal results.[87] Any country hosting this form may support a raft of laws and compacts about protection of the environment or treatment of labor, yet they will have agreed to create an area in which these very principles will be set aside. Perhaps more like the contagions described by Gabriel Tarde, decisions to create a zone are not always based on rational economic calculations. Decoupled from unfavorable economic assessments and the rule of law, the zone proliferates in order to conform to a currency of social habits—to provide what is believed to be the necessary entrée into global culture.

Mobile telephony may be the latest technology to inspire the dream of a universal shared platform, and yet despite the work of multiple international agencies since the mid-twentieth century, only recently has one of the most populous places on earth begun to receive international submarine cable. Broadband space is a social, political, and economic instrument of intergovernmental and international organizations like the UN, the World Bank, the IMF, and the ITU. Yet as well as providing leadership, these agents of global governance also tend to multiply contradictory authorities and bureaucracies. The messy and multivalent story on the ground in Kenya's technoscape is a case in point. Even as access to information becomes ubiquitous, there are new concentrations of power in a field that never resolves itself.

If international organizations have a universal language, it is arguably a language of standards. The ITU joined forces with the International Electrotechnical Commission (IEC) when it was established in 1906 as the world's first international standard-making organization to coordinate electrical equipment.[88]

---

87 Takeo, "Introduction," *AMPO: Japan-Asia Quarterly Review* (1977). Today the World Federation of Economic Free Zones (FEMOZA)—a non-profit NGO established in 1999 and headquartered in Geneva—convenes private entities and consults with UNIDO. The organization acts as a parastate parliament, collecting and sharing data about free zones in conventions and publications.

88 See itu.int.

The ITU is now also linked to ISO, the subject of the next chapter. As an attempt at universal consensus ISO is an international organization *par excellence*, devoted solely to setting standards for almost every conceivable exchange (shipping, electronics, photography, computing, etc.). Yet the organization now also presides over a catechism of management mottos like those of other inspirational gurus, and they whisper advice to the leaders of both corporations and countries. As will become clear, ISO demonstrates that some of the most rationalized corners of infrastructure space may harbor the most elaborate irrationalities.

Finally, it seems that, as Meyer and his colleagues observe, "Global society is a rationalized world, but not exactly what one could call a rational one." Some of the very behaviors that encourage conformity and compliance in an emergent world culture also lead to elaborate systems of belief as well as ponderous bureaucracies.[89]

Histories of infrastructure space are often drawn into the thrall of ideological stories about militarism, liberalism, or universal rationalization. These stories have the power to influence dispositions—political allegiances as well as physical arrangements—in infrastructure space. The stories themselves assume dispositions—competitive binaries or exclusive closed loops—that are often symptoms of a strategic elimination of information. An echo chamber helps to maintain faith in the stories; and to the degree that they support authoritarian power, the stories themselves are dangerous. Moreover, while they often demand of their followers pledges of vigilant adherence to principles, to the degree that those principles target a single incarnation of violence or authoritarian power (e.g., Capital), they are not vigilant enough.

Consequently, just like dispositions, the stories that are attached to infrastructure space are important diagnostics in the politics of extrastatecraft. Even as these stories create ideological collisions and confusions, organizations of every scale institutionalize techniques for overlooking or overriding the disconnect

---

89   Meyer, Drori, and Hwang, *Globalization and Organization*, 269, 273–4.

between what they are saying and what they are doing. While this decoupling helps to make the stories more durable, it also reveals a world that is more receptive to influential fictions and beliefs—creating a political opportunity for the shrewd operator in extrastatecraft.

CHAPTER 5

Quality

The phone-voice promises, "Your call will be monitored for *quality assurance purposes.*" Credit cards, all 0.76mm thin, slide into slots and readers all around the world. Screw threads conform to a given pitch. Every make of car shares the same dashboard pictograms. Batteries with consistent durations are sized to fit any device. Books, magazines, music, and audiovisual works are indexed with ISBN numbers. Paper sizes and the machines that handle them are standardized. RFID tags, transshipment containers, trucks, car seats, film speeds, protective clothing, book bindings, units of measure, personal identification numbers (PINs), and fasteners of all kinds conform to global standards.[1]

All of these shared standards emanate from the International Organization for Standardization, or ISO—a quintessential parliament of extrastatecraft. Founded in 1947, ISO is a private nongovernmental organization (NGO), but also a global meta-organization—an organization of organizations. It convenes a UN-style assembly of member nations as well as private entities, and is a crossroads for nearly every type of organization in the world (e.g., NATO, WTO, ILO, OECD, etc.), most of which maintain a currency in standard making.[2] ISO, like its strategic partners the ITU, the IEC, and the WTO, has its headquarters in Geneva—a Vatican of sorts for international organizations. Regarded by some as no less than the beginnings of a "world state," ISO formats the performance and calibration of many components of infrastructure space at every scale, from the

---

1 See iso.org and Thomas A. Loya and John Boli, "Standardization in the World Polity: Technical Rationality over Power," in John Boli and George M. Thomas, eds., *Constructing World Culture: International Nongovernmental Organizations since 1875* (Stanford: Stanford University Press, 1999), 169–97.

2 Goran Ahrne and Nils Brunsson, *Meta-organizations* (Cheltenham: Edward Elgar, 2008).

microscopic to the gigantic. The organization has been "steadily and energetically at work promoting the construction of a uniform built environment."[3] ISO presides over a multitude of technical standards that establish criteria for everything from roller bearings and refrigerants to lubricants and footwear. There are technical standards for the parameters of a JPEG (ISO/IEC: 15444) or an MPEG (ISO/IEC 21000), for cooking pasta (ISO 7304-2:2008), and even a standard glass for wine tastings (ISO 3591:1977).[4]

In addition to technical standards, ISO also develops management standards, and pins its hopes of universal engagement on a management standard addressing the mysterious term "quality." The ISO 9000 family of standards establishes principles of quality management—procedures for managing any industry to better satisfy customers and improve both production and market status. Quality standards do not dictate technical specifications for a product but rather offer management guidelines for a *process* or quality system. Using systemic processes of information gathering, quality promises to deliver a well-run company, with strong supplier relations and enhanced customer satisfaction.[5]

ISO's institutional disposition is at once evangelical and almost secretive. In zones all over the world, most companies sport ISO 9000 certification as a shibboleth or seal of approval. For any global project, like Kenya's LAPSSET highway, quality certification is regarded as a necessary signal to international contractors and governance agencies. In 1992, the European Union required ISO 9000 compliance as a condition within its trade policies.[6] Yet, while ISO may sometimes strike the profile of a public information source or an intergovernmental body, it is a private, voluntary, nongovernmental organization—a business

---

3   Loya and Boli, "Standardization in World Polity," 169.

4   See iso.org. JPEG is an acronym for Joint Photographic Expert Group; MPEG for Moving Picture Experts Group.

5   Staffan Furusten, "The Knowledge Base of Standards," in Nils Brunsson, Bengt Jacobsson, eds., *A World of Standards* (Oxford: Oxford University Press, 2000), 71–8.

6   Mendel, "The Making and Expansion of International Management Standards," 137–66.

that sells its standards, protects its clients, and maintains no public archive. Its history and its multi-scalar effects on the environment are difficult to track.

Broadening its reach, ISO has recently also developed new management standards for the environment, education, health, social responsibility, urban data, and even government itself. This private form of governance thus continues to enter and assert its authority in a public arena without a public political dialogue. Like its management consulting cousins at McKinsey & Co. or Booz Allen, ISO coaches companies as well as countries, influencing government policy, regional planning, and macro-urbanism.

Quality management has actually become something like a peculiar global custom—the unofficial patois of infrastructure space. Armies of businessmen speak its managementese in conference centers, breakout rooms, webinars, blogs, and books. Every utterance is worthy of an acronym, a bullet-pointed list, a mandala, or a pyramidal diagram. Any idea must be expressed in an unctuous, motivational aphorism. At its most extreme, quality management is exemplary of a supposedly rationalized set of practices serving as an ideal vessel of irrationality.

As important as it is to understand what quality management does, it is equally important to understand what it does not do— indeed what it obstructs. Despite being treated as a seal of approval, it does not set technical performance standards for some of the world's most pressing issues related to labor and the environment. Only its non-specific, non-binding management standards inch toward these issues. They may stimulate and leverage productive change, but they may also inoculate organizations against regulation while developing more expensive and opaque bureaucracies.

With its multitude of standards ISO speaks many technical languages, but it has no management standards that directly deploy spatial variables even though space itself is a technology and a medium of information. The matrix of repeatable spatial products like malls, resorts, golf courses, and suburbs, as well the urban formulas for zones or broadband networks, contributes to a global spatial operating system. Altering infrastructure space is often a matter of global concern, exceeding the reach of nations and businesses and requiring the scale and leverage of extrastatecraft, but it is ordinarily manipulated with non-spatial tools. The global zone and broadband networks, for instance, shape huge swaths of territory according to urban defaults dictated by econometrics or informatics. In environmental landscapes like rain forests, the technical language of the carbon market is used to galvanize the cooperation of groups of states. The global financial market recently collapsed over the proliferation of spatial products in the suburban housing market, but only legal and financial tools were available to address the crisis.

ISO's management standards provide an index of experiments attempted as well as questions unexplored in the design of global infrastructure space. Learning from both the successes and the absurdities of ISO, what kinds of spatial protocols—crafted not as standards but as an interplay of spatial variables—could be instrumental in the global parliaments of extrastatecraft?

Logos of strategic partners ISO, IEC, and ITU

Quality Has No Content

ISO evolved from a number of different gatherings before and after World War II—sometimes including NATO—that were needed to address regulations in manufacturing and defense.[7]

---

7   See iso.org. Since ISO was founded on February 23, 1947, and held its first

Standard making has long been an endeavor of industry, and ISO assembles national private standard-making bodies—parastate institutions deputized by governments but representing the interests of thousands of "businesses, professional societies and trade associations, standards developers, government agencies, and consumer and labor organizations."[8] The British Standards Institute (BSI), the American National Standards Institute (ANSI), and the Deutsches Institute für Normung (DIN), for instance, represent their respective countries, and as full members of ISO have one vote in the assembly. In the 1950s and '60s more and more developing countries became ISO members. Corresponding and subscriber members have less power and pay smaller dues than do full members, although most, especially those from developing countries, may have increasingly more at stake.[9] The voting members send large numbers of experts to work on the technical committees that develop the content of the standards.

In the 1970s, ISO began publishing its reports as "International Standards" rather than recommendations. At the beginning of 2014, ISO had published over 19,500 standards and had members representing 161 countries.[10] Caught between information withheld and shared, the standards are not in the public domain; they are strictly protected by copyright and only available at a price.[11]

---

general assembly in Paris in 1949, it has evolved a special position among organizations devoted to creating standards. In 1946, delegates from twenty-five countries met in London at the Institute for Civil Engineers to discuss cooperation among standard-making institutions that had been developing in many countries to regulate both manufacturing and defense. During World War II, the US Department of Defense also established standards.

8   See "FAQs" at ansi.org; Aseem Prakash and Matthew Potoski, *The Voluntary Environmentalists: Green Clubs, ISO 14001, and Voluntary Environmental Regulations* (Cambridge University Press, 2006), 83–84; and iso.org.

9   In response to increasing interest from developing countries, from 1968 on, corresponding members, while not able to vote in the assembly, were made privy to information about its decisions. Since 1992, subscriber members have paid only nominal membership fees, have no voting rights, and usually represent developing nations with less stake in the international market. Prakash and Potoski, *The Voluntary Environmentalists*, 83.

10   "The ISO Story," at iso.org; Loya and Boli, "Standardization in the World Polity," 176.

11   Revenues from these proprietary products and from member dues

First released in 1987, ISO's most popular standard, ISO 9000, perhaps derives its broad appeal and extensive voluntary compliance from a lack of content. Over a million organizations in 170 countries have been ISO 9000 certified, and yet no one can say what ISO 9000 actually is.[12] Since it is not a technical performance standard that directly addresses, for instance, emissions, fuel efficiency, durability, or dimensional precision, the standard only acquires content as it is applied to a specific industry.[13] As published, the standard is several pages long and written as a circular set of instructions. It sets out principles that are designed to apply to any organization from industrial production to food service.

Successful engagement with the standard is measured by evaluating whether an organization has addressed the objectives it set for itself. Quality, in this context, does not measure the value or performance of a product or service, but instead outlines a process for achieving internal goals related to the product. So a cheap product that might be considered by some to be of poor value can still meet all of the quality assurance criteria and satisfy customer expectations as established by the business organization in question.

The tone of the ISO public relations literature is earnest, even slightly juvenile, as if to overcome technical obscurity with overwhelming accessibility. The hyperlinked website offers an apparently endless branching network of information. The openness and accessibility seem designed to overcompensate for the

---

nevertheless give the organization a potentially productive independence from state influence.

12   See "Standards: ISO 9000" at iso.org; and Mendel, "The Making and Expansion of International Management Standards," 137. Mendel quotes the number of certificates in 2003 at 560,000.

13   The ISO 9000 series has been adapted for specific industries. For instance, other international standards include AS-9100 for the aerospace industry. In the Automotive industry QS-9000 is a set of techniques developed by Daimler-Chrysler, Ford, and GM to coordinate suppliers. The ISO/TS-16949 was developed for the global automotive industry. The ANSI and the ASQ have collaborated on standards for statistics. TL-9000 is a body of quality standards based on the ISO 9000 but adopted for the telecommunications industry.

central policy of the organization—namely, that its most instrumental information is only available to those willing to purchase
a standard.

After following multiple helpful links leading to additional
helpful links, each promising to boil the information down to
increasingly essential points, one can arrive at a link that reveals
the eight principles behind the standard: Customer focus;
Leadership; Involvement of people; Process approach; System
approach to management; Continual improvement; Factual
approach to decision making; and Mutually beneficial supplier
relationships. Another link goes deeper to access lists of the key
benefits and potential outcomes for each of these eight inter-
twined and self-referential principles. The simplest and most
durable motto and acronym attending ISO 9000 reflects its longer
history and usually appears within a mandala diagram as PDCA,
or "Plan Do Check Act."[14]

Even though the content of ISO 9000 is determined by each
individual industry, quality specialists must also be hired to
handle fulfillment of the process. Just as an educational or
medical institution is accredited, so too in industry a third
party—a so-called quality engineer—performs auditing and
certifying services that are often purchased along with access to
the standard. An audit often consists of interviews, with a set
questionnaire, so the size of the firm usually determines the
cost of the process. Small companies may spend tens of thousands of dollars and large companies may spend hundreds of
thousands and several months on completing the initial accred-
itation. The resulting certification is highly prized, and since
losing it can damage a company's reputation, it must be continually renewed. Since management standards apply to contractual
relationships, large companies also encourage their suppliers to
be certified.[15]

Quality is thus a product, but it is also a significant service

---

14   See iso.org.
15   Mendel, "The Making and Expansion of International Management
Standards," 140.

industry and quasi-profession. The BSI is now "a group" of companies that has acquired standard-making institutions in the United States and Singapore. The group also acquired KPMG, an ISO-registration business with its headquarters in the Netherlands. Now called a "superbrand," in 2009 the BSI Group earned $222 million dollars and operated in 147 countries. BSI's Entropy Software solution is one product it markets to businesses to help them succeed and manage risk.[16] Likewise, the American Society for Quality has crafted quality into a discipline or a professional activity. Their website is studded with phrases such as "We are your source for Quality," "Are you new to Quality?" or "Hot Topics in Quality."[17]

Quality is also a habit. As management researcher Staffan Furusten points out, management decisions are not usually responsible for the success or failure of an organization. Nor are they a gauge of an organization's efficiency or productivity. Feedback from customers is also not the primary reason why organizations change and develop.[18] Moreover, management consulting is a significant and ongoing expense for business. As Furusten suggests, "Order and clarity are not always typical of what really goes on in organizations." As it has developed over the last hundred years, "global popular management culture" has, at best, simply provided a common

---

16   See bsigroup.org.

17   The ASQ certifies quality operators and quality management systems. ASQ members may aspire to be auditors for ISO or for the Malcolm Baldrige National Quality Award (MBNQA), mandated by Congress in 1987 (the same year that the ISO 9000 appeared). The trade magazine and website, *Quality Digest*, convenes adherents from a number of quarters of the quality culture. The magazine airs issues related to technical subjects such as food safety, leaks, green technologies, or new industrial practices like 3D printing. It holds webinars and discussions sporting all of the quality jargon about, for instance, "zero defects" and "root cause analysis." Quality consultants find a forum there. Quality management specialist W. Edwards Deming still has a following, and among the speakers who attract quality professionals is a Deming impersonator, Mike Micklewright, who adopts a signature cadence and tone as well a familiar critique of business management in the United States—a country he characterizes as "underdeveloped." See asq.org and qualitydigest.com.

18   Furusten, "The Knowledge Base of Standards," 78–80.

set of practices.[19] At its core it may even provide a cohesive fellowship—the camaraderie of teams and an attitude-shifting congregation of actors—believing in the organization and the apotheosis of quality.

Quality Is Extra History

The history of "quality"—this common but nevertheless mysterious practice—is found in the literature of several strains of management thinking, each of which enthusiastically present reinvented wheels. Management culture flourishes in, perhaps even requires, this amnesic climate. Any scholarly attempt to chronicle this history must eventually encounter the ephemeral, repetitive pop culture that is its nourishing and rejuvenating medium.

Histories of management often start by examining the administration of large-scale communication and transportation organizations in the late nineteenth century. For instance, railroad and international construction companies developed technical expertise that exceeded that of the state, as well as management structures that were often independent of state jurisdictions. Managerial capitalism developed its own forms of governance to orchestrate and plan for future trade, production, distribution, and funding. Increased numbers of multinational corporations appearing at the end of nineteenth century began expanding their foreign investment networks.[20] When the Ford Motor Company adopted F. W. Taylor's 1911 principles of "scientific management" to increase assembly-line efficiencies, they

19   Ibid., 84, 80–3.
20   Siemens and Halske, United Fruit, Exxon, Royal Dutch Shell, Lever Brothers, J. & P. Coats, and Bayer are among these multinational enterprises. International banks also contributed managerial techniques and traditions that reinforced their authority and reputation. Ford Motor Company, established in 1903, was operating in Canada by its second year and by 1930 had plants in eighteen other countries. Business historian Mira Wilkins points out that by 1929–1930, after recovering from World War I, "American and European MNEs were ubiquitous, with many operating on six continents." See Mira Wilkins, "Multinational Enterprise to 1930," in Chandler and Mazlish, eds., *Leviathans*, 79.

helped to disseminate practices that were not only a fascination of US industries and the US government, but also part of a growing global management phenomenon.[21]

Two other mottos of scientific management prefigured the PDCA acronym. Henri Fayol's "Administration Industrielle et Générale" of 1916 may be one of the origins of the compulsion to create numbered lists and steps in contemporary managementese. Fayol offered the mantra "Planning, Organization, Command, Coordination, Control," or "POCCC," as well as fourteen synthetic principles for management that addressed fair remuneration, equity, and *esprit de corps*. In 1937, in a publication entitled *Papers on the Science of Administration*, Luther Gulick and Lyndall Urwick mixed social science with

---

21   Organizations similar to New York's Taylor Society were established in Germany and France. While the British adopted techniques of scientific management much later, in the 1940s and 1950s, the British Standards Institute (BSI) was founded very early, in 1901, to coordinate technical standards for, among other things, structural steel and railway gauges, and it provided an essential antecedent for quality management. The famous BSI logo or kitemark of 1903 became a seal of approval for consolidating technical standards in the British Commonwealth. See "Our History" at bsigroup.com. In Germany, the ideas of scientific management became part of an industrial and engineering discourse, but they were also a topic of discussion among the group of artists, architects, and engineers who had formed the German Werkbund in 1907. Peter Behrens, Hermann Muthesius, Walter Gropius, and Ludwig Hilberseimer circulated between several discussions about standardization in Germany. Gropius was associated with the Reichkuratorium für Wirtschaftlichkeit, or RKW, the German equivalent of the Taylor Society. A board member of AEG, for whom Behrens worked, was a member of the governing body of Germany's standard-making organization Deutsches Institut für Normung (DIN), which was established in 1917. The second incarnation, then called Deutscher Normenausschufs or DNA (The German Normalization Committee), collaborated with architects and Werkbund members Behrens and Muthesius. The avant-garde artists who traveled in some of the same circles took positions about "Qualitat" in Werkbund discussions and even in an avant-garde journal by the same name. Quality, however, was usually used to challenge technical standards and processes with attributes related to beauty, taste, style, and workmanship that engineering techniques could not measure. As Werkbund historian Frederic J. Schwartz has written, quality "is the result of the consumer's awareness of or involvement in the making of things, her or his physical closeness to production." Frederic J. Schwartz, *The Werkbund: Design Theory and Mass Culture Before the First World War* (New Haven: Yale University Press, 1996), 96; Detlef Mertins and Michael William Jennings, *G: An Avant-Garde Journal of Art, Architecture, Design, and Film, 1923–1926* (Los Angeles: Getty Research Institute, 2010).

organization science. Building on Fayol's work they offered another mantra: "POSDCORB (Planning, Organizing Staffing, Directing, Co-ordinating, Reporting, and Budgeting)."[22]

The practice of quality control through inspection of assembly-line goods began to evolve into an information science.[23] In the 1920s, Walter Shewhart, a statistician for Bell Labs, shifted the focus away from inspection of the final product toward an analysis of data generated during the *process* of production. Since not every item could be inspected, the new technique evaluated batches or lots. Shewhart's *Economic Control of Quality of Manufactured Product*, published in 1931, described a technical means of accounting—what would later be termed Statistical Process Control and Statistical Quality Control (SQC).[24]

Management theory around the world, although differing from country to country, increasingly began to incorporate the thinking of social scientists (e.g., Elton Mayo, Kurt Lewin, Douglas McGregor) and to consider worker motivation and other issues of human relations as well as larger structural factors related to the organization. These theories gave rise to both new industry practices as well as new academic modes of analysis, such as organization studies—the study of how organizations and social relations influence each other. Organization studies took industry as one of its subjects, even as industry was beginning to pursue its own internal organization studies. Eventually what was called quality assurance—an organization-wide

---

22   Furusten, "The Knowledge Base of Standards," 81.

23   During the world wars, to ensure consistency and safety of munitions, the BSI, the American National Standards Institute (ANSI, founded in 1918), and the American Society for Quality (ASQ, established in 1946), together with the US Department of Defense, all developed wartime standards for quality control through inspection. Indeed, the BSI claims that the Commonwealth Standards Conference in London in 1946 was essentially the founding meeting of ISO. The ANSI also brought standard-making organizations together in 1926 to create the International Standards Association, which they too claim was the precursor to ISO. See "About BSI" at bsigroup.com; "About ASQ" at http://asq.org; and "About ANSI" at ansi.org.

24   See "About ASQ" at http://asq.org.

assessment of company practices in relation to customer satisfaction—subsumed previous practices of quality control.[25]

Parallel strains of management thinking focused distinctly on knowledge economies—"restructuring the boardroom, not the shop floor."[26] By 1930, when *Business Week* declared the existence of a profession called management consulting, a number of different players such as cost accountants, advertisers, and engineers had already started to offer consultancy services to businesses.[27] The firm that would become Booz, Allen & Hamilton had its first incarnation in 1919. McKinsey & Company appeared in 1926 offering accounting expertise.[28] A number of professional organizations and business schools reflected serious interest in management practices.[29] In 1944, a *Fortune* article, "The Doctors of Management," reported that business advising had itself become big business. The number of firms had grown from 100 in 1930 to 400 by 1940.[30] Businesses subscribed to newsletters and hired advisors for banking, international

---

25   Management historian Mauro F. Guillén considers three major organizational paradigms related to scientific management, human relations, and structural analysis. Mauro F. Guillén, *Models of Management: Work, Authority, and Organization in a Comparative Perspective* (Chicago: University of Chicago Press, 1994).

26   Christopher D. McKenna, *The World's Newest Profession: Management Consulting in the Twentieth Century* (Cambridge: Cambridge University Press, 2006), 62.

27   For instance, advertising consultancy J. Walter Thompson was established in 1864. Efficiency engineering firms Arthur D. Little and Stone and Webster were founded in 1886 and 1889 respectively. See ibid., 49–50, 34.

28   Ibid., 47.

29   In 1925 the American Management Association was established, a few years after the journal *Management Review* was first published (1919). Business Schools in the major American universities began building curricula around new management practices. The American Association of Consulting Management Engineers (ACME) was established in 1929. The new manager was valuable in the 1930s as banks and businesses encountered federal regulation. In general, the new manager focused on a larger structural analysis of the organization in relation to not only goods but also new technologies, services, and regulation. See John Micklethwait and Adrian Woodridge, *The Witch Doctors: Making Sense of the Management Gurus* (New York: Random House 1996), 70; and McKenna, *The World's Newest Profession*, 47, 18.

30   McKenna, *The World's Newest Profession*, 62.

politics, and market research. *Fortune* claimed that "the consulting field is now so promising that executives may well give up industrial jobs for what will possibly be more lucrative and almost certainly will be more exhilarating careers acting as advisors to other executives."[31]

Consistent with the self-erasing history of management, Peter F. Drucker, the *eminence grise* of the contemporary management world, claimed in his 1946 book, *Concept of the Corporation*, that, at the time, "'management' as a discipline and as an object of study did not exist at all."[32] Drucker had observed the corporation during an extraordinary moment of wartime collaboration with the US government. Using Alfred P. Sloan's management of General Motors as paradigm, he profiled the corporation as an agile, intelligent, and transnational player—an emergent social institution within which labor was an asset.[33] Over the course of his career, Drucker would introduce a number of durable terms such as "privatization" or "knowledge worker."[34] Drucker argued that "a conflict between different concepts of big-business industrial society" were at the heart of global ideological conflicts between Fascism, Communism, and Western Democracy.[35]

---

31   "Doctors of Management," *Fortune*, July 1944.

32   Peter F. Drucker, *Concept of the Corporation* (New Brunswick, NJ: Transaction Publishers, 2008), xiii.

33   Ibid., 25.

34   John Micklethwait and Adrian Woodridge, in their analysis of contemporary management culture, suggest that Drucker incorporated not only structural and human relations thinking but also notions of scientific management, with the sense that the successful executive was one who set deliberate objectives and met them. In other words, there was still something to chart—still a kind of obsessive management accounting that could quantify benchmarks and goals. See Micklethwait and Woodridge, *The Witch Doctors*, 77, 74, 67–83.

35   By World War II, the manager had been characterized as a floor inspector, technical engineer, statistician, social engineer, a technocrat, and a mascot of classic economic liberalism. The technocracy theories of Thorstein Veblen, Walter Rautenstrauch, and others cast the engineer as a character able to manage global resources based on comprehensive databases or energy units that would replace currency. James Burnham's *The Managerial Revolution: What is Happening in the World* (New York: The John Day Company, 1941), projected that an elite strata of managers would become the new ruling class and that a "managerial state" would replace capitalism. Having swung from the radical left to an extremely conservative position, he suggested that indicators of this trend included Leninism and Stalinism

Drucker disagreed with his friend Karl Polanyi, a fellow émigré from Vienna and colleague at Bennington, that big business sustained itself through some form of collective planning, cooperation, or communitarianism. Though he found Polanyi's economic analysis to be "brilliant" and "profound," Drucker claimed that his own subject, General Motors, was an "essay in federalism."[36] The corporation was not a rival power but a patriotic partner of government.

While Drucker ennobled the corporation, he simultaneously generated a new authority for himself: that of the guru. His voice was not exactly that of a scholarly theorist, but nor was it that of a practical engineer of scientific management. As scholarship, he claimed, reviewers did not know how to assess his book. "It dealt with a business yet it wasn't 'economics.' It dealt with structure, organization, policy, constitutional principles, power relationships—and yet it wasn't 'government.'"[37] *Concept of the Corporation* was used to reorganize many corporations around the world, launching the "organization boom" of the ensuing twenty years.[38]

By 1950, an estimated 1,000 management firms portrayed themselves as viable partners to the nation, a "contractor state" asked to consult on governance, defense, Cold War tactics, and the Space Race. They joined the OECD, the IMF, the World Bank, and other IGOs—the new institutions of global coordination and cooperation. Many relocated to Washington, DC, and moved fluidly through ranks of authority advising both

---

as well as "New Dealism" and technocracy. Drucker dismissed Burnham's arguments as myopic misinterpretation. Drucker, *Concept of the Corporation*, xi, 9.

36   Drucker, *Concept of the Corporation*, 204, 214, 237, 256, 46. For Drucker, "collectivism—whether state socialism or state capitalism—is not the answer to the basic political problems of industrial society" (204). Quoted in full: "the essay in federalism—on the whole, was an exceedingly successful one. It attempted to combine the greatest corporate unity with the greatest divisional autonomy and responsibility; and like every true federation, it aimed at realizing unity through local self-government and vice versa"(46).

37   Ibid., xiii. The quote is from the Drucker's preface to the 1983 edition, included in the 2008 edition.

38   Ibid., 291.

businesses and governments domestically and abroad. In the 1960s, attired in conservative dress, these consultants were also legendary characters haunting the Yale Club and the University Club in Manhattan. The Marshall Plan ensured that their influence was now global as they were awarded more and more overseas contracts. Even the Bank of England was "McKinseyed," and in the 1970s, and Robert McNamara also hired McKinsey to advise the World Bank.[39]

Quality management practices were significantly transformed as they circulated through other countries, especially post-war Japan where *Concept of the Corporation* was a bestseller. Since Japan's manufacturing industries had a reputation for poorly made goods, the country was very receptive to notions of quality control as they began to rebuild their industry. To help in this effort, General MacArthur enlisted US quality-control experts and management consultants, among them W. Edwards Deming, Joseph Juran, Armand Feigenbaum, and Malcolm Baldrige. In dialogue with these theorists, Japanese management culture developed what would come to be called Total Quality Management (TQM)—a family of techniques that includes Quality Circles (QC), *kanban* or just-in-time production, zero defects, and suggestion systems, among other things.[40]

---

39 McKenna, *The World's Newest Profession*, 62, 181–6. Like Drucker, McKinsey adopted the authority of the academic with its own journal the *McKinsey Quarterly*. See Micklethwait and Woodridge, *The Witch Doctors*, 54.

40 Japan's own standard-making organization, the Japanese Union of Scientists and Engineers (JUSE), started a magazine, *Statistical Quality Control*, and in 1950 invited W. E. Deming to teach a seminar. He introduced his "Deming Cycle" (also called the Deming Wheel and the Shewhart Cycle), which is sometimes represented as "Design, Production, Sales, Research," and sometimes as "plan, do, study, act" (PDSA). It would inspire the Japanese version "plan, do, check, act" (PDCA). In the United States, Armand V. Feigenbaum used the phrase "Total Quality" in papers and in his 1951 book, *Quality Control: Principles, Practice, and Administration*, which when republished in 1961 was titled *Total Quality Control: Engineering and Management*. While the introduction of the term Total Quality Control is variously attributed, there is general agreement that when JUSE invited Juran was to speak in 1954, his lectures helped to move the idea of quality control past its technical application in heavy industries to a structural application in a broader range of industries. TQM may also be known as Total Quality Management, Total Quality Control, or Company-Wide Quality Control. See Masaaki Imai,

Management consultant Masaaki Imai has argued that the ethos of *kaizen* (continual improvement) distinguished the Japanese from the Western models of innovation and maintenance.[41] In the 1960s, Toyota became a high-profile workshop for many of these techniques, although they were also tried out at Nissan, Mitsubishi, and Komatsu, among others.[42]

As Japanese production techniques markedly improved in the 1970s, and as their management styles became more popular around the world, they began to challenge the supposedly dominant US paradigm. At first assuming that the Japanese were simply undercutting them in price, US businesses finally awoke to the competition and began to emulate Japanese techniques. In the 1970s, DIN, BSI, and the Canadian Standards Association (CSA) developed a strain of quality standards and urged ISO to do the same.[43] By the 1980s, ISO formed TC 176 (Technical Committee 176) to research and develop standards for "quality management and quality

---

Kaizen (Ky'zen): The Key to Japanese Competitive Success (New York: Random House Business Division, 1986); A. V. Feigenbaum, *Quality Control: Principles, Practice and Administration: An Industrial Management Tool for Improving Product Quality and Design and for Reducing Operating Costs and Losses* (New York: McGraw-Hill, 1951); and A. V. Feigenbaum, *Total Quality Control: Engineering and Management: The Technical and Managerial Field for Improving Product Quality, Including Its Reliability, and for Reducing Operating Costs and Losses* (New York: McGraw-Hill, 1961).

41 Imai, *Kaizen (Ky'zen)*, 4, 23, 43.

42 Konosuke Matsushita, a TCM guru, has written, "We will win and you will lose. You cannot do anything because your failure is an internal disease. Your companies are based on Taylor's principles. Worse your heads are Taylorized too. You firmly believe that sound management means executives on one side and workers on the other, on one side men who think and on the other side, men who only work." Quoted in J. Seddon, "Changing Management Thinking: The Key to Success with TQM," in Gopal K. Kanji, ed., *Total Quality Management: Proceedings of the First World Congress* (London: Chapman and Hall, 1995), 341.

43 Kristina Tamm Hallström, "Organizing the Process of Standardization," in *A World of Standards*, 86; bsigroup.com. In 1977, DIN submitted a proposal to ISO for a technical committee that would evaluate quality standards. The Canadian Standards Association issued quality guidelines CSA-Z299 in the mid-1970s. In December 1979, the United States issued ANSI/ASQC Z-1.15, *Generic Guidelines for Quality Systems*. In 1979, the BSI published BS 5750, which they claim as the first quality-management standard and the template for ISO 9000.

assurance."[44] The first ISO 9000 standard was published in 1987.[45]

The approach to quality management that ISO finally adopted reflects quality's antecedents in scientific management, statistics, structural, and human relations thinking, and global management cultures. ISO was now involved in all the myriad theories associated with the *process* of production, the procedures and practices of a company, and the social architecture of production, services, and corporate governance. Given its history, it is not surprising that even though ISO 9000 is not a technical standard, there is obsessive data gathering and metrics are used to quantify or prove that deliberate objectives have been met.

Accompanying this history there is no epic portrait of war, no depiction of a monstrous multi-cephalous Leviathan, not even a heroic engineer or scientist who intervenes to rationalize the world's economies. Rather, there is a seemingly innocuous set of incrementally developed conventions, perhaps accompanied only by a promotional photograph of a quality engineer holding up a framed copy of the ISO 9000 certification. Quality lends to infrastructure space part of its inherent disposition—a drive to habituate without specific content. Perhaps nothing could be more powerful.

Quality Multiplies in Infrastructure Space

Just as ISO was beginning to discover the ways in which quality management might enhance its global influence, the zone formula was being applied to a new crop of urban installations. ISO technical standards related to container shipping—for container sizes, construction specifications, and locking mechanisms—helped to

---

44   Ibid.; Mendel, "The Making and Expansion of International Management Standards," 141. ISO would later address TQM, defining it as "a management approach for an organization, centered on quality, based on the participation of all its members and aiming at long-term success through customer satisfaction, and benefits to all members of the organization and to society" (ISO 8402:1994).

45   "A Brief History of BSI," at bsieducation.org; Joseph M. Juran and Donald W. Marquardt, *The ISO 9000 Family of International Standards* (New York: McGraw-Hill Professional, 2001).

accelerate zone growth. By 1970, ISO had concluded negotiations over technical specifications to standardize Keith W. Tantlinger's famous 1958 invention of the corner locking mechanism (currently ISO 1161:1984) for Malcolm McLean's shipping container (currently ISO 6346).[46] The snap and lock of those boxes echoed across container populations that were now growing exponentially. To manage the avalanche of data tracking required for global trade, new generations of computing and broadband telecommunications were also delivered to new generations of zones and urban enclaves in more and more developing countries.

ISO became a global club for this new crop of urbanism, and the zone functioned as a multiplier of quality management practices. The "informational city" described by Manuel Castells in 1989 was a world in which technical standards as well as new management practices like ISO 9000 directly arranged not only the just-in-time factory and the zone but also the larger industrial and telecommunications landscape.[47] With just-in-time manufacturing and transshipment logistics, management made not things, but populations of things—things that flowed even more seamlessly as information rather than assembly-line objects.

Modern architects of the early twentieth century conceived of architecture and urbanism as a shared global platform, yet their titanic, utopian dreams were no match for the plodding bureaucracies of standard making. Modular proportional systems, flexible joints, minimum requirements for dwelling, or prefabrication technologies were among the proposals that architects offered in projects, books, exhibitions, or conferences like the meetings of the International Congresses of Modern Architecture (CIAM). Spatial variables, it was hoped, would shape a universal language.[48] Nevertheless, while infrastructure space may be the operating

46   Marc Levinson, *The Box: How the Shipping Container Made the World Smaller and the Economy Bigger* (Princeton: Princeton University Press, 2006), 137–49, 148.

47   Manuel Castells, *The Informational City: Information Technology, Economic Restructuring, and the Urban Regional Process* (Oxford: Blackwell, 1989).

48   Eric Mumford, *The CIAM Discourse on Urbanism, 1928–1960* (Cambridge, MA: MIT Press, 2002).

system for zones as well as other the generic spatial products—golf courses, resorts, retail, and suburbs among them—architects have usually not devised the rules. Corporate budgets and practices arguably shape this space, and within these practices, the language of standards is common and global.[49] Moreover most global construction firms, and some large design firms, necessarily implement quality-management programs and speak the ISO dialects.

Having used quality as a gambit to bring more and more corporations into the fold, ISO began authoring additional specialized quality-management standards. One of these was ISO 14000—a management standard addressing environmental issues. The ISO 14000 Technical Committee, TC 206, was established in 1993. The standard does not set explicit targets for emissions or waste. Rather, it is designed to change attitudes toward the environment.[50] It has been adopted by over half of the ISO members, and while certification is not mandatory, over 150,000 certificates have been issued in 148 countries.[51] ISO 14000 is part of what has been called a move "Beyond Total Quality"—management standards increasingly concerned with public issues like the environment, health care, education, corporate social responsibility, and even governance.[52] ISO standards have created a habit that has spread to almost every kind of endeavor, such that it would seem that management standards are the answer to any problem in any field. All the familiar practices—information gathering, feedback questionnaires, quantified progress reports, and other metrics—now attend each new incarnation of quality.

---

49   Architects have long developed their own technical standards, and some of these efforts have contributed to the work of ISO. For a history of the Architectural Graphic Standards, the common reference book for architectural standards, see Nader Vossoughian, "Standardization Reconsidered: *Normierung* in and after Ernst Neufert's *Bauentwurfslehre* (1936)," *Grey Room*, Winter 2014, 34–55.

50   See bsigroup.com and iso14000-iso14001-environmental-management. com/iso14000.htm.

51   "Environmental Management: The ISO 14000 Family of International Standards," Geneva: ISO, 2009.

52   In 1991, ISO established a Strategic Advisory Group on the Environment (SAGE). The BSI published the first environmental management standards in 1992 (BS 7750). The 1992 Rio Summit on the Environment was also a galvanizing event.

ISO's influence has been so pervasive that the management habit has been mimicked in non-ISO standards and certification programs. The same year that ISO established ISO 14000, the US Green Building Council (USGBC) inaugurated a certification process called LEED (Leadership in Energy and Environmental Design) that replicated ISO's jargon and metrics. LEED assumes a similar bureaucratic structure to that of ISO with its member organizations, technical committees, and audits. Buildings are rated according to their fulfillment of criteria on the LEED checklist for environmentally sensitive design (Certified, Silver, Gold, and Platinum). The USGBC hosts an international round table for the green councils of thirty nations and develops what it calls "Global Alternative Compliance Paths" for international work.[53] LEED certification is a badge that is prominently displayed among professionals in the design and construction industries.[54]

LEED in turn has its own imitators. The US Public Interest Design Institute offers training in SEED (Social Economic Environmental Design) certification—a set of standards for evaluating community design, established in 2005. Promising to move beyond LEED, SEED measures the success of projects with the "SEED metric." It also accounts for the "triple bottom line" (TBL)—a term used in relation to corporate social responsibility to indicate sensitivity to people, planet, and profit. The "SEED Evaluator 3.0" is another tool for gathering information and assessing "proof of concept" or adherence to SEED's five basic principles. Meetings in the network use questionnaires to gather participant responses, while access to the network and training is only available after taking a pledge to abide by the organization's five principles.[55]

---

53   See usgbc.org.

54   See "Executive Leadership" at m.gensler.com.

55   See publicinterestdesign.com and seed-network.org. SEED's five principles are: 1) Advocate for those who have a limited voice in public life. 2) Build structures for inclusion that engage stakeholders and allow communities to make decisions. 3) Promote social equality through discourse that reflects a range of values and social identities. 4) Generate ideas that grow from place and build local capacity. 5) Design to help conserve resources and minimize waste.

Recently, ISO has begun to consider building technologies and cities. The organization renders buildings not as enclosures but as assemblages of technical systems, components, and inhabitants. "Intelligent and Sustainable Buildings" was the theme of the ISO 2008 General Assembly in Dubai. The assembly recognized that buildings represent "a large share of the economic assets of individuals, organizations and nations," and that they are major sources of employment, consumers of energy, and producers of waste and emissions.[56] Sprawl, smart cities, zero carbon emission cities, and earthquakes were some of the topics discussed. Nearby Masdar City was held up as a model for future cities. The assembly's program consistently advanced global standards as the key to achieving this urban future. And ISO's 37120, a new standard for urban data collection, even identifies forty-six "performance indicators" for consistently comparing global cities.[57]

There is, however, no ISO technical committee specifically tasked with addressing the technologies of infrastructure space. Architecture and urban planning, as currently configured, may also be better at conforming to rather than confronting or renovating development practices around the world where ISO-style bureaucracies are often pulling the strings.

Quality Speaks Managementese

This new way of thinking involves not only free enterprise but also a veritable cult of enterprise, bordering on the religious, to the point where many firms have taken their desires for reality, their project of corporate development for internal democracy, their discourse

---

56 See "Buildings for a Sustainable Future, Dubai, 15 October 2008," and "Summary of Open Session Held on 15 October on Buildings for a Sustainable Future," both at iso.org.

57 Louise Cox, President of the International Union of Architects, advised that designers "should not be aiming to replicate New York or London throughout the emerging economies of Africa and South America." See Louise Cox, "Sustainable Building for the Global Village: The Vision and Standards Needs for Architects and Designers," ISO General Assembly, 2008, at iso.org; and "Finally, Clear Performance Data for Comparing the World's Cities" at citylab.com.

about new internal communications, for the advent of employee participation and mobilizations, and new forms of corporate self-organization for new means of personal realization.—Armand Mattelart[58]

In 1965, one in every hundred employees was a management consultant; by 1995 the ratio was one in every thirteen.[59] Consistent with the idea that management standards are the answer to everything, the last few decades have seen a new "frenzy of management fads."[60] Most of these fads share several common attributes. The guru, as a subject of modern mythologizing, is often present to lend human scale and promote discipleship. Charts and aphorisms are default requirements, reflecting the engineering, accounting, and motivational ingredients in management's longer history.

In motivational teamwork environments, Japanese models of Total Quality Management have cast their spell with incantatory slogans and mantras about striving for better results and eliminating error (e.g., "You are surrounded by mountains of treasures." Meaning: There are many problems from which to learn).[61] A number of Japanese management leaders offered signature techniques.[62] Among them the 3 MU checklist, the 5 S movement, the 4 M checklist, the Seven Statistical Tools, the 9 Wastes, or the 5 Ws and the 1 H (meaning: One needs to ask "Why" at least five times to determine the cause of a problem and then decide "how" to fix it.) From each of these gnomic postulates flow additional steps, diagrams, charts, and checklists.[63]

In the United States, managementese often assumes the tone of self-help literature. Established firms like McKinsey offer their own formulas and incubate new popular gurus (e.g.,

58   Mattelart, *Mapping World Communication*, 208–9.

59   McKenna, *The World's Newest Profession*, 8.

60   Micklethwait and Woodridge, *The Witch Doctors*, 62.

61   Ibid., 79; Guillén, *Models of Management*.

62   Including the professors/consultants Kaoru Ishikawa, Masao Kogure, and Yoji Akao.

63   See "Quality Management," at businessballs.com; Guillén, *Models of Management*; and Imai, *Kaizen (Ky'zen)*.

Kenichi Ohmae, Tom Peters, or Robert Waterman).[64] McKinsey & Co. has the McKinsey 7-S (Shared Value, Strategy, Structure, System, Staff, Style, Skill). Booz & Co. (a spinoff of Booz Allen) offers a mandala of interpenetrating circular arrows in which the phrases "way to play," "product and service fit," and "capabilities system" surround a central core with the phrase "right to win." Tom Peters, in the line of succession from Peter Drucker, is the author of nearly twenty books, and he further broadcasts his message in seminars, papers, a website, and tweets. Among the "free stuff" on the *tompeters!* website one finds "The Top 50 Have Yous," the "100 Ways to Succeed/Make Money," the "209 Irreducibles," among many others. Peters sometimes directly addresses quality systems. His "Quality and Excellence: The Quality 136" offers 136 "random thoughts" on quality. "Quality is saying thank you" appears twice as numbers 6 and 8 in the list. "Quality is strategy" and "Strategy is quality" appear as numbers 43 and 44. In a constant fount of jargon, sometimes created from other jargon, Peters encourages his devotees to be "blackbelt listeners," arguing that "quality is letting go of those who suffer from SED—Severe Enthusiasm Deficit."[65]

A sister to the quality industry, as sponsored by ISO and others, and one that shares many personnel in the quality world, is Six Sigma. Six Sigma, a term used in statistical analysis, refers to a set of quality techniques that Motorola developed and shared in 1988. Now broadly applied to many different kinds of organizations, it relies heavily on statistics to reduce defects in production and management. One can be certified as a quality auditor, a quality engineer, and even as something called a CSSBB, a Certified Six Sigma Black Belt. Numerous groups, like the International Six Sigma Institute and Secret Society for Imperious Professionals of Process Improvement (ISSISSIPPI), make up a secondary industry offering training in Six Sigma practices and certification processes.[66]

---

64 Micklethwait and Woodridge, *The Witch Doctors*, 55–6.
65 See tompeters.com.
66 See ississippi.org.

Some of the most powerful individuals and organizations in the world have partnered with management gurus or adopted management scripts. During the winter of 1994, President Bill Clinton went on a self-imposed retreat with Stephen Covey (*The Seven Habits of Highly Effective People*) and Anthony "Tony" Robbins (*Unlimited Power: The New Science Of Personal Achievement*). During his attempt to recapture power for the conservative right in the 1990s, Newt Gingrich made Drucker part of the reading list for his adherents and made the "Contract for America" a management theory document.[67] Global strategists like McKinsey or Booz Allen partner with governments to work on political campaigns, defense contracts, national infrastructure planning, and regional or macro-urban development strategies, among many other things. Developing countries hire these consultancies to provide advice about governance, organization, new technologies and industries, etc. It is then not surprising that, in the mid-1990s, examining, critiquing, or chronicling the practices of management and consulting firms became a new micro-industry.[68]

Since management consulting is in the business of "retailing" ideas, its principles must paradoxically maintain the fluidity and novelty of merchandise in rapid cycles of obsolescence. Like the promises of spiritual cults or recipes for celebrity, the message is continually refreshed with content, maintaining a forward

---

67   Micklethwait and Woodridge, *The Witch Doctors*, 291, 301–2.

68   In 1996, John Micklethwait and Adrian Woodridge published *The Witch Doctors: Making Sense of the Management Gurus*, claiming that it was the first such exposé. In 1997, James O'Shea and Charles Madigan published *Dangerous Company: Management Consultants and the Businesses They Save and Ruin*. Both were largely exposing management culture to its potential customers in large businesses. Subsequent treatments, among them Walter Kiechel's *The Lords of Strategy: The Secret Intellectual History of the New Corporate World* (2010), attempt to clarify historical developments in management or expose its false logics. Christopher D. McKenna's *The World's Newest Profession: Management Consulting in the Twentieth Century* argues that management should officially be considered a professional activity. Lewis Pinault's *Consulting Demons: Inside the Unscrupulous World of Global Corporate Consulting* (2000) and Martin Kihn's *House of Lies: How Management Consultants Steal Your Watch and Then Tell You the Time* (2005) are entertaining, absurdist exposés of management culture.

movement that is satisfying perhaps precisely because it cycles through familiar territory with only slight variations. All of this content must be constantly boiled down to essential steps that can be instantly absorbed. The result is a welter of books, seminars, lectures, heroes, bibles, acronyms, upbeat jargon, steps, take-aways, executive summaries, and "go-to" concepts. In this industry worth over $300 billion, speaking fees of $60,000 are routine.[69] The teasers for guru seminars resemble the infomercial that seems to provide everything but the one essential ingredient that must finally be purchased—or, as one seminar promised: "The Most Important Sentence in the English Language."[70]

Self-help management speak can be found throughout the literature on quality. Personal achievement is a recurring theme. Swooping arrows embellish the mandalas and pyramids that are a staple of the genre. Joining these might be, for instance, a classical edifice, a soft-focus photograph of an oyster shell opening to reveal its pearl, individuals in silhouette reaching the summit of a mountain, or others jumping up enthusiastically with arms outstretched.

Quality Is Extrastatecraft

However innocuous ISO may appear to be, the organization has universal ambitions. ISO hopes to certify more and more companies and draw an ever larger section of the global community into the management habit. Once this population of players is listening and committed to continually renewing its certification, the management protocol becomes a means of reconditioning any number of organizations with a new message or an inflection of the old one.

---

69   "Remembering Drucker," *Economist*, November 19, 2009.

70   Micklethwait and Woodridge, *The Witch Doctors*, 87, 84. The Transcendental Meditation Organization, led, until his recent death, by the Maharishi Mahesh Yogi, operates in precisely the same way, making very clear the similarity between religion and management culture. So close are the two that one of TM's enterprises is to run schools of management, which they have established all over the world. See Easterling, *Enduring Innocence*, 73–98.

Before 2000, European nations were the predominant subscribers to ISO management standards, but ISO 9000 certification doubled in the first decade of the twenty-first century, and when in 2009 the number of ISO 9000 certificates topped one million, one-quarter of those were from China.[71] The number of certified organizations in the United States and the UK has held steady. Regarding the adoption of ISO standards to be overly bureaucratic or constraining, US companies were initially less inclined to adopt them. Characterizing US management systems as much more susceptible to markets and management fads, the European management systems perhaps respond more positively to hierarchical coordination from international organizations like ISO.[72] To consider the needs of developing countries, ISO set up DEVCO—sometimes seen as a "missionary" organization bringing the secret signals of a capital market to the not-yet-initiated. Yet now, the latest trends in management culture are beginning to come from densely populated developing countries like India, Africa, and China. Coimbatore Krishnarao Prahalad or Vijay Govindarajan are perhaps edging out Tom Peters or the gurus of Total Quality Management.

With ISO 14000 and other Beyond Total Quality standards, ISO has begun to engage other international organizations involved in global governance. ISO 14000 was developed with the cooperation of a number of NGOs and IGOs including the World Health Organization, the WTO, the Global Ecolabelling Network, and the Sierra Club. ISO's new Guidelines for Social Responsibility, ISO 26000, recognize that management standards have potential responsibilities beyond those related to customer satisfaction. Addressing corporate as well as public institutions, ISO 26000 refers to a number of existing voluntary

---

71   "The ISO Survey of Certifications 2008," ISO, 2009.

72   Mendel, "The Making and Expansion of International Management Standards," 142–4. Mendel attempts to apply Weberian distinctions between material and formal actions and practices, assigning ease with the formal to the European and South American notions of civil society. See also Walter Mattli and Tim Bu, "Setting International Standards: Technological Rationality or Primacy of Power?," *World Politics* 56, no. 1 (2003), 23, 41–2.

guidelines from the ILO, the OECD, and the United Nations Global Compact Office (UNGCO). Implementation of these guidelines is encouraged but neither certified nor enforced.

Like LEED and SEED, the global activist group Social Accountability International (SAI) also mirrors the form of ISO 9000 protocols, this time precisely to piggyback on systems and habits already in place in an enormous number of organizations. In 1998, SAI—an NGO that claims a large global "citizenship"— launched SA8000. While SA8000 confronts issues of labor, the environment, and human rights more directly than any ISO standard, ISO provides it with the camouflage of a relatively conservative organization. SA8000 incorporates basic tenets of the ILO, the ICFTU, and the UN Global Compact of 2000—"ten universally accepted principles in the areas of human rights, labour, environment and anti-corruption."[73] However, the SA8000 codes have the benefit of operating independently from the regulation of any one country; so while the United States, for instance, may not have formally ratified principles concerning labor protection, Social Accountability International can approach US companies individually and attempt to extract a pledge.[74]

Even though SA8000 has acclimated to corporate practices, multinational corporations would nevertheless prefer to propose their own standards, regulations, and certification processes in response to pressure and criticism from labor and environmental activists, and national regulatory agencies. Corporations not only report their ethical code of conduct in promotional literature, they organize and submit to their own second- and third-party certification processes. Launched in 1998, the Fair Labor Association has a similar certification process. The FLA's audit of Foxconn was controversial largely because the organization is funded by some of the same companies, such as Apple, that it is charged with investigating. The OECD reports the existence of hundreds of such self-certifying codes of conduct in circulation.[75]

---

73   See unglobalcompact.org.

74   See "Certified Facilities List," at saasaccreditation.org.

75   Gary Gereffi, Ronie Garcia-Johnson, and Erika Sasser, "The NGO-Industrial Complex," *Foreign Policy*, no. 125 (2001).

A so-called NGO-Industrial Complex has evolved in which NGOs may operate either as a legitimate means of influencing corporate policy, or as a smoke screen for inoculating a business against any reckoning. A company like Apple, Nike, or Starbucks may undergo a number of certification processes, and display next to their logo a collection of badges and certificates representing 'universal principles'—all in lieu of adhering to the laws of a state. Compliance is voluntary, and the seal of approval may be self-constructed or internal to the corporation.[76]

Quality Inoculates

Perhaps because environmental standards provoke shared questions about performance, ISO 14000 has prompted research concerning both its efficacy and the intentions behind it. Invoking what they call "club theory," researchers have argued that industries requiring ISO 14000 certification from their suppliers act like multipliers spreading influence and encouraging compliance on the part of the other players in the club.[77] They have collected evidence suggesting that "ISO 14001-certified facilities have better environmental performance (lower pollution emissions, adjusted for their toxicity) than they would have had if they had not joined the club."[78] Some analysts project that the standard might become a carrier of additional guidelines, habits, or symbolic capital.[79]

---

76   See "Certified Facilities List," at saasaccreditation.org.

77   See Aseem Prakash and Matthew Potoski, "Racing to the Bottom? Trade, Environmental Governance, and ISO 14001," *American Journal of Political Science* 50, no. 2 (2006); Prakash and Potoski, *The Voluntary Environmentalists*, 90; and Yasuhumi Mori and Eric W. Welch, "The ISO 14001 Environmental Management Standard in Japan: Results from a National Survey of Facilities in Four Industries," *Journal of Environment Planning and Management* 51, no. 3 (2008).

78   Prakash and Potoski, *The Voluntary Environmentalists*, 186.

79   F. Orecchini and D. Sabatini, "Cars and the Environment: A New Approach to Assessment through ISO 14001 Certification of the Car Process," *Proceedings of the Institution of Mechanical Engineers–Part D–Journal of Automobile Engineering* 217, no. 1 (2003).

Sampling of logos for organizations offering certification programs
in the so-called NGO-Industrial Complex

As part of various governance collectives, ISO may be a
standard-bearer and facilitator of changing attitudes, or just
another proxy or disguise. Nils Brunsson, a researcher of business organization and administration, argues that standards
"may not only promote but also inhibit competition and
innovation."[80] Similarly, noting that standards can be used as
both "sword" and "shield," the international law scholar David
A. Wirth observes that as they become part of trade negotiations, they may be used by one country to challenge and exclude
the products of another, or to shield their own from critique.
They may also be used to inoculate organizations against binding and more consequential regulations, especially when
minimum guidelines are treated as maximum standards. Wirth
also raises questions about a regulatory consensus among
private organizations when those regulations create a

---

80 Nils Brunsson, "Organizations, Markets, and Standardization," in
Brunsson and Jacobsson, eds., *A World of Standards*, 31.

significant financial liability. Moreover, how does one evaluate private agreements about environmental issues without public input?[81]

For the environmental lawyer Judith Kimerling, ISO 14000 and the various programs of Corporate Social Responsibility are hardly innocuous, and they may only provide larger more established organizations or nations with techniques for protecting themselves against binding standards. Having witnessed some of the dangerous consequences of drilling in the oil fields of the Ecuadorian Amazon, she argues that oil companies in the region used "the cloak of international standards and corporate responsibility to wrap [their] operations in a veneer of environmental excellence and social responsibility." For Kimerling, "corporate responsibility" and "international standards" can be used to undermine the development of national environmental law and capacity by arbitrarily "legitimizing norms that have been defined by special interests, and reassuring government officials and other stakeholders that practices are improving, based on enigmatic standards that lie beyond the reach—or responsibility—of national authorities."[82] With her book *Amazon Crude* (1991), Kimerling, who has worked in the region for decades, inspired a lawsuit against Texaco that has still not been settled.[83]

As Kimerling points out, for all the activity in this burgeoning sphere of extrastate consensus, there are many signal absences, *primarily* related to environment and labor. She writes that the "imbalance in international governance is illustrated by the fact that under the rules governing trade today, there is a meaningful legal mechanism to hold a company accountable for pirating a Madonna video, but not for contaminating the

---

81   David A. Wirth, "The International Organization of Standardization: Private Voluntary Standards as Swords and Shields," *Boston College Environment Affairs Law Review* 36, no. 1 (2009).

82   Judith Kimerling, "International Standards in Ecuador's Amazon Oil Fields: The Privatization of Environmental Law," *Columbia Journal of Environmental Law* 26 (2001), 394.

83   Joe Kane, *Savages* (New York: Vintage, 1996); Judith Kimerling, *Amazon Crude* (National Resources Defense Council, 1991).

environment or using forced or child labor."[84] ISO developed a
technical standard so that different countries and agencies could
uniformly measure emissions of a ton of carbon, and they have
also developed techniques for monitoring the quality of air,
water, and soil. Still, they make no recommendations regarding
emissions.[85] Similarly, there are ISO standards for cold work-
places, protective clothing, and other safety issues, but no
standard regarding hours and wages, or conditions in tropical
climes. Quality management practices may bring labor into
dialogue with management (e.g., quality circles), but customer
satisfaction surveys may shield management when they only
address the services delivered by employees. Moreover, companies like Classic Fashion Apparel in the Jordanian QIZ are able to
sport ISO certifications as well as other awards and congratula-
tions on their website, even while being under investigation over
allegations of sexual abuse and predation.

ISO is devoted to the sharing and coordination of information, yet because it must treat its standards as a product, it cannot
be a clearinghouse for information. If it was a truly public institution with open archives, it could provide an amazing index of
the performance and compliance of every species of organization
in the world. While ISO is not in the auditing and certification
business, it does hire the research company Nielsen to keep track
of the number of certifications that have been issued. The
company produces a summary of this data and publishes it on
the web, but it does not include the names of the organizations
that are ISO certified—a list that is almost impossible to compile.
ISO keeps these records confidential so as not to reveal its clients
to competing companies in the certification business. The aspirations of engineers in the quality industry take precedence over
the public aspirations that the quality standards address.

In the oil fields of the Amazon forest or in the factories of
every ISO 9000-certified manufacturer, as in countless other

---

84   Kimerling, "International Standards in Ecuador's Amazon Oil Fields," 290.
85   "Reforms to Improve Service Delivery in the Public Sector," at planning.
go.ke.

situations around the world, it seems that, for all the strenuous efforts to develop standards, for all of the weight of mind-numbing organizational habit, or for all of the attempts to control the world from Geneva, in many places where it matters most, there are few tools for initiating change. The reasonable men and women in quality-management culture—all in attendance, all simultaneously translating, all balancing loyalties—seem to work on safer, less controversial issues. Quality practices of information gathering have taught them to repeatedly ask questions that will yield positive responses. "Have I answered all of your questions today?"; "Is there anything else I can help you with?"; "Have I responded to all of your needs with excellence?"

Technical and management standards are instructive if only because they have, in a matter of decades, changed the way people across the world talk to each other while also strengthening a layer of influential intermediate authority operating in between the market and the state. The strategic indeterminacy of these standards, offering fluid goals to a global audience, is politically shrewd, demonstrating the power of disposition or pure activity divorced from content. Quality is a practice that is *doing* something as it habituates, and *saying* almost nothing as it avoids controversial political stances. Yet its absurdly self-reflexive forms of consensus can mask the gravest political problems facing its adherents—cultivating what philosopher Jacques Rancière calls the "diseases of consensus."[86]

Quality Meets Interplay

ISO is a powerful multiplier among corporate networks and urban incubators like the zone. As such it may be a possible, if unlikely, source of inspiration for alternative urban design projects using the ISO network as an undisclosed carrier. Rather than focusing on the design of a building as object form, the designer might work on a component detail for anything from a skyscraper to an automobile—a detail strategically

---

86   Jacques Rancière, *On the Shores of Politics* (London: Verso, 1995), 106.

placed as a multiplier or germ of change in a population of buildings, disguised as inoffensively banal, but amplified by ISO's global reach.

Yet, despite the widespread faith in management standards, infrastructure space offers the possibility of a new global habit that is potentially more powerful—not standards but software and protocols for simple interdependencies or linkages between spatial variables. As was discussed in the preceding accounts of zone and broadband urbanism, spatial software is different from a master plan that often acts as a container for spatial products, but it is also different from standards that merely manage and often inoculate. Software offers neither plan nor solution, but rather an expression of relationships—a means to leverage change in infrastructure space with interdependent constraints and offsets. Floating and adaptable protocols, establishing not fixed content but rather an interplay of active forms, might become customary bargains in global exchanges.

In crafting global agreements, organs of interdependence and reciprocity are different from the organs of consensus that surrounds quality. Spatial software can mix remote abstract values together with the values of a complex local context, without requiring that all parties conform to a single universal principle. After all, institutions that do so often develop elaborate rituals to demonstrate that they are adhering to such principles when in fact they are departing or decoupling from them. As a political apparatus, the interplay of spatial software, by contrast, potentially benefits from the balance and exchange of distinct, remote, or divergent values.

Various bargaining instruments are already in play in global development. The Emirates largely accepted the zone as a prepackaged formula to be deployed in exchange for trade, education, or technology. Yet the UAE also made exploitation of its resources contingent on an offset investment in other industries that it needed, from desalination and fish farming to tourism. The country was then able to curate the broader composition of its offerings to the world while becoming more self-reliant.[87] Across the world, any number of banking products also organize investments to leverage new assets. Can a city like Nairobi similarly link zone incentives to public transit investment? Or in Kenya's digital villages, can roadways and broadband capacities be linked in a way that preserves wilderness and attracts remote educational or tourist assets? All of these linkages might engender a sustaining give-and-take, and a spatial software for simple interdependencies has the potential to become as contagious as a standard.

Consider global landscapes as different as suburban sprawl and the rain forest. Both landscapes involve national and international players, their problems are politically intractable, and they cannot be adequately addressed with the prevailing tools of standards or master plans. Both landscapes are also abstractly valued: In suburban sprawl, the global financial industry generates complex mortgage products and derivatives to represent the house, while in the rain forest the global carbon market assigns carbon credits to represent the forest. REDD (Reducing Emissions from Deforestation and Degradation) is a protocol for calculating the carbon value of resources like the rain forest, so that forest owners who choose not to deforest can be compensated for preserving a global asset.[88] Additional environmental assets may be commoditized as a Payment for Environmental Services (PES), where corporations pay for a resource like clean water.[89]

In both suburb and forest, rather than merely being

---

87   See tec.tawazun.ae. See also Easterling, "Extrastatecraft," *Perspecta 39, Re_ Urbanism: Transforming Capitals* (2007), 2–16. The author is also indebted to Yale Global Fellow Raheela Khan for sharing knowledge of Islamic banking instruments. Interview, December 4, 2013.

88   See *The Little Redd Book*, at amazonconservation.org.

89   R. Arriagada et al., "Do Payments for Environmental Services Affect Forest Cover? A Farm-Level Evaluation from Costa Rica," *Land Economics* 88.2 (2012), 382–99; J. Farley and R. Constanza, "Payments for Ecosystem Services: From Local to Global," *Ecological Economics* 69 (2010), 20, 60–8; J. Hauck et al., "Benefits and Limitations of the Ecosystem Services Concept in Environmental Policy and Decision Making: Some Stakeholder Perspectives," *Environmental Science & Policy* 25 (2013), 13–21; K. Jax, "Ecosystem Services and Ethics," *Ecological Economics* 93 (2013), 260–8. The author is indebted to Gina La Cerva, graduate student at Yale's School of Forestry, for sharing research about Payment for Environmental Services.

monetized, how might a diverse portfolio of spatial assets and values associated with any property (the land, home, agriculture, soil, climate, resources, culture, symbolic capital) become variables in in a parallel market? Trading in abstract values can lead to volatility, with lasting physical effects on the ground and there is a need to instrumentalize alternative values. Global deals crafted as an interplay of spatial variables operate with risks and rewards that are more tangible and transparent.

A spatial software of active forms may be able to deliver what a world of weak standards and weak urban design cannot. For instance, often what is needed in these landscapes is not a way to drive the development machine forward but a way to put it in reverse. The standards, incentives, and regulations of environmental management are often there to facilitate development. Similarly, the object form that most architects and urbanists are trained to work with often only results in the addition of more buildings. Could an active form be instrumental in the removal of buildings or roads? Is it possible to develop a spatial protocol, like a governor, that can not only add to development but also shrink, concentrate, or reverse it? A subtraction protocol might be popular in many parts of the world where, for instance, over-development has produced distended or failed markets, where development confronts environmental issues, where it would be wise to retreat from exhausted land or flood plains, or where special land preserves are valued.

In an elementary ecology of properties—whether McMansions in the suburban sprawl or ranches in the Amazon—a subtraction protocol would be something like the Savannah software in reverse. It might play out through an accumulation of simple moves within which densifying suburban properties or preserved areas of forest are linked to properties where development might best be deleted. Sites of densification provide revenues for the sites of subtraction. The latter can also generate revenue, if, for instance, the contraction of development in the forest sponsors the growth of alternative industries like tourism. The same contraction in the suburb may provide room for alternative energy or transit industries on land that would otherwise be difficult for a city to acquire. The counterbalancing relationship between properties can create a ratchet effect capable of reconditioning urban space.

Perhaps more important than the content of the interplay in all these scenarios is the disposition of interplay as distinct from that of standard making in global negotiations and compacts. Spatial software recognizes and builds intelligence with the information that resides in urban space. It also recognizes the possibility of parallel markets of exchange. Offering no redemptive prescription or easy stamp of approval, an interplay of active forms exists only to be adjusted. It is unfolding and indeterminate. Like the signals that aid in the navigation of a river, it provides only markers or tools with which a global network of players can engage.

Quality Is Irrational

How can it be that the confused and contentious bumblers who populate the pages of organizational case studies and theories combine to construct the elaborate and well-proportioned social edifice that macrotheorists describe?—Paul J. Dimaggio and Walter W. Powell[90]

ISO is often regarded as a model of rational activity. The sociologists John Boli and George M. Thomas assign lofty aspirations and projections to the increasing number of organizations like ISO, which they regard as indicators of a "world polity" or "world-cultural authority."[91] They have looked at ISO from the perspectives of neo-realist, state-competition, world-system, and neoliberal institutionalist theories of globalization, and claim to

---

90   Paul J. Dimaggio and Walter W. Powell, "The Iron Cage Revisited: Institutional Isomorphism and Collective Rationality in Organizational Fields," *American Sociological Review* 48, April (1983), 156–7. Reprinted in Walter W. Powell and Paul J. Dimaggio, *The New Institutionalism in Orgainzational Analysis* (Chicago: University of Chicago Press, 1991), 63–82.

91   John Boli and George M. Thomas, "INGOs and the Organization of World Culture," in Boli and Thomas, eds., *Constructing World Culture*, 13–49, 13, 48, 45.

have discovered something that is not reducible to any of them: Global standard-making organizations are "are a constitutive part of world society. An analysis that treats them as such can teach us much about a transcendent level of social reality."[92]

Demonstrating the power of social stories as active forms in infrastructure space, organizations like ISO also beget more global organizations all of which thrive on shared languages and rituals. Sociologist Peter Mendel argues that "international standards bodies constitute an extensive yet mundane and, to now, rather silent force of social rationalization across the globe." ISO is evidence of an "expanding global society."[93] Suggesting that the organization is a "peculiarly modern social actor," Mendel continues:

> Thus, the spread of modern managerial ideologies contains not only specific organizational models, but the underlying cultural blueprint and rationale for creating organizations and imbuing them with the capacity for independent agency. Where this assumption of organizational actorhood lands and takes hold, the outcome is a constant hunger for all types of discourse and reforms to rationalize and improve the organization as a social actor, especially universal paradigms and programs legitimated at the global level.[94]

John W. Meyer suggests that the organization is regarded as a special actor, one not serving traditional families, bureaucracies, or regimes, and operating within a context that exceeds Weberian explanations. It has become a "modern myth" to replace that of the "national state and society."[95] For Meyer, the very notion of globalization seems to inspire a desire for common platforms

---

92   Boli and Thomas, "Standardization in the World Polity: Technical Rationality over Power," in Boli and Thomas, eds., *Constructing World Culture*, 169–97, 170.

93   Mendel, "The Making and Expansion of International Management Standards," 162–3, 164.

94   Ibid., 161.

95   Meyer, Drori, and Hwang, "World Society and the Proliferation of Formal Organization" and "Introduction" in *Globalization and Organization*, 41, 15–16.

celebrated with "highly elaborated and scripted forms." In fact, "organizations wear the protective armor of rationalization and formalization" as part of the procedural regalia of quasi-sovereignty.[96] People "play the roles of small gods as they carry universal visions of rationality and empowered human actorhood in a very lawful, increasingly global world." Meyer identifies many of these "organization-as-religion" phenomena as he assesses the foibles, failures, successes, heroes, and gurus of the "modern binge of organization."[97] He and his colleagues write: "Like traditional religious movements, it is not the practical people, but the modern-day incarnations of priesthoods— professors, scientists, consulting gurus, and theorists—and their scientized homilies that carry the movement on."[98] It is worth repeating the observation of Meyer and his colleagues that "Global society is a rationalized world, but not exactly what one could call a rational one."[99]

ISO harbors or encounters many paradoxes. It is a nonstate actor that advises state governments. It strives for universal impact, but must operate as a somewhat secretive institution with no truly public dimension—no appeal to a citizen who is not also a consumer. It is an overachiever that believes in the superior fitness of its plans, but portrays itself as inoffensive and subservient. Its rather obscure processes are largely unknown to the general public but nevertheless attract a broad consensus—a consensus for a platform that does not originate in a political dialogue. It is treated as an institution more agile than state bureaucracy, and yet it perpetuates layers of procedural ritual and regulation. Its practice of standard making demonstrates that the most easily shared dialogue is the one that is the most meaningless, while its capacity to leverage

---

96 Meyer, Drori, and Hwang, "Introduction," in *Globalization and Organization*, 49, 16.

97 Meyer, Drori, and Hwang, "Conclusion," in *Globalization and Organization*, 262, 273.

98 Ibid., 262.

99 John W. Meyer, Gili Drori, and Hokyu Hwang, "Conclusion," in John W. Meyer, Gili Drori and Hokyu Hwang, eds. *Globalization and Organization: World Society and Organizational Change*, 269.

change in consequential areas related to labor and the environment remains elusive.

Nevertheless, ironically, ISO's most instrumental and inspiring attribute may be its irrationality. Quality standards demonstrate the power that non-state organizations can have in the world—an authority that does not precisely correspond to the familiar modes of legal, historical, or political analysis. Quality demonstrates the power of contagion and conformity over the presumed imperatives of economic science or technocracy. ISO 9000, the most universal standard, is based not on technical compliance but emotional, motivational belief systems. Promises of a comprehensive, rationalizing, universalizing intelligence accompany the idea of global governance. Such ideologies have been powerfully shaping the thickening bureaucracies that currently preside over global development. Institutions like ISO provide firm technical and economic foundations for both the public and the private players in development. Yet with its quality-management programs, ISO demonstrates the currency of immaterial habits and stories. In the reflected light of this relatively elaborate form of irrationality, many of the sound, reasoned decisions of global development take on a similar color.

ISO, in short, models not a practice to be emulated but a territory to be occupied by extrastatecraft. As the word suggests, extrastatecraft plots to bypass bureaucracies with an effective spatial practice at the global scale. Global influence need not wait for the construction of a comprehensive, singular, or totalizing form of governance. On the contrary, such consensus often threatens to deaden political positions. No one is waiting for the Kyoto Protocols of urbanism as crafted by a Union of International Architects meeting somewhere in Switzerland. Designing an interplay of spatial variables that values and maximizes the countervailing and counterbalancing desires of different parties is the business of artful, entrepreneurial spatial practitioners who can exploit the currency of new habits in infrastructure space.

CHAPTER 6

Extrastatecraft

The 1999 Battle of Seattle launched an ongoing protest against the WTO and globalization, yet the zone continues as the engine room of globalization, immune from any protest or significant regulation.[1] The "No Blood for Oil" marches of 2003 brought millions of people all over the world into the streets to protest the war in Iraq. Yet, largely unaffected, the Bush Administration proceeded with the war, swaying sentiment with claims of weapons of mass destruction that did not exist. The demonstrations of the Arab Spring spread across North Africa and the Middle East demanding democratic reforms in government. Yet governments could shut down the protests simply by switching off the internet that had been used to organize them. In 2011, the Occupy movement stood up to represent the 99 percent against the 1 percent in the United States who enjoy excessive power and wealth. Even as their resistance mobilizes global unrest around similar issues, the 1 percent maintains its control over elections and legislation.

In countering authoritarian forces, familiar forms of activism are often galvanized around at least a provisional declaration. Assembling and standing firm together, the activists reject abusive policies and protect those who are the target of abuse. Dissent, as resistance and refusal, must often assume an oppositional stance. Activists may fight and die for their principles, employing tactics that often require enormous courage to enact. The most lauded activist takes a stand, fights for what is right, chooses sides, and decides who is and is not sympathetic to the cause. Strongly held, forthright beliefs support the vigilant maintenance of solidarity, decency, and justice. David must kill Goliath.

---

1   Alexander Cockburn, Jeffrey St. Clair, and Allan Sekula, *5 Days that Shook the World: Seattle and Beyond* (London and New York: Verso, 2000).

Yet many powerful players that these activists oppose maintain fluid or *undeclared* intentions by saying something different
from what they are doing. It is easy to toy with or trick activist
resistance if declaration is all that qualifies as information. When
targeted, the powerful wander away from the bull's-eye, arrang-
ing for shelter or immunity elsewhere. They may successfully
propagate a rumor (e.g., that there is evidence of WMD, that
climate change is hoax, that Obama is not a US citizen) to capture
the world's attention. Switching the characters in the story, they
may even come costumed as resisters. Goliath finds a way to pose
as David.

Dissent is then often left shaking its fist at an effigy. Activists
who show up at the barricade, the border crossing, or the battle-
ground with familiar political scripts sometimes find that the
real fight or the stealthier forms of violence are happening somewhere else. Attempting to cure its failures with "purification," the
left consolidates, and expels those who seem to compromise its
values.[2] And it must make of its opponent an even more dangerous ur-force—an "Unspecified Enemy" like Capital, Empire, or
Neoliberalism.

In this way, assumptions regarding the proper techniques
and territories for political work may ironically generate some of
activism's most significant internal constraints, foreclosing on
the very insurgency that it wishes to instigate. Righteous ultima-
tums or binaries of enemies and innocents that offer only
collusion or refusal might present a structural obstacle greater
than any quasi-mythical opponent. In these tragic endgames, the
idea that there is a proper realm of political negotiation may even
act as the perfect camouflage for undeclared political power.

Still, any deviation from the accepted techniques, even in an
attempt to aid and broaden activism, may be interpreted as a
betrayal of principles. Entering the market as an entrepreneur,
even if only to manipulate that market, is mistaken for collusion.
Giving positive attention to agents of systemic change rather

---

2   Todd Gitlin, "The Self-Inflicted Wounds of the Academic Left," *The
Chronicle Review* 52, no. 35 (2006), B6, at http://chronicle.com.

than negative opposition to a series of enemies is mistaken for an uncritical stance. Relinquishing overt resistance is mistaken for capitulation or ethical relativism. Answering duplicity with duplicity is mistaken for equivocation or lack of conviction rather than a technique to avoid disclosing a deliberate strategy.[3] In the end, righteous and combative narratives may exhaust themselves and escalate tensions. Dissent, in these instances, is inconsolable.

An Expanded Activist Repertoire in Infrastructure Space

The binary division between resistance and non-resistance is an unreal one.—Colin Gordon[4]

There are times to stand up, name an opponent, or assume a binary stance of resistance against authoritarian power, but supplementing these forms of dissent are activist stances that are both harder to target and less interested in being right. Just as many of the most powerful regimes in the world find it expedient to operate with proxies and doubles in infrastructure space, the most familiar forms of activism might similarly benefit from using undisclosed partners or *unorthodox* auxiliaries, if only to soften up the ground and offer a better chance of success.

An unorthodox auxiliary entertains techniques that are less heroic, less automatically oppositional, more effective, and sneakier—techniques like gossip, rumor, gift-giving, compliance, mimicry, comedy, remote control, meaninglessness, misdirection, distraction, hacking, or entrepreneurialism. Working together in different constellations, these techniques cannot be

---

3 Architecture discourses often drift toward tragic or stock narratives. For instance, with its attraction to tragic ultimates and endgames, Manfredo Tafuri's critique of the "impotent and ineffectual myths" of a political architecture is apt if architecture sees as its only tools object form and ideology. See Manfredo Tafuri, *Architecture and Utopia: Design and Capitalist Development* (Cambridge, MA: MIT Press, 1979), 178, 182.

4 Colin Gordon, "Afterword" in Michel Foucault and Colin Gordon, ed., *Power/Knowledge: Selected Interviews and Other Writings 1972–977* (New York: Pantheon Books, 1972) 256–7.

isolated or pedantically defined. While they are long-standing practices, for designers accustomed to making object forms or for activists accustomed to making declarations, this alternative aesthetic and political repertoire is perhaps unfamiliar.

Such techniques are politically inflected incarnations of the active forms discussed throughout this book. In infrastructure space, the crucial information about a political bearing is often found not in declaration but in disposition—in an immanent activity and organization. All the active forms that shape spatial products, free zones, broadband technoscapes, and other networks—the multipliers, remotes, interdependencies, or topological adjustments—are both the markers of a disposition and the means to tune or alter it. To hack the operating system by, for instance, breaking up monopolies, increasing access to broadband, or exposing enclaves to richer forms of urbanity is to engage the political power of disposition in infrastructure space.

Redesigning disposition in infrastructure space is not a duel. Given the broad foundational space of infrastructure, the active forms that generate dispositions are capable of effecting significant changes to the operating system. The activist need not face off against every weed in the field but rather, unannounced, alter the chemistry of the soil. Dispositional capacities invite an approach to both form-making and activism that is more performative than prescriptive. While some political traditions call for inversions, revolutions, or the absolute annihilation of the old system, a shift in disposition may sponsor the *ongoing* reconditioning or revolutionizing of a spatio-political climate. Such adjustments may reduce tensions and violence, and because they are undeclared, they need not call up the prevailing dogmas that must, if named, square up for a symmetrical fight.

An alternative activist repertoire exploits the cultural stories as well as the organizational attributes that inflect disposition. The discrepancies between story and disposition—the ways in which power says something different from what it is doing— offer the first political opening. Discrepancy is always present in the ever-changing dialogue between humans and technologies. It may be a symptom of an organization in denial, with its activities decoupled from its story. It may expose the distance between reality and an overused or degraded ideological story like liberalism. Or it may be the result of a deliberate deception. Focusing on discrepancy is then not only useful in detecting an underlying but undeclared disposition, it is also an opportunity to launch a counter-narrative. It tutors an activism in which the forthright may be less important than the fictional or the sly.

Releasing the tense grip of binary resistance, the auxiliary activist never turns around for the duel but continues pacing away into a new field of extrastatecraft.

Gossip/Rumor/Hoax

There is no manager more powerful than consumption, nor, as a result, any factor more powerful—albeit indirect—in production than the chatter of individuals in their idle hours.—Gabriel Tarde[5]

Gossip, rumor, and hoax are common tools for destabilizing power, and all of the multipliers present in infrastructure space facilitate such trickery.

In *Domination and the Arts of Resistance*, James C. Scott argues against enshrining the techniques of politics proper, looking instead at the actual tools most frequently used by the politically oppressed. Referencing figures from Balzac to Brer Rabbit, he writes, "Most of the political life of subordinate groups is to be found neither in overt collective defiance of power holders nor in complete hegemonic compliance, but in the vast territory between these two polar opposites."[6]

Scott identifies rumor and gossip as tools of aggression among the powerless. The servant gossips about the master; the underlings can, with anonymity, stir up public opinion about the boss. Gossip, he wrote, never starts anywhere. The

---

5   Bruno Latour and Vincent Antoni Lépinay, *The Science of Passionate Interests: An Introduction to Gabriel Tarde's Economic Anthropology* (Chicago: Prickly Paradigm Press, 2009).

6   See James C. Scott, *Domination and the Arts of Resistance: Hidden Transcripts* (New Haven: Yale University Press, 1990), 136.

"linguistic equivalent and forerunner of witchcraft," it magically multiplies without attribution, and it cannot be contained.[7] It is a technique of "infrapolitics," the invisible, subterranean territory of subordinate groups.[8] In this way, gossip and rumor are similar to the disguises, tricks, and *perruques*—the "art of the weak"—about which the scholar and theorist Michel de Certeau writes.[9]

Still, rumor and gossip are also available to the powerful as well as the weak. Hoax and spin are the raw material of politics. They fuel everyday mischief while also being a practical technique of markets and governments. For the last decade, James Inhofe, a Republican congressman from Oklahoma, has led a dogged campaign to convince the world that climate change is a hoax. In a 2003 senate committee speech, Inhofe claimed that the elaborate climate change hoax was designed to "satisfy the ever-growing demand of environmental groups for money and power and other extremists who simply don't like capitalism, free markets, and freedom."[10] Media personalities like Rush Limbaugh provided the story with its necessary multiplier. Limbaugh is what is variously known in pop-culture marketing terms as a "connector" or a "sneezer"—someone with the capacity to contact a large number of people.[11] After nearly ten years of broadcasting and embellishing the argument, he claims that the left is finally also convinced that global warming was all an elaborate ruse.[12]

During the US presidential election of 2008, since it was very easy to demonstrate that Barack Obama was Christian, claiming

---

7   Ibid., 143–4.

8   Ibid., 19.

9   See Michel de Certeau, *The Practice of Everyday Life* (Berkeley: University of California Press, 1984), 37, 29–44, 142–3.

10   "Sen. Inhofe Delivers Major Speech on the Science of Climate Change," at inhofe.senate.gov.

11   Two examples of pop-culture books about marketing are Seth Godin, *Unleashing the Idea Virus* (New York: Do You Zoom, 2001); and Malcolm Gladwell, *The Tipping Point* (New York: Little Brown, 2002).

12   Rush Limbaugh, "Left Just Now Discovering Global Warming Hoax," April 1, 2013, at rushlimbaugh.com.

that he was a Muslim was a very effective rumor. It found a compelling multiplier that thrived even on its own falsehood. Being false, it was kept alive even longer and repeated twice over—first to spread the falsehood and then to refute it. Rumor and gossip are less reliant on content than on the way that content behaves, so that what must be designed is not only the content, but also the *bounce* of the rumor—its active forms.

In the extrastatecraft of infrastructure space, tuning a multiplier is like crafting rumor or gossip. Designers can alter the repertoire of a technology to be more suited to certain populations just as the construction of suburban homes was designed as an assembly-line process. Similarly, a new spatial protocol will be more powerful if it finds a carrier that multiplies it. Infrastructure space is thick with technologies that are potential multipliers: populations of suburban houses, skyscrapers, vehicles, spatial products, zones, mobile phones, or global standards.

As with rumors, active forms are also social or narrative forms, and the designer can enhance the spatial consequences of a multiplier with the non-spatial stories that accompany it. Just as the US suburban house was popularized in part through narratives about family and patriotism, a persuasion or ideology attached to a technology may deliver it to a ready audience or a powerful political machine. The cell phone, for example, is characterized as a source of freedom, a political right, and a tool of economic liberalization. A new free zone, even before completion, is rumored to be a world city *fait accompli* in an attempt to capture a slice of the global market. The most official communiqué or the most hard-boiled business plan, while purporting to rely on facts, often marshals evidence in a pliable reality that relies on fiction.

Just as the ideological stories that accompany infrastructure space, however immaterial, can have enormous physical consequences, so a counter-story, even a deceptive one, may be the most immaterial yet most effective way to move mountains in infrastructure space. Discussing "energy narratives," David E. Nye cites the moment when, despite a domestic oil crisis, President Reagan persisted in sending out sunny messages about "abundance."[13] Similarly, rather than reveal the dangers surrounding oil extraction, oil companies adopt the imagery of green technologies. Using a story to different ends, the graphic design firm Pentagram countered the assumption that green energy policy is the province of leftist politics by associating it with early American patriotism. Their posters for Cleveland's new energy policies portrayed a green revolutionary soldier or minuteman who became a memorable icon in the city's conservation campaign.[14] And the activist organization Greenpeace dramatizes environmental abuse with media-genic "mind bombs" in an alternative form of war.[15]

Perhaps only a design that combines organizational active forms with narrative active forms has any chance of successfully engaging the world's powerful spatial products. For example, when Wal-Mart replaced electric lighting with day lighting, sales actually increased.[16] Here a spatial rumor could find a multiplier in the roof areas and megawatts of power-usage in Wal-Mart stores worldwide, but the environmentally sensitive designer might also embellish this with a narrative rumor—mixture of fact and fiction or what Hollywood calls "faction." A day-light roof is then reported as being an essential new condition for all big box stores, and whether this is true or false is less important than how the rumor will bounce within its audience. While utopian or visionary projections offer comprehensive, reasonable, even righteous, reforms, the less resolute factions in the global confidence game offer rumors that may be more contagious.[17]

---

13   Nye, "Energy Narratives," in *Narratives and Spaces*, 85–6.

14   "Green Machines," at http://new.pentagram.com.

15   See "History" at greenpeace.org.

16   "Some Facts About Wal-Mart's Energy Conservation Measures," at http://news.walmart.com.

17   For an exhibition of architectural rumors see *Some True Stories: Researches in the Field of Flexible Truth*, Storefront for Art and Architecture, New York City, November 2008, at storefrontnews.org.

Pandas

Another powerful technique of extrastatecraft, seemingly very different from resistance, is that of the gift. In 2005, China offered Taiwan two pandas named Tuan Tuan and Yuan Yuan. The names, when translated, mean "unity"—referring to the unity with mainland China that Taiwan has passionately refused. The pandas were used here to deploy a fiction of friendship, replacing opposition with conciliatory flattery, while the undisclosed disposition may actually reflect a low-grade but persistent form of aggression. Excessively soft and cute, the panda is a steam-roller of sweetness and kindness—an arm-twisting handshake that disarms and controls with apparent benevolence. The pandas were thus used to exert political leverage by exploiting a currency in values, social signals, and sentiments not usually quantified in the marketplace or treated in economic theory.

Infrastructure space—with its free zones, broadband networks, oil exploration, and spatial products—offers many pandas, or gifts that cannot be refused. The zone itself was a "gift" from developed countries to developing countries, one that promised to rescue them from poverty and bestow upon them membership in a global economic club. Yet when global corporations offer to developing countries the gift of mobile telephony or social networking, they are often actually giving themselves a gift—a large amount of data about the world's next big crop of consumers. Oil exploration in the Ecuadorian Amazon promised to bring progress to the region, just as development formulas like LAPSSET come with promises of economic solvency, global fluency, and signature architecture. These sorts of gifts have often leveraged from their host countries billions of consumers, exploitative cheap labor, and immunity from regulation even in the face of labor and environmental abuses.

Gifts of another sort try to temper such abuse by using awards or prizes as incentives for productive behavior or self-regulation. The Mo Ibrahim Prize for Achievement uses profits from mobile telephony to grant 5 million dollars over ten years and $200,000 per year for life to an elected African official who has served their term and demonstrated strong leadership.[18] The Global Citizen Award, sponsored by Clinton's Global Initiative, the Aga Khan Awards, the XPrize, and the targeted philanthropy of the Bill and Melinda Gates Foundation are among countless examples of awards used to incentivize socially responsible individuals and projects. Certification systems like ISO or Social Accountability International also similarly reward selected behaviors.

In extrastatecraft, however, the give-and-take designed into an interplay of spatial variables may offer active forms like governors—pandas more powerful than awards and self-congratulatory certificates. Governors can establish a counterbalancing interdependency that may remain in place to extract more benefits for labor or the environment. They can be designed to yield more than inferior jobs in global free zones. Like the offsets that were part of Dubai's deal with foreign investors, the offerings of workers, urbanity, natural resources, and consumers can be used more effectively to leverage access to education, technology transfers, wilderness preservation, and better labor practices.

Exaggerated Compliance

In *Domination and the Arts of Resistance*, Scott draws attention to a passage in Milan Kundera's *The Joke* in which the prisoners in the story are challenged to a relay race against the camp guards. The prisoners decide to run very slowly, while wildly cheering each other on. Their compliance brings them together in an act of defiance that does not diminish their energies as would competing or fighting. Compliance can disarm and deliver independence from authority.[19] It can destabilize an enemy that is bracing for opposition rather than an obedient response.

---

18   "Celtel Chief Unveils $5 Million Award for Governance," *Property Kenya*, October 31, 2006, at propertykenya.com. Ibrahim founded Celtel International (subsequently bought by Zain and Bahari Airtel) and turned it into one of the continent's largest mobile phone operators. He is one of the most successful African businessmen.

19   Scott, *Domination and the Arts of Resistance*, 139–40; Milan Kundera, *The Joke* (New York: Harper, 1992), 139–40.

When the mayor of Copenhagen, Ritt Bjerregaard, made a campaign promise of 5,000 affordable apartments for the city, the Danish architecture firm PLOT (later BIG and JDS Architects) appeared to rush to her aid by producing designs for the buildings in advance. Their designs kept the issue in the press, making it hard for the mayor to break her promise and forcing a design competition for the housing. In this way, compliant activism can mobilize resources for change in advance of political will—submitting to and even congratulating power on intentions it never had.

The New York City Occupy movement generated symbolic capital by demonstrating that the Occupy Kitchen set up to feed the protestors was actually better at delivering food to the needy than many of the municipal agencies paid to do the job. Winning over their potential critics, they got the upper hand. Like good children whose perfect grades and model behavior strip their parents of all authority, the compliant activist can run rings around supposedly more powerful players.

Responding to the Taksim Square protests of 2013 in Istanbul, Turkish Prime Minister Recep Tayyip Erdoğan delivered a speech in which he referred to the protesters as çapulcu or "looters." The protesters responded by embracing the insult, using it on social media, and printing it on T-shirts and bags. The label served as both a protective camouflage and call to arms. Made into a verb, çapuling even came to mean standing up for your rights.[20]

Exaggerated compliance is central to the tactical bluffs of infrastructure deal-making. Infrastructure contractors have long operated under the banner of economic liberalism, and their access to new territories is often characterized as a struggle with regulation. The companies laying terrestrial or submarine fiber-optic cable in Kenya were all competing against each other for market share while being forced to "submit" to regulations from

---

20 Sebnem Arsu, "Protest Group Gives Turkish Officials Demands," *New York Times*, June 6, 2013. The author is indebted to A. J. Artemel for sharing his research on the 2013 anti-government protests in Turkey.

the host nation, the World Bank, or some other organization. They would all characterize each other as monopolists and competitors at any one moment in the game. Yet, the smartest entrepreneurs discovered that if they stayed together in a reciprocal game, alternating between resistance to regulation and compliance, they generated collective advantages. And the open, competitive system to which they appeared to submit would yield a larger market.

In extrastatecraft, picking one's submissions rather than one's battles is an almost invisible, noncontroversial means of gaining advantage in the field without drawing attention to a broader strategy.

Doubling

Head-to-head confrontations are marked by competition and symmetrical mimicry that often leads to violence. Another kind of mimicry, the double, can be not only a source of competition but also an opportunity for confusion and disguise. The double is a shill or proxy that, like twin siblings, can sometimes fool the world or launder an identity. A double can also simply hijack the place or power of its counterpart to increase its territory in the world.

Employing the double as imposter or caricature has long been a tactic in exposing the absurdities of authority. In 2007, a member of the activist group The Yes Men posed on the BBC as an executive from Dow Chemical (which owns Union Carbide) and announced that the company had, after years of evasion, finally decided to make full restitution for all of the suffering they had caused in Bhopal. A Yes Men member also posed as speaker in the US Chamber of Commerce, promoting green policies that the organization lobbies against. Another member appeared at a Wharton Business School conference suggesting that "full private stewardry of labor," or the buying and selling of human beings, was a realistic approach to economic stability in Africa. The Yes Men could then report that this advocacy of slavery, smothered in jargon, had been politely received without questions or challenges from the floor.[21]

The Dutch non-profit organization Women on Waves (WoW), founded in 1999, is a double that addresses women's reproductive rights by adopting the imbricated sovereignties and shifting political identities used in commercial maritime trade. Commercial ships move between legal jurisdictions as they cross from national to international waters. When in international waters, they are subject to the laws of the country in which they are registered. Many shipping companies select legal responsibilities that work to their advantage by registering in a country with, for instance, lax labor or environmental laws. Exploiting this freedom, WoW funds a medical ship that conducts abortions for women from countries where abortion is illegal by sailing into international waters where only Dutch law has jurisdiction.[22]

On their day off, domestic workers in Hong Kong meet by the hundreds in the central public spaces of the city that are otherwise inhabited by their employers. Taking over these open spaces, they sit, talk, prepare meals, and reconnect to their home culture. Their occupation is entirely peaceful and yet is a way for the workers to stand their ground and establish themselves as a group of professionals, rather than invisible servants. The doubling is passive but resolute.

The Tea Party movement used the label "fascist" to describe Obama, thus hijacking a marker that had been used defensively by the left to refer to power seized through the exploitation of fear and hatred. The Tea Party double was used offensively to instigate the same kind of fear and hatred that might have been originally anticipated. The double simultaneously defanged the term in its previous usage and inoculated the present user against the accusation.

The doubled and redoubled ideological stories that attend infrastructure space can be used to commandeer political

---

21   See http://theyesmen.org.
22   See womenonwaves.org.

support. FDR appropriated the liberal label to sway right-wing sentiment for his New Deal policies—to capture territory and either confuse or neutralize the arguments of laissez-faire. Sentiments surrounding liberalization have fueled contemporary development patterns related to the zone or to broadband urbanism. The neoliberal label is yet another doubling used to expose the inequities of liberalization and privatization, and something like a libertarian strain of liberalism now attends the "free" exchange of information in social media and the communities they sponsor.

Market platforms like Jana are doubles of the activist crowdsourcing platform Ushahidi. Jana comes cloaked in ideas about the well-being of the collective and a rerouting of compensation from big business to billions of cell phone customers. Yet it remains to be seen whether Jana will leverage useful income and other assets for developing countries or whether it will be used primarily to shape a consumer market—whether its primary research will be conducted for the UN or for Unilever.

Just as the privateer was a shadow for the state, zone urbanism has served as the double for Hong Kong in Shenzhen, Mumbai in Navi Mumbai, Seoul in New Songdo City, and Almaty in Astana. Each major city or capital has a camouflaging agent able to conduct business with relaxed laws and less accountability, allowing it to operate in more fluid or profitable global networks.

The double can also engineer a replacement for abusive or unproductive situations by creating a twin enterprise that satisfies or exceeds projected revenues while being a carrier of alternative politics. When the zone doubles the city, it becomes the city, potentially adopting the politics and public accountability that the city offers without reducing revenues. The interplay of spatial variables in the new broadband digital village and the new financial portfolio for subtracting development are doubles—parallel markets designed to slip into and displace existing markets, social habits, and desires.

Extrastatecraft as an alternative activist repertoire is, in some ways, a doubling of the kind of extrastatecraft practiced by the world's most powerful. It creates not a binary—an enemy and an innocent—but rather countless mirrorings of power in a world where no one is innocent. It monitors the sleight of hand of any double in the world even as it manipulates these twists and turns of identity with doubles of its own.

Comedy

As an expert on internet dissent in China recently said, "humor works as a natural form of encryption."[23] Comedy presents contradictions that can, without direct confrontation, topple the logic of dominant organizations. With irreverent cheekiness, it interrupts the rigidities that characterize both concentrations of power and resistances to power. Comedy may engage in a direct satirical address, as do The Yes Men. It may rely on wordplay or a single punch line. It may simply effect an inversion, as in the case of the BLO or Barbie Liberation Organization—a project to covertly switch the voice chips of Barbies and GI Joes in toy stores (Barbie: "Eat lead, Cobra." GI Joe: "Let's plan our dream wedding").[24]

Infrastructural space itself is often a carrier of comedy that is perhaps most powerful when, like the humor of Ryle's clown, it is dispositional, unfolding, and undeclared.[25] Erandi De

---

23   Hu Yong quoted in Brook Larmer, "Where an Internet Joke Is Not Just a Joke," *New York Times Magazine*, October 30, 2011, 38.

24   Cheekiness—the *kynicism* about which philosopher Peter Sloterdijk writes—resists a self-satisfied cynicism or consensus. See Peter Sloterdijk, *Critique of Cynical Reason* (Minneapolis: University of Minnesota Press, 1987), 101–33; and rtmark.com.

25   Usually producing the humor of "knowing that" rather than "knowing how," the architecture culture that called itself "postmodern" created compositions from various architectural tropes that were to be consciously read as witticisms and ironies within fixed object forms and one-to-one correspondences of meaning— "one-liners" in comedy jargon. The counter-culture demonstrations and satires of Ant Farm or Archigram entered into other print, film, and performance media with mixtures of object and active forms. Some were designed to reference a specific antecedent upon which the humor relied. Others carried non-specific references that were both funny and disruptive. While there was specific content in the comics that Archigram designed, the very act of depicting architecture with comic books was itself an active form with many associations. Ant Farm's *Cadillac Ranch*, a sculpture

Silva's comic design work *Logopelago* satirizes "The World"—
Dubai's familiar archipelago of artificial islands constructed in
the shape of a world map. De Silva's cartoons of similar island
formations take the shape of gigantic logos—a Nike swish, a
Mickey Mouse head, a Ralph Lauren horse, or the double Cs of
Chanel. All these logo islands are populated with the villas, golf
courses, and other spatial products that fill up infrastructure
space. Yet "The World" itself may be its own best satire. In its
hyperbole, the island formation is already a joke about global
real estate conquest or the migration of global power into
islands of exemption. Preempting its own critique, or stealing
the punch line, each micro-nation is not unlike the city-state of
Dubai itself. The comedy now continues in a different vein
since, after the financial crisis of 2008, the sea has been reclaim-
ing the dissolving islands.

Similarly, François Roche's *DustyRelief/B_mu*, a 2002 design
for a building in Bangkok, avoids the single punch line in favor
of a longer comedic performance. The building was designed to
attract dust electrostatically from the surrounding polluted
air.[26] Its continual, obliging willingness to clean its surround-
ings, coupled with its slow miniscule advance toward becoming
a gigantic and adorably flocked fuzz ball, are actively comic in
visual, temporal, and cognitive registers. It critiques pollution
with a sympathetic, resourceful, and enthusiastic remedy. Yet it
associates this desire for cleaner air with hapless self-
deprecation rather than the piety and belt-tightening that often
accompany green initiatives.

Deadpan reportage of the comedies of infrastructure space
might often be sufficient to achieve the desired political effect. Yet
another promotional video for yet another zone that begins, as
have dozens before it, with a zoom from outer space, exposes the
entire PR apparatus with its canned fanfares and toy architectures.
A simple comparison of the acronyms for management mottos

---

of Cadillacs half buried in the ground, or its *Media Burn* performance featuring a
collision of a car with a pyramid of TVs, travel as active form with no one specific
antecedent.

26   See new-territories.com.

and creeds—PDCA, POCCC, POSDCORB, CSSBB, ISSISSIPPI among them—together with their buoyant narratives and sober metrics also requires very little effort from the comedian.

Remotes

A remote control effects change indirectly or from some distance away, often without being detected. Jerry, the soft cartoon mouse, presses down on the plunger labeled "TNT" with Tom at the receiving end of a long fuse. He catapults Tom into the air by dropping an anvil on the opposite end of a seesaw where the cat is sitting. Objects in one part of the house ricochet until they eventually hit Tom over the head. In similar fashion, a nation indirectly floods a city when it builds a dam downstream. A hacker drops a pebble in the internet waters with collateral effects. A mass-produced suburb, remote from the center, drains the city of its population. Any switch in any of the networks of infrastructure space can act like a remote—as a valve that may control flows of cars, electricity, microwaves, or broadband capacity somewhere down the line.

The activist often longs to directly confront and cure a problem just as the designer often longs to address urban issues with object form. Political engagement is typically scripted with concerns about the environment, natural resources, labor, or human rights, accompanied by persuasions about volunteerism and self-sacrifice, or dramatized with grave manifestos and sci-fi dystopias. Showing up at the local site and getting one's hands dirty is considered to be a sign of political authenticity.

Yet there may be no great virtue in exclusively local action on the ground when the powerful remote controls in the networks of extrastatecraft may be businesses, governments, or international organizations halfway around the world. These remotes lend extra leverage to the bargaining of "pandas" since, alongside the multinationals, there are now extra players in the game— NGOs, IGOs, and coalitions of all sorts. Saving a wilderness, for instance, relies on direct advocacy as well as remote pressures and incentives from research institutions, distant markets, regulations, and compacts. Advocates who cannot provoke action from their own state can look to NGOs or IGOs in another state or in the international community, creating "governance triangles" that leverage influence or exert pressure on the home state—what has been called a "boomerang effect."[27]

Remotes are essential to designing an interplay of spatial variables rather than a single prescription. The designer and urbanist Rahul Mehrotra approached the slums of Mumbai not with a master plan to reorganize the entire territory but with a simple public toilet that was designed to have remote effects throughout the slum. Solar panels allowed the toilets to operate off the grid, eliminating a charge for electricity and maintaining consistent power. Women and children were then not fearful to use the toilet at night. A caretaker's apartment above the toilet further ensured its cleanliness and safety, and an open-air porch on the top floor provided a panoramic view, to relieve the limited, congested perspective of streets.[28]

In the same way that a confidence man needs to find a way to look completely normal, the remote can also be camouflaged in a seemingly nonpolitical, non-spatial, self-serving project with an undisclosed political intent. The most conscientious consumers already check the labels on clothing or packs of coffee and boycott those products that have been manufactured in abusive conditions. Yet without overt political declaration, a remote might simply work on the prevalent tastes of, for instance, fashion or food. Companies that make clothes poorly with mediocre materials and cuts usually also search for the cheapest labor. A new articulation in desire, seemingly pursued for self-serving, even frivolous reasons, may deliberately deflate the market for disposable clothes or food produced under abusive conditions.

---

27 Kenneth W. Abbott and Duncan Snidal, "The Governance Triangle: Regulatory Standards Institutions and the Shadow of the State," in Walter Mattli and Ngaire Woods, eds., *The Politics of Global Regulation* (Princeton: Princeton University Press, 2009), 50; Margaret E. Keck and Kathryn Sikkink, *Activists Beyond Borders: Advocacy Networks in International Politics* (Ithaca: Cornell University Press, 1998), 23–4, 12–13.

28 "Conversation with Rahul Mehrotra," at http://harvardmagazine.com.

These remotes can indirectly retool the disposition of manufacturing and agricultural spaces, buying time before the race to the bottom begins again.

Distraction/Meaninglessness/Irrationality

Activism cast as resistance typically goes head-to-head with an oppressing power, facing off in a symmetrical opposing position. Yet rather than engaging in the fight, with the risk of it escalating or being drawn into its vortex, the activist may distract from it with misdirection and surprise—often by creating a third thing that is supposedly neutral to the opposing forces. The comedian already knows something about the power of distraction to defuse tension. Warring countries are brought together over ping-pong, chess, or music. In Tirana, Albania, mayor Edi Rama transformed the exhausted post-war city by first simply painting the facades with very bright colors—a move sufficiently strange to refresh the terms of development, even governance, in the city.

Meaninglessness can continue the work begun by distraction, crafting the initial moment of destabilization into a condition that must be continually maintained. Generally considered by the forthright activist to be an evacuation of principles and an indication of crisis, meaningless can be the opposite—a tool with enormous political instrumentality. Just as the bait and switch relies on distraction, the longer confidence game relies on a series of distracting stories that draw attention away from the real details of the transaction, which is, of course, never declared. Hustlers lead their suckers down the garden path with countless little courtesies and unimportant details that become collectively untraceable but are inescapable. The absence of a single coherent story is the compelling factor, convincing the victims that they do not see what is in front of them.[29]

---

29   In *Empire*, Hardt and Negri discuss a number of techniques of political craft, including the refusal of characters like Herman Melville's Bartleby or J. M. Coetzee's Michael K., paying particular attention to Michael K. as a gardener whose constant movement is mimetic of the vines he wishes to be tending. This serpentine disposition eases the dangerous stakes embodied in defiant refusal and enhances his

Many of the most powerful political operations in the world are lubricated with obfuscations and irrational desires that have anesthetizing effects, keeping at bay the dogma that incites conflict. In Jerzy Kosinski's novel *Being There*, Chauncey Gardiner is at once a comedian and a beautiful soul whose meaningless statements about the growth of the garden or the inevitability of the seasons allow him to become a confidant of the US president. However transparent, some hypnotizing fictions may form a strong web capable of holding together opposing forces or diffusing cruel forms of authority.

Meaninglessness, like simplemindedness, can be powerful because it is not burdened with information. Leaders like Ronald Reagan often resisted intelligence as a matter of duty and principle. In a now famous story, at one G-7 summit Reagan failed to study the briefing books, choosing instead to stay up and watch his favorite movie, *The Sound of Music*. His aid, David Gergen remembered that the next day Reagan was in top form—able to grasp the "big picture" free of complicating facts.[30] Apparent oblivion—a kind of special stupidity—nourishes resilient forms of power and attends many of the most successful political strategies.[31]

However powerful and monolithic it may seem to be, infrastructure space trades on ephemeral desires and irrational aspirations. Organizations of every kind—from celebrity golf suburbs to retail chains to zones—attempt to profit, govern, or otherwise maintain power with instrumental forms of meaninglessness. Quality management attracts a large following with principles that lack any binding content. Managementese is often a form of babble used in isomorphic organizations. It means very little, but it can be used to create consensus around almost anything. Typically these organizations find collective beliefs and rationalizing formulas galvanizing, but they must

chances of success. See Hardt and Negri, *Empire*, 203–4.

30 *PBS Newshour*, "Remembering Ronald Reagan," airdate June 7, 2004, at pbs.org.

31 For a discussion of "special stupidity," see Easterling, *Enduring Innocence*, 195.

also develop techniques for overlooking the evidence that contradicts their formulations. They must find ways of decoupling errant events from controlling logics. Rationalizing formulas can also engender nonsensical beliefs to which the group is sentimentally obedient.

For extrastatecraft, the long con is instructive. Just as fictitious rumors can be successful, so too can the stubbornly circuitous unfolding story. The day of reckoning can always be delayed. Diaphanous fairy tales can replace hard-nosed logics. The auxiliary activist learns that through any combination of new technologies, new spatial software, or new persuasions, a snaking chain of moves can worm into an infrastructure space and gradually generate leverage against intractable politics.

Hackers/Entrepreneurs

To ask, "How can one escape the market?" is one of those questions whose principal virtue is one's pleasure in declaring it insoluble.— Jacques Rancière[32]

Hackers and entrepreneurs—whether as social, political, or commercial agents—understand the power of multipliers, rumors, remotes, and distractions.[33] Understanding the currencies of all kinds of value, these characters play social and market networks with the viral dissemination of pandas and persuasions as well as products in infrastructure space. Both operate very differently from the utopian activist or designer. The utopian often imagines a transcendent and singular moment of change—a comprehensive reform or a soulful masterpiece. Like the activism of declarations, the designs of architects and urbanists are often presented as a corrective program. Even when, moving away from the object or master

---

32 Jacques Rancière, "The Art of the Possible: Fulvia Carnevale and John Kelsey in Conversation with Jacques Rancière," *Artforum International* 45 no. 7 (March 2007): 256–60.

33 Mattli and Woods, eds., *The Politics of Global Regulation*, x–xi.

plan, design has borrowed extradisciplinary techniques from, for instance, the social sciences, cybernetics, or mathematics, the desire has often still been to declare—to find data or equations that deliver the right answer. The fact that the world never seems to adopt the utopian schemes of planners can then be portrayed as a sad mistake, or a lack of purity.

The hacker/entrepreneur does not value purity but rather relies on multiple cycles of innovation, updating platforms, and tracking changeable desires that supersede, refresh, or reverse the products and plans they introduce into the world. Entrepreneurs cannot survive unless they are always on the way to becoming obsolete. Finding fertile territory in inversion—an inversion that is often considered to be unreasonable—entrepreneurs will be most successful if they renovate what is considered to be practical. They vigorously engage the world looking for multipliers that will amplify their influence.

The cagey and enterprising bargains of the most productive hacker/entrepreneur may not measure their productivity in moral terms—on a determination of what is good. Just as Bateson assessed political temperament in terms of information flow, productive change might constitute those moves that release and mix more information than they hoard or deny—breaking deadlocks, undoing isomorphisms, unwinding authoritarian concentrations of power to generate less violent, more resilient political dispositions. The utopian's binary righteousness and refusal may even be the least desirable disposition if it means arresting the flow of information.

For the hacker/entrepreneur of extrastatecraft, space is the underexploited opportunity or the low-hanging fruit. Not products and technologies circulating in space but space itself is the operating system to manipulate or overwrite. Spatial variables are the crucial active forms in an extensive shared platform—at once information, technology, product, and pawn. The space that has always been available for manipulation, when seen in this way, becomes a fresh territory for political action.

Inadmissible Evidence

I would rather talk about dissensus than resistance.—Jacques Rancière[34]

Dissensus, as the opposite of consensus, is usually seen as a condition that needs remedying, but it can also be a positive engine. Dissensus disrupts the self-reflexive consensus that only considers compatible evidence. It also suggests a general unrest, a confusion in order that is more widespread than a single target of dissent. For Jacques Rancière, "The work of dissensus is to always reexamine the boundaries between what is supposed to be normal and what is supposed to be subversive, between what is supposed to be active, and therefore political, and what is supposed to be passive or distant, and therefore apolitical."[35] For Rancière, "inadmissible" evidence generates dissensus.[36] For instance, the immigrant worker, a character for whom there is often no relevant national or international law, is something like inadmissible evidence. Rancière describes the immigrant as a

> wordless victim, object of an unquenchable hatred. The immigrant is first and foremost a worker who has lost his name, a worker who is no longer perceptible as such. Instead of the worker or proletarian who is the object of an acknowledged wrong and a subject who vents his grievance in struggle and disputation, the immigrant appears as at once the perpetrator of an inexplicable wrong and the cause of a problem calling for the round-table treatment.[37]

---

34   Jacques Rancière, "The Art of the Possible: Fulvia Carnevale and John Kelsey in Conversation with Jacques Rancière," *Artforum International* 45, no. 7 (2007), 256–60.

35   Ibid.

36   Jacques Rancière, *The Politics of Aesthetics* (London: Continuum, 2004), 85.

37   Rancière, *On the Shores of Politics*, 105.

The immigrant worker returns again and again in the evidence of infrastructure space as the subject of an uneasy or false consensus—"the round-table treatment." Dissensus always exposes this inadmissible evidence, forwarding and highlighting it within the consensus that tries to explain it away.

Looking beyond the sanctioned plotlines of the proper political story, inadmissible evidence identifies the category leftovers, or the butterflies that are not pinned to the board. Political change often pivots around less dramatic turning points that are not taxonomized by either the left or the right. Unlikely evidence may be the real cause of shifts in sentiment, changes in economic fortune, or escalations and suspensions of violence. Just as consensus may deliver the worst and most destructive leaders or juridical forms, an opponent may be strong-armed with a gift. The biggest changes may result from a seemingly innocuous detail that sneaks in when no one is paying attention. The most productive move may be the selfishly motivated innovation of the most abusive player. An abundance of fiction may make a supposedly impossible option, whether productive or unproductive, suddenly inoffensive and plausible. Waters may part inexplicably because of an indirect bargain made over a remote problem.

Extrastatecraft plunges into the field of contradictory or inadmissible evidence. The hacker/entrepreneur looks for openings in a bit of code or a stray desire that will unsettle the status quo and release more information. The scholar looks for the extra history sidelined by the dominant ideologies. The innovative economists, sociologists, information specialists, and urbanists are often looking beyond the master narratives and assumptions of their disciplines for more actors, more complex contexts, and more information for problem solving. The auxiliary activist hopes to engage all kinds of values and concentrations of authoritarian power, not just those celebrated in the political theologies of Capital or Neoliberalism.

Dissensus is not only about identifying the inadmissible and navigating the ripples and dimples on the water; it is also about creating some of those ripples. Space can embody dissensus when it scripts an interplay for multiple opposing or counterbalancing players and when it returns to that game of the laws and people that the market has erased or excluded for its convenience. The dissensus of extrastatecraft troubles the waters.

English

English is a word used when playing pool or billiards, in phrases such as "put a little english on the ball" or "give it some english." Grazing the cue ball in a particular way imparts a bit of spin that transfers to the numbered ball, perhaps to overcome a bad angle and help the ball slip into the pocket. Apart from the general direction and intent of the shot, which may even be announced by the player, the ball delivers another unannounced agency that is much harder to control, one that even sometimes seems to be a matter between the balls themselves.

In *The Politics of Aesthetics*, Rancière does not discuss the aesthetics of politics, but the politics surrounding a work of art. He does not describe, for instance, the pageant of goose-stepping soldiers in a Zeppelin field, or the aestheticizing of resistance as fervid disappointment. Instead he describes the scatter of associations that attend art or design as they are received and used in political action. For instance, discussing the ways in which art both inflects and generates political activity, he mentions Flaubert:

> When *Madame Bovary* was published, or *Sentimental Education*, these works were immediately perceived as "democracy in literature" despite Flaubert's aristocratic situation and political conformism. His very refusal to entrust literature with any message whatsoever was considered to be evidence of democratic equality.[38]

Somehow the novels relayed to their audience a liberating disposition despite Flaubert's conservative politics. The books had "english," or an indirect political spin in culture.

---

38   Rancière, *The Politics of Aesthetics*, 14.

Bob Dylan's "Like a Rolling Stone" was something of an accident—the result of a single take after a two-day recording session filled with false starts in June of 1965. The snarling song seemed to be addressed to a rich girl, and it had no explicit political content. Yet for whatever reason—the opening "pistol shot" of drums, Dylan's association with Woody Guthrie, or his strained voice crying "how does it feel?"—the song became an anthem of the counter-culture during the wars and assassinations of the 1960s. It introduced a kind of english that helped to ignite the song for political use.[39]

Political disposition often relies on a bit of english or aesthetic spin. Rancière outlines an aesthetics that "does not refer to a theory of sensibility, taste, and pleasure for art amateurs." Rather than treating aesthetics as a codified set of guides or rules that culture carefully tends and maintains, he focuses on "aesthetic practices" that both "depict" and enact, that articulate "ways of doing and making." Aesthetics exists as a changing regime of forms that are full of meaning but not determinate meaning. Rancière describes the ways in which forms are "distributed" into various strata of the sensible.[40] Just as Foucault's *dispositif* is a matter of "the said as much as the unsaid," for Rancière, "Politics revolves around what is seen and what can be said about it, around who has the ability to see and the talent to speak, around the properties of spaces and the possibilities of time."[41]

"English" is an advanced technique in pool and in infrastructure space. It is deployed deliberately but it is not entirely

---

39   Greil Marcus, *Like a Rolling Stone: Bob Dylan at the Crossroads* (New York: Faber and Faber, 2005), 80, 224, 3.

40   In response to selected media and installation work of the 1990s, art critic Nicolas Bourriaud developed a notion of "relational form" that described art as a "state of encounter" rather than "the assertion of an independent and private symbolic space." In his manifesto, *Relational Aesthetics*, Bourriaud writes that this new "policy" of form "points to a radical upheaval of the aesthetic, cultural and political goals introduced by modern art." Rancière's broader framework describes a politics of aesthetics that does not rely on these new forms of media and performance art as a radical or inaugural moment. See Nicolas Bourriaud, *Relational Aesthetics* (Paris: Les Presses du Réel, 2002).

41   Foucault, "The Confession of the Flesh," in *Power/Knowledge*, 194; Rancière, *The Politics of Aesthetics*, 22–3, 12–14.

under the user's control. Its intelligent use lies in the recognition that a special kind of spin is *possible* beyond the straightforward dynamics of the ball. In the crafting of infrastructure space, it is not possible to control the consequences of technologies and their interactions with humans in space. Being able to control the english in infrastructure space would be like inventing the cell phone knowing that it would go from being a "yuppy toy" to a tool of development in the world's poorest countries. If it is not possible to control the english, it is nevertheless possible to be at ease with the presence of errant spin, to anticipate it, spot it, and use it to advantage. While perhaps a source of disappointment to those with the fixed anticipations of a proper political program, swerves, unexpected consequences, and the shadings of disposition are the raw material of a political performance in extrastatecraft.

Knowing How

A refreshed activist repertoire learns from a number of characters—pirates, prisoners, hackers, comedians—who, considering themselves too smart to be right, successfully pursue more slippery political practices. Like actors in theater, their job is to create mixtures of opposing intentions—playing actions that are different from the stated text. The operation need not be overt or declared. It may be remote or invisible. The Invisible Man was only powerful because he both appeared and disappeared. When the man himself was not visible, a drink was drained from a glass or doors were opened and closed and only the space that he disturbed was visible. In this context, a sneakier David—happy that Goliath is big—would never go to the trouble of killing the giant. He would see in infrastructure space not defeat but rather opportunity. Why kill the giant when it can be put to work, and when it's great size, like a multiplier, can amplify that work?

The indeterminacy of these alternative activist techniques is ultimately what is most practical about them. Erving Goffman was fascinated by discrepant characters like confidence men and go-betweens, just as he was fascinated by the discrepancy between what people say and what they do in their everyday performances. He wondered how they learned their art.[42] Most disciplines train their practitioners to reconcile and verify evidence using their own disciplinary standards, laws, and tests for what constitutes information. One does not ordinarily train in discrepancy or trickery. Discrepancy is the supernatural counterpart of forthright communication, the wispy smoke that passes between the supposedly solid fields of signifiers. Training to be a hustler, a con man, or a shill is learning to be responsive to change. It is dispositional. It relies on practical knowledge and improvisation—what James C. Scott calls *mētis*.[43] The techniques of extrastatecraft are rehearsed in preparation for a performance that one can only know *how* to do.

An auxiliary activism is enacted. The declarative and the enacted approaches to activism both map onto an ethical Möbius. One aligns with the maintenance of consensus around stated principles; the other, in a partial inversion, describes the maintenance of dissensus around a necessarily indeterminate struggle with undeclared but consequential activity. Each—while moving on opposite sites of the same surface and approaching from different directions—supports and challenges the other. The two together describe both the solid, stable state and the state of encounter. The galvanized and the atomized. The moment of certainty and the moment of uncertainty. The prescription and the epidemiology. The fix and the wager. The condition of "knowing that" and the evolving activities of "knowing how."

---

42   Goffman, *The Presentation of Self in Everyday Life*, 73–4.
43   Scott, *Seeing Like a State*, 6–7, 340.

Afterword

Fast-forward again through the images found at the beginning of this book—the repetitive matrix of spatial products and networks of infrastructure space. Like an operating system managing activities in the background, space is a technology, a carrier of information, and a medium of polity. Exposing the workings of this operating system—in free zones, broadband technoscapes, or global standards—is as important as rehearsing the skills to hack into it.

Many disciplines are questioning their own presumptions and searching for alternative ways to adjust the global political landscape. Infrastructure space is a good test bed for these experiments—a complex matrix harboring of all kinds of social habits, cultural values, economies, and technologies.

A web of active forms contributes to the disposition of infrastructure space—its immanent capacity, propensity, or political bearing. The active forms that make it powerful—its multipliers, switches, or topologies, among many others—can also be spatial variables or levers for manipulating it. The pervasiveness of infrastructure space may even offer the means to amplify an adjustment or make it contagious.

While the world looks to master plans, metrics, standards, and bottom lines, the preceding discussions have suggested an expanded repertoire for design—not fixed plans but an interplay of active forms that act like spatial software. Interdependent spatial variables can operate like little machines to continually adjust disposition within a context. The object of design is not a single form but an apparatus for shaping many forms. A vessel of dissensus rather than consensus, interplay favors counterbalancing differences that leverage benefits for multiple players over time. This kind of interplay can rewire a city, as in the case of the zone transplanted to the metropolis. It can be a governor, as in the case of the broadband village that balances enhanced global networks with landscape preservation. It can even direct the subtraction as well as the addition of development in many economically or environmentally exhausted sites around the world. In these ways, spatial variables, underexploited in global political negotiations, might be tools of an unorthodox form of spatio-political activism.

The stories that accompany infrastructure space are also active forms that propel and inflect its disposition. While some stories remain fluid, others become fixed ideologies that, however decoupled from reality, hold sway over politics. Stories about infrastructure space as a military apparatus, for example, perpetuate unnecessary binaries and may even obscure evidence of some of the most insidious violence against labor and environment. The ideological stories of economic liberalism that attach to infrastructure space and commandeer political policy can, ironically, profoundly compromise liberty. Meanwhile, some spatial software that avoids associations with freedom may demonstrate that interdependent *obligation* can yield expanded capacity and greater choice. Despite the stories of universal logic and rationality that prevail throughout infrastructure space, *irrationality* rules in a world that is susceptible to the most immaterial rumors and unlikely events.

In infrastructure space, discrepancy may be a better tutor than certainty. The misregistration between stated intentions and undeclared activity makes more palpable active forms and the underlying dispositions they shape. Discrepancy trains a crafty political imagination to anticipate the twists, deceptions, or fictions that usually outrun or outwit utopias.

Disposition is also political temperament. The way in which organizations encourage or inhibit the exchange of information is an important marker of this temperament. Designers can tune dispositions in infrastructure space by discouraging the violence that comes from excluding information and encouraging the stability that comes from enriching it. Design activism may even deliberately avoid the most righteous resistance if it is reductive and competitive, looking instead for ways to release tensions by releasing information.

There is often more power in "knowing how" rather than "knowing that." The markers used to navigate a river are indeterminate in order to be practical. Similarly, in the fluid organizations of infrastructure space, the manipulation of active forms in an unfolding process is more practical than prescriptions or declarations of urban reform. The aim is to offer not solutions but rather mechanisms for generating solutions. Beyond those cautions offered in the most familiar political theories, infrastructure space draws attention to broad, dynamic markers of danger associated with obstructions of information and concentrations of authoritarian power.

Whether deploying cunning, banality, or absurdity, infrastructure space is a tool of some of the most powerful forces in the world. But two can play at this game—in an art of extrastatecraft.

Index

Page numbers in *italics* refer to illustrations

Abu Dhabi 46, 58
active forms
    and disposition 21, 72–3, 81–5, 92, 214,
        239
    information management 86, 232
    interplay 78–81, 132–6, 203, 205–6
    multipliers 68, 73–5
    stories 89–91, 207, 217–18, 240
    switches and remote controls 75–6, 227–9
activism
    and declaration 22–3, 211–14, 231–2,
        240–1
    and discrepancy 214–15, 237–8
    and institutions 197, 227–9, 234
    middle class 43
    techniques 221, 222–3, 225, 229
actor-network theory (ANT) 89–91, 131
"Administration Industrielle et Générale"
        (Fayol) 180
aesthetics 235–6
Africa
    LAPSSET 128–9
    management culture 196
    submarine cables 110–14, *112*
    telecommunications 96–7, 99–106,
        117n60, 122
    terrestrial cables 114–17, *115*
    zones 66
    see also Kenya; Mauritius; Sudan
African Union 103
Agamben, Giorgio 53n76
airport cities 38n36
Al-Hassan Industrial Estate 63–4
Al Qaeda 147
Alcatel-Lucent S.A. 101–2, 111
Alexander, Christopher 84n15
AllianceTexas 63
Almogran 58
Amazon Crude (Kimerling) 200
American National Standards Institute
        (ANSI) 175, 181n23
American Society for Quality (ASQ) 178,
        181n23
Angevine, Robert 153n48

Annan, Kofi 104
Ant Farm 225n25
Appadurai, Arjun 110
Apple Inc. 58, 197–8
Archigram 225n25
architecture
    and active forms 81, 83–4
    and information 12–13
    international design principles 163,
        188–9, 191
    political 213n3
    postmodern 225n25
ARPAnet 71, 143
Arquilla, John 144–7
Astana 51–3, 52
AT&T Corp. 100–1
Athi River EPZ 126–7, *127*
authoritarianism 157–8, 168, 211
awards 219–20

Banerjee, Abhijit Vinayak 132
Bangladesh 54, 149
banking 17, 40–1n43, 60, 121, 204
    see also finance
Baran, Paul 144
Bateson, Gregory 85–8
Being There (Kosinski) 230
Benkler, Yochai 92, 159
Biemann, Ursula 64
binary patterns 86–8, 147–9, 212–13, 240
Bjerregaard, Ritt 221
BLO (Barbie Liberation Organization) 225
Boli, John 206–7
Bolin, Richard 32n19, 57
Booz Allen Hamilton Inc. 182, 193–4
Border Industrial Program (BIP) 30
Bourdieu, Pierre 89n26
Bourriaud, Nicholas 236n40
Brenner, Neil 49n63
A Brief History of Neoliberalism (Harvey) 157
Britain 99–100, 154–5
British Cable and Wireless Company 101
British territories 60
broadband
    access to 95–8, 104–6, 109, 125–6, 167
    companies 100–3

development 129, 130–1, 136
networks 17–18, 124–5
pricing 117–19
spatial variables 97–9, 132
submarine cables 110–14, *112*
terrestrial cables 114–17, *115*
villages 134–5, 224
and zones 37–8, 126–7, 133–4
see also internet; mobile telephony
Broadband Commission for Digital
    Development 105–6, 119
Brunsson, Nils 199
BSI (British Standards Institute) 175, 178,
    180n21, 181n23, 186
buildings
    DustyRelief/B_mu 226
    form 14, 81
    as reproducible products 11–12, 73–4
    standards 188–191
    subtraction protocols 205–6, 240
bureaucracy
    and economic liberalism 107–8
    and governance 167–8, 173, 196, 208–9
    and zones 27, 66–7, 160–1
Burnham, Jack 84n15
Burnham, James 183n35
business schools 182
    see also universities

Canadian Standards Association (CSA) 186
capitalism 146, 151–4, 179–80, 183n35
    see also market economics
carbon market 174, 204
Castells, Manuel 41, 188
CCK (Communications Commission of
    Kenya) 106–7, 111, 116–17
certification programs *199*
    as corporate PR 19, 65, 176–7, 197–8
    global reach 196–7
    incentivizing 220
    non-ISO 190, 193
    see also ISO
Chandler, Alfred D. 152–4
Chen, Xiangming 39
China
    and Africa 66, 127
    and ISO 196
    and Taiwan 219
    zones 26, 35–7, 42–4, 59, 62
China Daily (newspaper) 49
Churchill, Winston 155
CIDCO (City and Industrial Development
    Company of Maharashtra) 48
cities
    charter 66n110
    doubles 48–53, 224

free 27–8
    and infrastructure space 13, 191
    internet of things 81n6
    multipliers 74–5, 90
    as transnational product 12, 62–3
    Vision 2030 127–8
    and zones 26, 37–8, 42–8, 68–9, 133–4
class 43, 157
Classic Fashion Apparel Industry Ltd. 64–5,
    201
Clausewitz, Claude von 139–40, 147
climate change 216
Clinton, Bill 194
Colón Free Trade Zone 29–30
comedy 225–7
compliance
    ISO 19, 168, 172, 195–7, 209
    and power 215, 220–2
    as a smoke-screen 197–201
The Concept of Mind (Ryle) 81–3
Concept of the Corporation (Drucker) 183–4
Constitution of Liberty (Hayek) 158n65
construction industry 38, 152–3, 179, 189,
    190
content
    and activity 13–15
    and mobile telephony 121
    and quality management 176–7, 187,
        194–5, 202, 230
    and rumor 217
convergence 125n87
corporate social responsibility 65, 189–90,
    196–8, 200, 219–20
corporations
    and developing countries 219
    global governance 184–7, 196–201, 221–2
    global telecommunications 100–2, 106–7
    infrastructure building 150–4
    management thinking 179–85, 192–4
    offshore practices 60–1
    and zones 38, 40, 67, 160
Covey, Stephen 194
Cox, Louise 191n57
crowd-sourcing 96–7, 122–3, 131
Cyberjaya 15, 38

Dabba 122
Dariush Grand Hotel, Kish 61–2, *61*
Deleuze, Gilles 80, 145–7
Delhi Mumbai Industrial Corridor 66
Deming, W. Edwards 178n17, 185
design
    active forms 81, 84–5, 91, 218
    and broadband 132–3
    and comedy 226
    disposition 92, 240–1

environmentally sensitive 190, 205
international 163
multipliers 74–5, 84, 202–3, 217
as software 80, 84n15, 239
utopian 231–2
DEVCO 196
Dhaka EPZ 54, 149
Diamond, Walter H. and Dorothy B. 40
digital media 81, 85, 119, 163
DiMaggio, Paul J. 206
DIN (Deutsches Institut für Normung) 175,
180n21, 186
discrepancy 91, 212, 214–15, 237–8, 240
disposition
broadband 124
description 21–2, 71–2, 81–3, 92–3
interplay of active forms 78–81, 206
markers 72–3, 77–8
in sociology 89n26, 91
and stories 88, 90, 138, 168–9, 214–15
switches 75–6
and temperament 86–8, 240–1
dissensus 233–5, 238–9
distraction 15, 229–30
Domination and the Arts of Resistance (Scott)
215–16, 220
doubling 26, 48–51, 222–5
Drucker, Peter F. 57, 183–4, 194
Dubai *14*, 42
workers' rights 56–7
"The World" islands 226
zones 26, 41n42, 45–6, 59
Duflo, Esther 132
DustyRelief/B_mu (design work) 226
Dylan, Bob 235–6

Eagle, Nathan 123
EASSy (East Africa Submarine Cable
System) 105, 110–11, 113–14, 118n67
Ebene Cybercity 37, 105
*Economic Control of Quality of Manufactured
Product* (Shewhart) 181
economic liberalism
in Africa 106–9, 160–1
and infrastructure 138, 150–4, 221–2
and political ideology 154–60, 166n85,
224, 240
and zones 27, 35–6, 39–40, 65–6, 90, 160
see also neoliberalism
economic theory 130–2, 151, 154–5, 159–61
Economist (magazine) 119
Ecuador 66, 200, 219
Egypt 63–4
elevators 74–5
The Emergence of Noopolitik (Arquilla and
Ronfeldt) 145

Empire (Hardt and Negri) 148, 229n29
enclaves 25–6, 35–6, 68, 97–8, 125–6
see also zones
The End of the Nation State (Ohmae) 40
english 235–7
entrepreneurialism 125, 129, 212, 231–2, 234
environment
abuse 16, 43, 54
climate change 216
and development 204–6, 240
green energy 46, 218
regulation 34, 167
social responsibility 200, 219–20
and standards 19, 189–91, 197–8, 200–1
EPZs (Export Processing Zones)
development 25, 29–30, 32–3, 36–8, 39
Dhaka 54, 149
disadvantages 34–5
diversity 40–1
in Kenya 126–7
Shekou Industrial Zone 43
WEPZA 32–33nn18–19, 39–40, 57
see also zones
Erdoğan, Recep Tayyip 221
Euler, Leonhard 76–7
extrastatecraft (definition) 15

Facebook 71, 77
Fair Labor Association (FLA) 58, 197–8
fascism 155, 157–8
Fayol, Henri 180
Feigenbaum, Armand V. 185
fiber-optic cable
contracts 118n67
development 100–1, 104–5, 126
as a network switch 17–18, 76
submarine cables 95–6, 110–14, *112*
terrestrial cables 98, 114–17, *115*
finance 60–1, 150–4, 174
see also banking
Flaubert, Gustave 235
Ford Motor Company 179–80
form 14, 21, 74–5, 79–82, 89–90, 205
see also active forms
Fortune (magazine) 182–3
Foster, Norman 46, 52
Foucault, Michel 92, 141
Foxconn 57–8
free ports 27–8, 39, 43
free zones *see* zones
Friedman, Milton 157n62
FTZs (Foreign Trade Zones) 28–9, 34, 59, 63
see also zones
Furusten, Staffan 178

Gale, Stanley 50

General Motors Co. 183–4
Georgia 66, *67*
Germany 28, 53n76, 151n39, 180n21
gifts 219–20
Gingrich, Newt 194
globalization
    of governance 18–19, 100, 161–2, 164–5,
        167–8, 206–9
    of infrastructure 12, 162–4, 173–4
    interdependencies 203–6
    management standards 184–5, 187–9,
        195–6
    of markets 25–6, 31, 40, 135
    and protest 211
    "scapes" 110
Globalization and Organization (Drori,
    Meyer and Hwang eds.) 207–8
Go (game) 145–7
Goffman, Erving 89n24, 90–1, 237–8
golf courses 79–80
Google 77, 122
Gordon, Colin 213
gossip 213, 215–17
governors 78–80, 84, 86, 134–5, 205–6, 220
Govindarajan, Vijay 109, 196
Graham, Stephen 142
Gray, John 150
The Great Transformation (Polanyi) 150–1,
    155–6
green energy 46, 218
Grima, Joseph 81n6
Guattari, Félix 80, 145–7
Gulick, Luther 180–1

hackers 231–2, 234
Hall, Peter 41
Hamburg 27, 28
Hanseatic League 27
Hardt, Michael 148, 229n29
Harvey, David 157
Hayek, Frederick A. 156–7, 158n65
Heeks, Richard 130–1
Herlihy, Brian 109, 121
highways *see* roads
Hill, Charles 140n4
history
    of management 179–87
    military and civil society 21–2, 139–45,
        150–4
    political 154–8
    of telecommunications 99–106, 137,
        161–3
    of zones 27–31
HITEC City 15, 37
hoax 215–6
homo economicus 151, 158–60

Hong Kong 28–9, 43, 49, 223
Hoover, Herbert 155
Huawei Technologies Co. Ltd. 102, 109, 116
Hughes, Thomas P. 143
Hugo, Victor 12
Hundred Years' Peace 150–1

Ibrahim Prize for Achievement 219–20
ICT4D 130–2
ideologies
    conflict 183–4
    and disposition 168
    economic liberalism 160, 223–4, 240
    and ISO 209
    and technology 21–2, 93, 138, 217
    see also politics
IEC (International Electrotechnical
    Commission) 167–8, *174*
ILO (International Labor Organization) 56,
    64, 197
Imai, Masaaki 186
IMF (International Monetary Fund) 103, 106
inadmissible evidence 233–5
Incheon FEZ 30, 50
India 30, 37, 57, 66, 196, 228
information
    access 17–18, 109, 133–6, 164
    and activity 85–6, 91
    circulation 67, 77–8, 240–1
    flows 41, 88, 188, 232
    and infrastructure space 13–14, 71, 98
    and ISO 201–2
    technologies 36–8, 96–7, 119–24, 130–2,
        136
The Informational City (Castells) 41
infrastructure
    and comedy 225–7
    description 11–14, 17–20, 239
    disposition 21, 71–3, 78, 80–1, 92, 214–15
    and extrastatecraft 15, *174*
    military and civilian 139–45, 148–9
    narratives 22, 137–8, 168–9, 217–18, 240
    organization and development 150–4,
        161–4
    see also broadband; quality standards;
        space; zones
Inhofe, James 216
"Institutionalized Organizations: Formal
    Structure as Myth and Ceremony"
    (Meyer and Rowan) 166
intergovernmental agencies 18, 103, 110–14,
    165, 184–5, 196
International Congresses of Modern
    Architecture 163, 188
international organizations
    and broadband 96

contradictions 166–7, 207–9
and free market liberalization 106–7
global governance 100, 161–2, 196–8
growth 164–5
leverage 227–8
and standards 18, 167–8
and zones 32–3, 55–6
see also ISO; ITU
International Textile Garment and Leather
    Workers Federation 56
International Trade Union Confederation
    (ITUC) 56
internet
    access 96, 107, 109, 125–6
    control 77, 164, 211
    military narratives 143–5
    pricing 117–19
    see also broadband
internet of things 81n6, 119–24
interplay 78–81, 133–6, 203–6, 220, 228,
    239–40
Iraq 147, 211
island zones 59–61
ISO (International Organization for
    Standardization) *174*
    container shipping 187–8
    description 18–19, 171–3, 201–3, 206–8
    global ambitions 195–6
    inception 174–5, 181n23
    irrationality 167–8, 209
    ISO 9000 19, 172, 176–7, 186–7
    ISO 14000 189, 196, 198, 200
    ISO 26000 196–7
    as a smoke-screen 199–201
    and technologies 191
    see also quality standards
ISPs (internet service providers) 117–19, 125–6
Israel 58, 63
ITU (International Telegraph Union) *174*
    and broadband infrastructure 105–6
    first meeting 137–8, *139*, 150, 161
    and governance 100, 107, 167–8
    as international mediator 162
    and teledensity 103–4, 119

Jana Mobile Inc. 123–4, 224
Jansen, Ludger 81
Japan 37, 163, 185–6, 192
Japan Port Consultants Ltd. 129
Jeju Island 59
Jobs, Steve 58
The Joke (Kundera) 220
Jordan 63–5
Juran, Joseph M. 185
JUSE (Japanese Union of Scientists and
    Engineers) 185n40

just-in-time production 185, 188

KAEC (King Abdullah Economic City) 15,
    47–8, *47*, *54*
Kaohsiung Export Processing Zone 30, 32
Kazakhstan 51–3
KDN (Kenya Data Networks) 114–17
Kelly, Kevin 41
Kenya *108*, *120*, *127*
    access to telecommunications 95–9, 100,
        103–4, 110–11, 117–20, 125
    business innovation 17–18, 65, 121–4
    cable 111–17
    development 126–9, 133–6, 204
and economic liberalism 106–9, 160–1
    and intergovernmental agencies 103
    telecommunications companies 101–2
Keynes, John Maynard 155, 157n62
Kimerling, Judith 200
Kish Island 61–2
Kissinger, Henry 140, 147
"knowing how" 81–3, 85, 92, 225n25, 237–8,
    241
Konigsberg Bridge Problem 76–7
Konza Technology City 127–8
Kosinski, Jerzy 230
KP&TC (Kenya Post and
    Telecommunications Corp.) 101–2,
    106, 107
KPMG International 178
Krasner, Stephen D. 48–9
Kundera, Milan 220
Kurokawa, Kisho 52

La Fontaine, Henri 164–5
labor
    abuse 16, 27, 54–8, 200–1, 219, 222–3
    cheap 25, 30, 37, 43–5, 64
    and economic liberalism 39
    immigrant workers 233–4
    protection 19, 33–4, 160, 167, 197
    sexual harassment 64–5
    see also Rana Plaza
laissez-faire *see* economic liberalism
LAPSSET (Lamu Port–Southern Sudan–
    Ethiopia Transport) 128–9, 219
Latour, Bruno 81n5, 88–91, 159–60
law
    and labor 56, 160
    maritime 223
    and standards 18, 199–201
    and state sovereignty 49
    and zones 15–16, 26, 33–4, 45–6, 51, 53
Lazika city 66–7
LEED (Leadership in Energy and
    Environmental Design) 190

Lekki Free Zone 66
Lépinay, Vincent Antonin 159–60
Levine, Les 84n15
Levitt, William 73–4, 90
liberalism 108–9, 150, 154–61, 166n85, 224
    see also economic liberalism;
    neoliberalism
"Like a Rolling Stone" (Dylan) 235–6
Limbaugh, Rush 216
Linder, Marc 152
Logopelago (design work) 225–6
Lotringer, Sylvère 141
Lyons, Thomas E. 30

M-PESA 17, 121–2
Macau 59
Madigan, Charles 194n68
"The Making and Expansion of International
    Management Standards" (Mendel)
    196n72, 207
Malaysia 38, 42, 57
management culture
    history 153–4, 179–82
    Japanese 185–6, 192
    jargon 173, 192–3, 195, 226–7, 230
    management consulting 182–5, 192–5
    new trends 196
    significance 178–9
management standards
    globalization 187–9, 195–6
    ISO 9000 172, 176–7, 186–7
    ISO 14000 189, 196, 198–200
    significance 173–4, 201–3
    social responsibility 196–8, 200–1
    see also quality standards
The Managerial Revolution (Burnham)
    183n35
manufacturing
    standards 174–5, 181, 185–6
    supply chain cities 44
    in zones 28–9, 30, 39, 48, 63–5
maquiladoras 30, 31, 39
markers 72–3, 77–8, 88, 214, 240–1
market economics
    in Africa 106–9, 160–1
    development and regulation 151–6,
        158–60
    and zones 35–6, 39–40, 65–6
    see also economic liberalism
Masdar City 46, 191
Mattelart, Armand 140, 143, 161, 191–2
Mauritius 37–8, 104–5
McCormick, Joseph P. 158
McKenna, Christopher D. 194n68
McKinsey & Company, Inc. 103, 130, 182,
    185, 192–4

McLuhan, Marshall 13
meaninglessness 229–31
Mehrotra, Rahul 228
Mendel, Peter 196n72, 207
Meng, Guanwen 39n36, 40–41n43
Mexico 30, 63, 145
Meyer, John W. 165–6, 207–8
Micklethwait, John 183n34, 194n68
military
    administration 153–4
    conflict 58
    and infrastructure 138, 141–5, 148–9,
        240
    and realpolitik 139–41
    war machine 146–8, 152
    see also war
Millennium Development Goals 106, 126
mimicry 87, 190, 222–3
Mind and Nature (Bateson) 86
Mises, Ludwig von 156–7
The Missing Link (ITU report) 103–4
Mo Ibrahim Prize for Achievement 219–20
mobile telephony 108, 120
    advertisements 95
    entrepreneurialism 125, 129
    internet of things 119–24
    pricing 109, 118–19
    ubiquity 17–18, 96–8, 163, 167
    see also broadband
Morozov, Evgeny 164
MTN Group 109, 122
Multimedia Super Corridor (MSC) 38, 42
multinational industries see corporations;
    international organizations
multipliers
    cell phones 98–9, 120–1, 133
    gossip and rumor 215–18
    hackers/entrepreneurs 231–2
    ISO 198, 202–3
    topologies 77–8
    urban space 73–5, 78–9, 84, 90, 134
    zones 27, 68, 188
Mumbai 48, 228

Nairobi 98, 103, 116n58, 126, 134
    see also Kenya
National Optical Fibre Backbone
    Infrastructure (NOFBI) 115, 116–17
Navi Mumbai 48
Nazarbayev, Nursultan 51, 53
Ndemo, Bitange 111, 118n67, 128
Negri, Antonio 148, 229n27
Negroponte, Nicholas 84n14
neoliberalism
    and governance 55–6
    and liberalism 158–9, 224

"Washington consensus" economics 66,
        106–8, 157, 160–1
WEPZA 33n18, 39–40
NEPAD (New Partnership for Africa's
        Development) 103, 110–11, 113
networks
    broadband 17, 98–9, 133–5
    financial 60
    information 119–24, 164–5
    rail 152–4
    and security 144–5, 147
    social 143, 159–60
    socio-technical 20, 22n5, 88–90, 124–5
    switches 75–6, 97–8, 227
    telegraph 99–100, 137
    topologies 77–8
Networks and Netwars (Arquilla and
        Ronfeldt) 144–5, 147
New Deal 155, 224
*The New Institutionalism in Organizational
        Analysis* (Powell and DiMaggio) 206
New Songdo City 15, 26, 50–1, *50*
NGO-Industrial Complex 198, *199*
NGOs *199*
    FEMOZA 167n87
    power 144, 227–8
    proliferation 18, 165
WEPZA 32nn17–18, 39–40, 40–41n43, 57
    and workers' rights 55–6, 58, 197–8
    see also intergovernmental agencies;
        ISO
Nigeria 66
Noam, Eli 104
Nomadology (Deleuze and Guattari) 145
North Korea 62
Notre Dame de Paris (Hugo) 12
Nye, David E. 218

OAU (Organization of African Unity) 103
Obama, Barack 216–17, 223
object forms 14, 74, 81–2, 84, 133
Occupy movement 211, 221
O'Connell, Charles 153n49
OECD (Organization for Economic
        Cooperation and Development) 35, 41,
        197, 198
offshore banking 40–41n43, 60
Ohmae, Kenichi 40
oil and petrochemicals 44–5, 48, 200, 218,
        219
"On Distributed Communications" (Baran)
        144
On the Shores of Politics (Rancière) 233
Ong, Aihwa 55–6, 158–9
"Open Source Architecture (OSArc)" (Ratti,
        Grima et al.) 81n6

operating system
    forms as code 72–3, 92
    infrastructure space as 12–14, 173–4, 232,
        239
    see also software
Ordos, Inner Mongolia *16*
organization studies 181
O'Shea, James 194n68
Otlet, Paul 164

Palen, Ronen 49
Palestine 58, 64
pandas 219
Papers on the Science of Administration
        (Gulick) 180–1
PDCA (Plan Do Check Act) 177, 185n40
peace 137, 150–1
    see also war
Pentagram Design 218
Peters, Tom 193, 196
PLOT architects 221
Polanyi, Karl 150–1, 155–6, 184
political activism *see* activism
politics
    and art 235–6
    binary oppositions 86–7
    British 154–5
    and disposition 77–8, 92, 214, 240–1
    and infrastructure 137–8, 168–9
    and meaninglessness 229–30
    and mobile platforms 122–3
    and power 212, 215–16
    undeclared outcomes 71, 73
    US 155–8
    and war 139–41, 144–8
    and zones 16–17, 27, 55–6, 67–8, 90, 148
    see also activism; ideologies; liberalism;
        neoliberalism
The Politics of Aesthetics (Rancière) 235–6
Powell, Walter W. 206
power
    and comedy 225–6
    and design 84–5
    destabilizing 215–16
    and disposition 73, 168, 214
    industrial 99–100, 137–8, 152–3
    and infrastructure space 15, 22–3, 230
    relationships 87–8
    state 49, 55
    see also politics
Prahalad, Coimbatore Krishnarao 109, 196
Price, Cedric 84n15
protocols 78–9, 137, 203–6
Pudong SEZ 44
Puerto Rico 29, 30n11

Qatar 46
QIZs (Qualifying Industrial Zones) 63–4, 201
    see also zones
Quality Digest (magazine) 178n17
quality standards
    content 176, 187, 201–2, 230
    description 19, 172–4, 209
    globalization 187–9, 195–6
    history 179–82
    intentions 198–201
    and management gurus 192–4
    as a service industry 177–8
    Total Quality Management 185–6, 192
    see also ISO

rail 48, 152–4, 163, 179
rainforest 174, 204–5
Rana Plaza 54, 149
Rancière, Jacques 202, 231, 233, 235–6
RAND Corporation 144–5
rationalization
    and irrationality 12, 27, 65, 168, 173,
        230–1
    organizations 207–8
    universal 163, 166n85
Ratti, Carlo 81n5
Reagan, Ronald 157, 218, 230
realpolitik 139–41, 148
Reassembling the Social (Latour) 89–90
REDD (Reducing Emissions from
        Deforestation and Degradation) 204
regulation
    of markets 107–8, 154, 155–6
    of money transfer services 121n74
    and multinational industries 197–201,
        221–2
    and standards 173
    of zones 27, 33–4, 49, 54, 167
    see also quality standards
remote controls 75–6, 133, 227–9
Republic of Panama 29–30
resorts 58–61
The Road to Serfdom (Hayek) 157, 158n65
roads 76, 98, 128, 135
    see also transportation
Robbins, Anthony 194
Roche, Francoise 226
Ronfeldt, David 144–7
Roosevelt, Franklin Delano 155, 224
Rowan, Brian 166
rumor 212–3, 215–18
Russia 62
Ryle, Gilbert 81–3, 91

Safaricom 107, 109, 111, 117–18, 121
    see also M-PESA

SAI (Social Accountability International)
    197
satellite technology 95, 97, 113n53, 117, 163
Saudi Arabia 47–8
Savannah, Georgia 78–80, 79, 133
Schmitt, Carl 53n75, 55, 157–8
Schwartz, Frederic J. 180n21
The Science of Passionate Interests (Latour
        and Lépinay) 159–60
scientific management 179–81, 183n34, 187
Scott, James C. 164, 215–16, 220
Seacom Ltd. 113, 117, 118n67
SEED (Social Economic Environmental
        Design) 190
Seigel, Jerrold 158
Seoul 30, 50
SEZs (Special Economic Zones) 35–9, 42–4,
        51, 59, 62
    see also Shenzhen SEZ; zones
Shanghai 44
Shannon Free Zone 29, 32
Shaxson, Nicholas 60
Shenzhen SEZ 36, 43–4, 49, 57–8, 102
Shewhart, Walter A. 181
shipping 31, 38, 187–8, 223
Siemens AG 101
Silva, Erandi De 225–6
SIPs (Science Industrial Parks) 36–9
    see also zones
Six Sigma 193
Skolkovo 62
socialism 155, 157
software
    active forms as code 14, 79–81
    crowd-sourcing 122–3
    and design 84n14, 239
    spatial 20, 27, 98, 134–6, 203–6
    see also operating system
Software Technology Parks of India (STPI) 37
Songdo *see* New Songdo City
South Korea 30, 37, 50–1, 59
South Sudan 58, 128, 129
sovereignty
    bifurcation 49, 148
    exemption 15, 51, 53, 55–6, 223
    and liberalism 159
space
    and activism 232
    and broadband infrastructure 97
    description 11–12, 14, 22–3
    disposition 72, 124–5, 214
    as information 13, 19–20, 173–4
    interdependencies 203–6, 239–40
    militarization 142, 148
    spatial products 26, 37, 38n36, 62, 74–5,
        188–9

stories 90, 218
  urban 15–18, 78–80, 133–6
spin 216, 235–7
standards *see* management standards; quality
  standards
Stanford Research Park 36
Starr, Paul 143
state of exception 53, 55
states
  conflict 58, 129, 139–43, 146–8
  and international companies 152, 161–2,
    179, 183–4
  region states 40
  and standards 199, 202, 208
  and zones 15–17, 26–7, 34–5, 48–9, 66–7
Steps to an Ecology of Mind (Bateson) 85, 87
Sterling, Bruce 143
stories
  active forms 90–1, 207, 240
  and counter-stories 217–18
  and disposition 21–2, 88, 92–3, 168–9,
    214–15
  of globalization 110, 163–6
  military 143–9
  power 137–8
subtraction protocols 205–6, 240
suburban housing 73–5, 80, 84, 90, 204–6, 217
Sudan 58, 105, 129
switches 75–7, 86, 133–4, 227

Taiwan 30, 37, 219
Taksim Square protests 221
Tarde, Gabriel 159–60, 215
tax
  havens 59–60, 160
  incentives 15, 25, 29, 33, 43, 48
Taylor, Frederick W. 179–80
Tea Party movement 158n65, 223
TEAMS (The East African Marine System)
  111, 113, 116–17, 118n67
technology
  as actant 88–90
  building 188, 191
  and disposition 21, 71, 92–3
  international 163–4
  military and civilian 142–4
  printing 12
  satellite 95, 97
  zones 36–9, 42, 127–8
  see also information
TECHNOPARK-Allianz 62
Technopoles of the World (Castells and Hall)
  41
telecommunications
  development 18, 95–6, 99–106, 124–5,
    136–7

and economic liberalism 106–7, 110–11
  see also ITU; mobile telephony
Telkom Kenya 106–7, 111
temperament 86–8, 240
terrorism 142n12, 144, 146–7
The Third Wave (Toffler) 97n6
Thomas, George M. 206–7
Toffler, Alvin 97n6
topologies 76–8, 98, 144–5
tourism 58–61, 128–9, 134, 205
TQM (Total Quality Management) 185–6,
  187n44, 192
trade
  ethical 131, 204–5
  historic free ports 27–8
  role of standards 172, 199–201
  shipping 31, 38
  see also manufacturing; market
    economics; zones
trade unions 39, 44n49, 56, 160
traffic engineering 76, 164
trafficking 64
Transcendental Meditation movement
  195n70
transportation
  and broadband 98, 134–5
  corridors 128–9
  networks 11, 20, 76, 126
  and organizational power 152–4, 179
  technologies 46
"Treatise on Nomadology" (Deleuze and
  Guattari) 146
Twain, Mark 21

UAE (United Arab Emirates) 40–41n43,
  44–6, 111, 203–4
  see also Dubai
UIA (Union of International Associations)
  164–5
UNIDO (United Nations Industrial
  Development Organization) 32, 34–5,
  167
United Nations Global Compact 197
universities 46, 98, 134
urbanism
  broadband 18, 98–9, 124–5, 133–6
  global 12, 163–4, 188–9, 191
  incentivized 15–16, 26, 38, 62, 68
  and the military 140–2
  subtraction protocols 205–6
  zone 40–1, 66–7, 224
Urwick, Lyndall 180–1
US Green Building Council (USGBC) 190
USA
  industry 77, 99, 152–4, 179–80, 185–6
  labor standards 56, 197

management systems 182n29, 183, 192–3, 196
politics 140, 155–8, 194, 211, 216–17
zones 28–9, 33, 36, 59, 63
Ushahidi, Inc. 122–3, 224
USSR 37

villages 117, 126, 134–5, 164
violence 54, 58, 88, 148–9
  see also war
Virilio, Paul 139, 140–1
The Visible Hand (Chandler) 152–4
Vision 2030 126–9, 134

Wal-Mart Stores, Inc. 54, 218
war 54, 58, 139–43, 145–7, 211
  see also military; peace
The Wealth of Networks (Benkler) 92, 159
Weizman, Eyal 142
WEPZA (World Economic Processing Zone
    Association) 32–33nn18–19, 39–40,
    40–41n43, 57
Werkbund 180n21
Wirth, David A. 199–200
women 61, 64–5, 223
Woodridge, Adrian 183n34, 194n68
workers *see* labor
World Bank
  and broadband 96, 110–11, 117n60, 130,
    167
  and free market liberalization 106–8

and Kenya 103
and management consulting 184–5
and zones 25, 32
WoW (Women on Waves) 223
WTO (World Trade Organization) 56, 106,
    211

Yes Men 222–3

Zain Kenya 107, 118, 121n73
Zapatistas 145
zones
  antidote 68–9, 78, 133–4
  as cities 42–8
  cross-border 39, 40–41n43, 53
  description 15–17, 25–7
  disadvantages 34–5, 66–8, 148–9
  as doubles 48–53, 224
  growth and development 32–3, 35–41,
    65–6, 167
  history 27–31
  incentives 33–4, 43, 45, 48
  in Kenya 98, 126–9
  and laundering 62–4
  leverage 203–4
  and quality management 172, 187–9
  as resorts 58–61
  as state of exception 53–4
  workers' rights 55–8, 64–5, 160
ZTE Corp. 102